A Beginner's Guide to Meditation

A Shambhala Sun Book

A BEGINNER'S GUIDE TO
Meditation

Practical Advice and Inspiration from
Contemporary Buddhist Teachers

Edited by Rod Meade Sperry
and the Editors of the *Shambhala Sun*

SHAMBHALA
Boston & London 2014

Shambhala Publications, Inc.
Horticultural Hall
300 Massachusetts Avenue
Boston, Massachusetts 02115
www.shambhala.com

9 8 7 6 5 4 3 2

Printed in the United States of America

♾ This edition is printed on acid-free paper that meets the
American National Standards Institute Z39.48 Standard.
♻ This book is printed on 30% postconsumer recycled paper.
For more information please visit www.shambhala.com.

Distributed in the United States by Penguin Random House LLC
and in Canada by Random House of Canada Ltd

Designed by James D. Skatges

Library of Congress Cataloging-in-Publication Data

A beginner's guide to meditation: practical advice and inspiration from
contemporary Buddhist teachers / edited by Rod Meade Sperry and the
Editors of the Shambhala Sun.—First edition.
pages   cm
ISBN 978-1-61180-057-9 (pbk.: alk. paper)
1. Meditation—Buddhism. I. Meade Sperry, Rod. II. Shambhala Sun.
BQ5625.B45 2014
294.3'4435—dc23
2013024625

CONTENTS

ACKNOWLEDGMENTS

I wish to thank so many people for the inspiration and guidance—direct and indirect—that made the honor of working on this book possible for me.

Thank you to Beth Frankl, my editor at Shambhala Publications, and to Melvin McLeod, Andrea Miller, Jim Gimian, Andy Karr, and all my colleagues at the Shambhala Sun Foundation.

Thank you to John Golebiewski and Oliver Glosband at Shambhala Publications for all their assistance. Thanks also to Tracy Davis for her copy editing and to Liza Matthews and André Slob for their cover work.

Thanks to all the fantastic teachers whose essays are collected in this book.

Thank you, James Ishmael Ford, Larry Rosenberg, Barry Boyce, Josh Bartok, Thanissaro Bhikkhu, Tsoknyi Rinpoche, Maddy Klyne, and Dzongsar Jamyang Khyentse Rinpoche. Thanks too to those who've come into my life one way or another (some, over the Internet!) who, while not formal dharma teachers, have been inspiring if only by example.

This book is dedicated to all beings, not least of all dogs and "worst horses," those among us who feel we have a long, long way to go when it comes to the meditator's path.

Lastly, thanks to Maura Meade Sperry, for your loving, good heart. You are the best.

INTRODUCTION

Welcome to *A Beginner's Guide to Meditation*. This is not an advanced meditation book, nor is it a complete, definitive presentation of all the possible approaches to Buddhist meditation. Such a thing might not be possible in a hundred books, let alone one. Instead, what this book is meant to be is *sufficient,* meaning that these writings by eminent contemporary Buddhist teachers should be more than enough to get you started meditating with regularity and confidence. What you'll find here is meant to help you to get clearer about meditation—even excited about it—without becoming overwhelmed.

Many books on Buddhist meditation focus on a particular school, approach, or technique. *A Beginner's Guide to Meditation* keeps in mind that there are so many different practices under the rubric of Buddhist meditation because there are so many kinds of people. What might work best for one person might not work well for another. My hope is that the sampling of teachings gathered here will help you find an approach that works for *you.*

If you're just getting started, it might be helpful to reflect on the reasons people want to meditate. Meditation is, of course, a time-tested method for reducing anxiety and coming to terms with the short- and long-term mental afflictions that we all face. Ultimately, though, there's more to get from it than just an increased sense of calm. The more you stick with the practice, the more you stand to gain insight into what makes you tick and find more cohesion and connection with the people in your life, too. A meditation practice can help you in a number of ways:

- slow down and break patterns of obsessive or compulsive behavior
- connect more with loved ones and be more present with others in general
- come to terms with loss, addiction, and ill health
- foster better health and body awareness
- create a foundation for further investigation into Buddhist concepts

Part 1, "Let's Get Started," presents the practice in its simplest form so that you can see from the beginning that meditation is entirely doable and really not anything extraordinary. From there, you'll get advice and guidance to help you start your practice off right.

In part 2, "Cultivating Calm and Insight (and More)," you'll be introduced to the two basic forms of Buddhist meditation—*shamatha*, or tranquillity meditation, and *vipashyana*, or insight meditation—as well as other classic practices for cultivating a more spacious and friendly attitude toward others.

You'll get a glimpse into the world of Zen in part 3, which explains the practices of *shikantaza*, or "just sitting," and koan introspection, which is perhaps the best-known and yet most misunderstood meditation approach found here.

Part 4, "Indo-Tibetan Innovations," shares teachings that spread from the regions of India and Tibet. These practices involve methods of cultivating loving-kindness and compassion, training the mind through the use of ancient and powerful slogans, and looking directly at the mind to analyze what we see.

Finally, part 5, "Keep Your Practice Going," gives you what you need to do just that, so that you can practice at home or with others at a practice center or extended retreat with enthusiasm, engagement, and confidence. There are even helpful yoga tips to keep you limber and refreshed.

Having originated in northern India more than 2,500 years ago and then spread across the globe, Buddhism has a sprawling terminology that draws from many languages, with much of its terminology from Pali, Sanskrit, Japanese, and Tibetan. Different traditions use terms from different languages, so you'll see, for example, that the Buddhist teachings themselves may be referred to with the Sanskrit word *dharma* or the Pali word *dhamma*. The practice of insight meditation is called *vipassana* (a Pali word) in the Theravada tradition; others use the Sanskrit term *vipashyana*. Zen Buddhism has its own specialized lexicon from the Japanese. There's a glossary in the back to help you.

The wide range of meditation practices, approaches, and teachings presented in *A Beginner's Guide to Meditation* represent the many schools of Buddhist thought. Don't let it all overwhelm you. There's no need to worry that you have to "get it" all. Keep in mind that in Buddhist meditation, curiosity—the spirit of inquiry—is key. In that spirit, sample the various teachings here, note what resonates with you (and what doesn't), and see if you can *enjoy* playing with meditation. And if you have a day when can't enjoy it, for whatever reason, remember that this just happens sometimes. After all, that's what our minds are in the habit of doing: they lead us to make things more complicated than they are. Ultimately, it's meditation practice itself that helps us train (or *untrain*) our minds so that we don't have to follow these same old, tired patterns automatically.

As countless meditators have learned firsthand, the rewards of practice can positively transform the way we see and participate in our lives.

So let's get started.

PART I

Let's Get Started

We can start the practice of mindfulness meditation with the simple observation and feeling of each breath. Breathing in, we know we're breathing in; breathing out, we know we're breathing out. It's very simple, although not easy. After just a few breaths, we hop on trains of association, getting lost in plans, memories, judgments and fantasies. This habit of wandering mind is very strong, even though our reveries are often not pleasant and sometimes not even true. As Mark Twain so aptly put it, "Some of the worst things in my life never happened." So we need to train our minds, coming back again and again to the breath, simply beginning again.

—JOSEPH GOLDSTEIN

SITTING, STANDING, WALKING, LYING DOWN: these are the four modes, the Buddha said, in which we should be able to conduct meditation practice. Take the breath out of the equation and we're not sitting, standing, walking, or lying down. We're dead.

Meditation instructions, on the other hand, are about liberating ourselves so that we're more fully alive. As such, they're centered on the breath. The breath, if we let it, can anchor us to our awareness. Simple enough, yet not always so easy. But it's worth it—as generations of those who've tried and stuck with meditation will tell you.

Now's your chance to try it, starting with instructions for basic meditation on the breath—the fundamental practice at the root of all you'll encounter in this book—that are as simple and doable as can be. From there you'll learn more about what meditation is, what it isn't, some of the essential concepts behind it all, and some tips to get you started with confidence.

Basic Breath Meditation: It Doesn't Get Simpler Than This

Melvin McLeod

Although there are seemingly countless approaches to the practice, Buddhist meditation generally starts with the cultivation of mindfulness, in which the breath often serves as a guide for the mind. The Shambhala Sun's editor-in-chief, Melvin McLeod, offers the following mindfulness meditation instructions, which show just how universally achievable the most basic form of meditation really is. Read this and give it a try. There's no need to think about having the right cushion or the perfect meditation spot or all the little nuances you might be wondering about. We'll talk about all of that soon enough.

CHOOSE A QUIET and uplifted place to do your meditation practice. Sit cross-legged on a meditation cushion, or, if that's difficult, sit on a straight-backed chair with your feet flat on the floor, without leaning against the back of the chair.

Place your hands palms-down on your thighs and take an upright posture with a straight back, relaxed yet dignified. With your eyes open, let your gaze rest comfortably as you look slightly downward about six feet in front of you.

Place your attention lightly on your out-breath, while remaining aware of the environment around you. Be with each breath as the air goes out through your mouth and nostrils and dissolves into the space around you. At the end of each out-breath, simply rest until the next breath goes out. For a more focused meditation, you can follow both the out-breaths and in-breaths.

Whenever you notice that a thought has taken your attention away from the breath, just say to yourself, "thinking," and return to following the breath. In this context, any thought, feeling, or perception that distracts you is labeled "thinking." Thoughts are not judged as good or bad. When a thought arises, just gently note it and return your attention to your breath and posture.

At the end of your meditation session, bring calm, mindfulness, and openness into the rest of your day.

On Motivation: Meditate as a Hobby, Not as a Career

Clark Strand

Clark Strand explains how to let go of pressures that can hinder meditation practice.

THE WHOLE IDEA OF A HOBBY is to let go and experience something for itself, for the satisfaction and pleasure you take simply from doing it. You don't do it for your self-esteem, for the world, or for inner peace. Your relationship to it is simple, natural, and not self-conscious at all. If it were self-conscious, it wouldn't give you so much pleasure. It wouldn't be a hobby anymore.

Like a hobby, meditation ought to be a time when you can occupy your mind with something for its own sake, without getting caught up in any of your usual preoccupations: Am I doing this right? Are the others doing it better? I'll probably fail at this, just like everything else. It ought to be an area of your life where you can let go of the obsessive desire to improve yourself, to get ahead, or to do better than anybody else. And yet, without realizing it, this is exactly what many meditators do.

Some feel neurotically driven to achieve a higher level of self-esteem, as if meditating were synonymous with "being good." Others meditate for psychological health or for a lower pulse rate. Still others for better karma or a more exalted spiritual state. They go off for long retreats to find themselves, leaving their families behind. But where are they going to find themselves if not in the lives they have?

Meditating as a hobby is actually a far more honest approach to meditation than treating it like an obligation, a moral responsibility, or a job. When people tell me they are meditating for peace or to improve the world, I always think they don't know what meditation is about. Not that meditating doesn't make us more peaceful or give us a generally more positive outlook on the world, but it is impossible to meditate with such a goal in mind. I am always more impressed when people tell me they meditate because they like it, or because their lives are so busy that once a day, for a few minutes at least, they just want to have some peace of mind. In my opinion, this is a lighter, more open approach. Ultimately, it is also more direct.

Once meditation rises above the level of play, its possibilities are diminished. Why? Because when meditation loses its lightness, it becomes like everything else—another object of desire. When we meditate for something other than meditating, we only become further ensnared in the endless cycle of getting and spending, whereby every activity in every moment has to have a goal. Reaching that goal yields fulfillment or happiness; failing brings disappointment. To treat meditation in this way is not only ineffective, it actually makes matters worse, because then there really is no hope for peace or happiness, fulfillment or love, because these things, when they happen, always come from within us, and always happen now.

Meditation ought to decrease the drivenness of our lives, not make it worse. That is why I say meditate for its own sake, as a hobby, without losing the lightness of your first approach. That is why I say don't become an expert, but stay a beginner instead. If you treat meditation as a career, then it becomes concerned with achievement. And when that happens, meditation becomes fundamentally no different from the desire to get ahead, to get more money, or get a better job.

The person who meditates—whether for five minutes or five hours a day—wants to keep one area of his or her life that is not driven, that does not draw them ceaselessly away from the fundamental enoughness, sanity, and beauty of the world. The person who truly meditates, and is not caught up in some neurotic game, knows that peace, love, happiness, contentment—everything happens now.

Getting Started

Norman Fischer

You want to meditate, but all sorts of questions arise: Where will I do it? When will I do it? Am I doing it right? Norman Fischer helps you dispense with these concerns and get started on a commonsense, two-week trial run.

THOUSANDS OF PEOPLE over the years have asked me for advice about how to establish a daily meditation practice at home. Although there are thousands of Buddhist meditation centers around the country, most meditators do some or all of their practice at home on their own. In many cases, this is a practical matter. Most people don't live close enough to a Buddhist center to meditate there regularly. Or, for one reason or another, they don't feel comfortable with any of the local centers available to them. Or they feel that for them meditation is a private and personal matter, not a communal religious practice. Anyway, most meditators, for a variety of reasons, meditate at home. I do myself.

It wasn't that way when I began Zen practice. The conventional wisdom then was that you could never practice on your own. You needed to practice with others—that was the way it was done. You needed instructions from a teacher. You needed support—

maintaining the discipline to sit on your own would be too difficult. Besides, meditating alone could be dangerous.

Conventional wisdom has changed. These days many people
find that it is entirely possible to meditate on their own. Not that
lack of discipline is unknown—keeping up with regular practice
remains a struggle for some. But many go beyond struggle to find
enjoyment and ease in their daily practice.

When people ask me how to get a home meditation practice
started, here is what I tell them: the practice begins the night before.
Before you go to sleep, set the alarm for half an hour earlier than
usual and say to yourself: "Tomorrow morning I am going to get up
to sit. I want to do this, and it is going to be pleasant and helpful."
Hold that thought in your mind. Then, as you are falling asleep, say
this: "Am I actually going to wake up early and meditate?" And
answer yourself: "Yes, I am." And then question yourself again:
"Really?" Take this seriously. Think a little more and answer yourself honestly. If the answer is, "Yes, really," then you will get up. You
are serious about it. But if the answer is, "No, I have to admit that I
am probably going to reset the alarm and turn over to get that delicious extra half hour of sleep," then save yourself the trouble. Reset
the alarm now and don't even try to get up.

This little exercise may sound silly, but it is very important. It
addresses the main difficulty we have with self-discipline: we are
ambivalent. We both do and don't want to do what we think we
want to do in our own best interests. We find it difficult to take our
good intentions seriously, especially when it comes to our spiritual
lives. We have confusion at our core about whether we are capable
of confronting ourselves at the deepest possible human level—
maybe if we do we will find ourselves to be unworthy, trivial people.
Since we imagine that meditation promises a self-confrontation at
this level, we are deeply ambivalent.

Most of this convoluted thinking is not conscious. This is why
the before-bed self-dialogue is important. It provides a simple way
of confronting the issue. "Really?" It's a way to surface what we

really feel and, gently and honestly, deal with it. Otherwise our long habit of sneaky self-deception will likely prevail. We will not do what we're not really clear we want to do, which will give us further evidence that we can't do it.

Assuming you do get out of bed in the morning, splash cold water on your face, rinse out your mouth, put on some comfortable clothes (or stay in your sleeping clothes if you want), and immediately sit on your cushion. Do this before you have coffee, before you turn on the computer, before you activate your day and realize you don't have time for this. Burn a stick of incense to time yourself, or use a clock or one of the many excellent meditation timers now on the market (which will prevent clock-watching). Decide in advance to sit for twenty to thirty minutes. A bit more is good if you can do it.

Try this for two weeks, taking a day or so off each week. If you miss a day, that's OK. Don't fall into the unconscious trap that "Since I missed a day, I guess I can't do this, so I might as well not even try, or try less hard tomorrow because this missed day has weakened me." This is the way we think! So anticipate this and don't fall for it. Be gentle with yourself, but firm. Imagine that you are training a child, or a puppy—a cute little creature who means well but definitely needs adult guidance.

Decide in advance that you will meditate for two weeks. It is much easier to commit to meditating almost every day for two weeks than to commit yourself to meditating every day for the rest of your life. After two weeks, stop and ask yourself, "How was that? Was it pleasant or unpleasant? What impact did it have on my morning, on the rest of my day, on my week?" Usually positive results are apparent, and, seeing that the practice has been beneficial, you develop a stronger intention to return to it. So then, after a hiatus, commit again to practice, maybe now for a month, with the same break built in for evaluation. In this way, little by little, you can become a regular meditator. Taking breaks from time to time doesn't change that.

Many people ask, "Is it necessary to do this in the morning? Is there some magic to the morning? I am not a morning person." Yes, I think there is magic to the morning. Monastic schedules the world over include early morning practice. Practice seems most beneficial at that time of day, when your psyche is in a liminal state and the world around you has not quite awakened. Also, you are more likely to do it in the morning, before your day gets engaged and you remember all the things you need to do. In the middle of the day it is harder to rein yourself in, and at the end of the day you may be too tired or wound up. You may feel more like a glass of wine than meditation practice, which will likely feel pretty uncomfortable as your body notices all the aches and strains and kinks of the day. Actually, practice at the end of the day is very good for just this reason—while often uncomfortable, it does help you process all your stress and feel calmer afterward. But if you are trying to establish a fledgling practice, thinking you will sit restfully at the end of the day is probably not going to work as well as catching yourself at your weakest (which is to say your strongest): in the morning, when you are both more and less yourself, before you have fully assumed the armored, heroic personality with which you feel you must approach the world of work and family. (I must note here the obvious fact that all of this might not be true for you: we differ enormously as individuals, and in these intimate matters one size does not fit all. I am describing what I have found to be true for myself and for many other meditators.)

There are many approaches to meditation. In my tradition, the Soto Zen tradition, meditation is not considered a skill that we are supposed to master. It is a practice that we devote ourselves to. So if you are meditating in the morning feeling half asleep, with dream-snatches passing by, and your mind not crisply focused precisely on the breath, the way you think it is supposed to be . . . this is perfectly all right. It is considered normal and possibly even beneficial. The biggest obstacle to establishing a meditation practice is the erroneous idea (firmly held by most people who want to establish a meditation practice) that meditation should calm and focus the mind.

Therefore, if your mind is not calm and focused, you are certainly doing it wrong. Struggling with something that you are consistently doing wrong, and in your frustration can't seem to get right, does not inspire you to continue (unless you are a masochist, and there are more than a few meditating masochists).

Better to assume the Soto Zen attitude that meditation is what you do when you meditate. There is no doing it wrong or right. That is not to say that there is no effort, no calm, no focus. Of course there is. The point is to avoid falling into the trap of defining meditation too narrowly, and then judging yourself based on that definition, and so sabotaging yourself. You evaluate your practice on a much wider and more generous calculus. Not: Is my mind concentrated while I am sitting? But: How is my attention during the day? Not: Am I peaceful and still as I sit? But: Is my habit of flying off the handle reducing somewhat? In other words, the test of meditation isn't meditation. It's your life.

Dealing with the various practical obstacles to regular meditation is easy compared with the deeper self-deception issues I have been talking about. Once you get a handle on these, the practical problems are easy. Kids get up early? Then get up half an hour earlier than they do. But that's not enough sleep? Well, that half hour of sitting will be much more important for your rest and well-being than the lost half hour of sleep. Or you can just go to bed half an hour earlier.

No place to meditate? There is always somewhere—all you need is the space for a cushion on the floor. But better to have a clean and well-cared-for spot, even if only in a corner of an otherwise busy, messy room. Keeping that corner neat and clear is a preliminary to the meditation practice itself.

Your spouse doesn't want to meditate and resents you sneaking out of bed to sit? Patiently explain to your spouse that the main reason you are meditating is to become a more loving and helpful person. You are sneaking out of bed not to assert your independence but for the opposite reason: to be more loving. Have that conversation (lovingly) with your spouse. Ask them to help you do this two-week experiment and evaluate the results: have you been more loving, have you helped around the house, with the kids, etc., more than usual, with more willingness, more cheerfulness? (Of course, having had this conversation, you now have to do these things.)

In short, if you want to meditate there is virtually no excuse not to. But human confusion is very clever, so it is still possible to talk yourself out of it. If so, be my guest. Sometimes that's the way to finally begin serious meditation practice: by not doing it for ten or twenty years, until finally there is no choice.

As the world speeds up and history's trajectory becomes more drastic, more people are feeling the need to do something to promote well-being and foster a sustainable attitude. It is difficult to remain cheerful if you are under stress, difficult to believe in goodness and happiness if the world you live in doesn't offer much support for them. Gentle and realistic, meditation practice can provide the powerful attitudinal boost we need. It doesn't require preexisting faith or excessive effort; simply sitting in silence, returning to the present moment of body and breath, will naturally bring you closer to gratitude, closer to kindness. And as you commit yourself to these virtues, you will begin to notice, to your surprise, that many people in your life are also doing this, so there is plenty of companionship along the way.

What Meditation Isn't

Bhante Gunaratana

*In this encouraging, plain-English reality check, Bhante Gunaratana
reassures us that meditation is simply about developing awareness—
and it doesn't involve hypnosis, supernatural powers, or anything
else otherworldly.*

THE THINKING PROCESS operates by association, and all sorts of
ideas are associated with the word *meditation*. Some are probably
accurate and others, hogwash. Some of them pertain more to other
systems of meditation and have nothing to do with, for example,
vipassana practice. Before we proceed, it behooves us to blast some
of that residue out of our own neuronal circuits so that new information can pass unimpeded. Let us start with some of the most obvious stuff.

We are not going to teach you to conquer demons or harness
invisible energies. There are no colored belts given for your performance, and you don't have to shave your head or wear a turban. You
don't even have to give away all your belongings and move to a
monastery. In fact, unless your life is immoral and chaotic, you can
probably get started right away and make some sort of progress.
Sounds fairly encouraging, wouldn't you say?

Many teachings on the subject of meditation are written from a
point of view which lies squarely within one particular religious or

philosophical tradition. Here we are dealing exclusively with the vipassana system of meditation. The goal is awareness, an awareness so intense, concentrated, and finely tuned that you will be able to pierce the inner workings of reality itself.

There are a number of common misconceptions about meditation. We are going to take these misconceptions one at a time and dissolve them.

Misconception I: Meditation Is Just a Relaxation Technique

The bugaboo here is the word *just*. Relaxation is a key component of meditation, but vipassana-style meditation aims at a much loftier goal. Do it strongly and thoroughly enough, and you achieve a deep and blissful relaxation which is called *jhana*. It is a state of such supreme tranquillity that it amounts to rapture. It is a form of pleasure which lies above and beyond anything that can be experienced in the normal state of consciousness. Most systems stop right there. That is the goal, and when you attain that, you simply repeat the experience for the rest of your life. Not so with vipassana meditation. Vipassana seeks another goal: awareness. Concentration and relaxation are required precursors, handy tools, and beneficial by-products. But they are not the goal. The goal is insight.

Misconception 2: Meditation Means Going into a Trance

Here again the statement could be applied accurately to certain systems of meditation, but not to vipassana. Insight meditation is not a form of hypnosis. You are not trying to black out your mind. If anything, the reverse is true. You will become more and more attuned to your own emotional changes. Through the use of this technique, certain states do occur which may appear trance-like to the observer. But they are really quite the opposite. In hypnotic trance, the subject is susceptible to control by another party, whereas in deep concentration the meditator remains very much under his own control. If you find that you are becoming unconscious in meditation, then you aren't meditating, according to the definition of that word as used in the vipassana system. It is that simple.

Misconception 3: Meditation Is a Mysterious Practice That Cannot Be Understood

Some of the data about meditation just won't fit into words. That does not mean, however, that it cannot be understood. There are deeper ways to understand things than by the use of words. You understand how to walk. You probably can't describe the exact order in which your nerve fibers and your muscles contract during that process. But you can do it. Meditation needs to be understood that same way, by doing it. It is something to be experienced. Meditation is not a mindless formula which gives automatic and predictable results. You can never really predict exactly what will come up during any particular session. It is an adventure every time. In fact, this is so true that when you do reach a feeling of predictability and sameness in your practice, you use that as an indicator. It means that you have gotten off the track somewhere and you are headed for stagnation. Learning to look at each second as if it were the first and only second in the universe is most essential in vipassana meditation.

Misconception 4: The Purpose of Meditation Is to Become a Psychic Superbeing

The purpose of meditation is to develop awareness. Learning to read minds is not the point. Levitation is not the goal. The goal is liberation. There is a link between psychic phenomena and meditation, but the relationship is somewhat complex. During early stages of the meditator's career, such phenomena may or may not arise. Some people may experience some intuitive understanding or memories from past lives; others do not. In any case, these are not regarded as well-developed and reliable psychic abilities. Nor should they be given undue importance. Such phenomena are in fact fairly dangerous to new meditators in that they are quite seductive. They can be an ego trap which can lure you right off the track. Your best approach is not to place any emphasis on these phenomena. If they come up, that's fine. If they don't, that's fine, too. Don't worry about it. Just concentrate on developing more and more awareness. If voices and visions pop up, just notice them and let them go. Don't get involved.

Misconception 5: Meditation Is Dangerous, and a Prudent Person Should Avoid It

Everything is dangerous. Walk across the street and you may get hit by a bus. Take a shower and you could break your neck. Meditate and you will probably dredge up various nasty matters from your past. The suppressed material that has been buried there for quite some time can be scary. It is also highly profitable. Vipassana is development of awareness. That in itself is not dangerous; on the contrary, increased awareness is the safeguard against danger. Take it slow and easy, and the development of your practice will occur very naturally. Nothing should be forced. Later, when you are under the close scrutiny and protective wisdom of a competent teacher, you can accelerate your rate of growth by taking a period of intensive meditation. In the beginning, though, easy does it. Work gently and everything will be fine.

Misconception 6: Meditation Is for Saints and Holy Men, Not for Regular People

You find this attitude very prevalent in Asia, where monks and holy men are accorded an enormous amount of ritualized reverence. Even in the West, we expect the meditator to be some extraordinarily pious figure in whose mouth butter would never dare to melt. A little personal contact with such people will quickly dispel this illusion. They usually prove to be people of enormous energy and gusto, people who live their lives with amazing vigor.

It is true, of course, that most holy men meditate, but they don't meditate because they are holy men. They are holy men because they meditate. And they started meditating before they became holy, otherwise they would not be holy! A sizable number of students seem to feel that a person should be completely moral before he begins meditation. This is an unworkable strategy. You can't follow any set of moral precepts without at least a little self-control, and if your mind is perpetually spinning like a cylinder in a one-armed bandit, self-control is highly unlikely. So mental culture has to come first.

There are three integral factors in Buddhist meditation: morality, concentration, and wisdom. Those three factors grow together as your practice deepens. Each one influences the other, so you cultivate the three of them together, not one at a time. When you have the wisdom to truly understand a situation, compassion toward all the parties involved is automatic, and compassion means that you automatically restrain yourself from any thought, word, or deed that might harm yourself or others. Thus your behavior is automatically moral. It is only when you don't understand things deeply that you create problems. The person who waits to become totally moral before beginning to meditate is waiting for a "but" that will never come.

To understand this relationship more fully, let us propose that there are levels of morality. The lowest level is adherence to a set of rules and regulations laid down by somebody else. It could be a prophet, the state, a parent. No matter who generates the rules, all you've got to do at this level is know and follow them. A robot can do that. This level requires no meditation at all.

The next level of morality consists of obeying the same rules even in the absence of somebody watching over you. You obey because you have internalized the rules. You smack yourself every time you break one. This level requires a bit of mind control. If your thought pattern is chaotic, your behavior will be chaotic, too. Mental cultivation reduces mental chaos.

There is a third level of morality, but it might be better termed ethics. This is a leap up the scale, a real paradigm shift in orienta-

tion. At the level of ethics, a person does not follow hard-and-fast
rules dictated by authority. A person chooses to follow a path dictated by mindfulness, wisdom, and compassion. This level requires
real intelligence and an ability to juggle all the factors in every situation to arrive at a unique, creative, and appropriate response each
time. Furthermore, the individual making these decisions needs to
have dug himself out of his own limited personal viewpoint. He has
to see the entire situation from an objective point of view, giving
equal weight to his own needs and those of others. In other words,
he has to be free from greed, hatred, envy, and all the other selfish
junk that ordinarily keeps us from seeing the other guy's side of the
issue. Only then can he choose that precise set of actions which will
be truly optimal for that situation. This level of morality absolutely
demands meditation, unless you were born a saint. There is no
other way to acquire the skill. Furthermore, the sorting process required at this level is exhausting. If you tried to juggle all those factors in every situation with your conscious mind, you'd wear
yourself out. The intellect just can't keep that many balls in the air
at once. It is an overload. Luckily, a deeper level of consciousness
can do this sort of processing with ease. Meditation can accomplish
the sorting process for you.

One day you've got a problem—let's say, to handle Uncle Herman's latest divorce. It looks absolutely unsolvable, an enormous
muddle of maybes that would give King Solomon himself a head-
ache. The next day you are washing the dishes, thinking about
something else entirely, and suddenly the solution is there. It just
pops out of the deep mind and you say, "Aha!" and the whole thing
is solved. This sort of intuition can only occur when you disengage
the logic circuits from the problem and give the deep mind the opportunity to cook up the solution. The conscious mind gets in the
way. Meditation teaches the mental art of stepping out of your own
way, and that's a pretty useful skill in everyday life.

Unfortunately, certain students enter the practice expecting instantaneous cosmic revelation, complete with angelic choirs. What
they usually get is a more efficient way to take out the trash and

better ways to deal with Uncle Herman. They are needlessly disappointed. The trash solution comes first. The voices of archangels take a bit longer.

Misconception 7:   Meditation Is Running Away from Reality

Meditation is running straight into reality. It allows you to delve so deeply into life and all its aspects that you pierce the pain barrier and go beyond suffering. It allows you to blow aside the illusions and free yourself from all those polite little lies you tell yourself all the time. Meditation is not an attempt to forget yourself or to cover up your troubles. It is learning to look at yourself exactly as you are to see what is there and accept it fully. Only then can you change it.

Misconception 8:   Meditation Is a Great Way to Get High

Meditation does produce lovely blissful feelings sometimes. But they are not the purpose, and they don't always occur. Furthermore, if you practice meditation with that purpose in mind, they are less likely to occur than if you just meditate for the actual purpose of meditation, which is increased awareness. Bliss results from relaxation, and relaxation results from release of tension. Seeking bliss from meditation introduces tension into the process, which blows the whole chain of events. Still, it is a very pleasant side effect, and it becomes more frequent the longer you meditate. You won't hear any disagreement about this from advanced practitioners.

Misconception 9:   Meditation Is Selfish

It certainly looks that way. There sits the meditator parked on her little cushion. Is she out giving blood? No. Is she busy working with disaster victims? No. Why is she doing this? She is actively engaged in the process of getting rid of greed, tension, and insensitivity. Those are the very items which obstruct her compassion for others. Until they are gone, any good works that she does are likely to be just an extension of her own ego and of no real help in the long run. Cleansing yourself of selfishness is not a selfish activity.

Misconception 10: When You Meditate, You Sit Around Thinking Lofty Thoughts

Of course, such thoughts may arise during your practice. They are certainly not to be avoided. Neither are they to be sought. They are just pleasant side effects. Vipassana is seeing your life unfold from moment to moment without biases. What comes up, comes up. It is very simple.

Misconception 11: A Couple of Weeks of Meditation and All My Problems Will Go Away

Sorry, meditation is not a quick cure-all. You will start seeing changes right away, but really profound effects are years down the line. Nothing worthwhile is achieved overnight.

Meditation is tough in some respects. It requires long discipline and sometimes a painful process of practice. At each sitting you gain some results, but those results are often very subtle. They occur deep within the mind, and only manifest much later. And if you are sitting there constantly looking for some huge instantaneous changes, you will miss the subtle shifts altogether. You will get discouraged, give up, and swear that no such changes will ever occur. Patience is the key. Patience. If you learn nothing else from meditation, you will learn patience, and patience is essential for any profound change.

Dedicating Your Practice

Sharon Salzberg

For many Buddhist meditators, the benefits and aspirations associated with practice are concisely addressed in dedications, which are often recited internally or aloud at the end of a meditation session. The meditation teacher Sharon Salzberg explains the purpose of dedication and offers a simple example. Its universally applicable, nonreligious wording makes it suitable for anyone who might be joining you.

As you come to the close of your practice session, feel the pleasure that comes from caring for yourself, paying attention, taking risks, and being willing to begin again. To do so isn't conceited or vain; you're experiencing the joy of making healthy choices.

And because the inner work we do is never for ourselves alone, make a point of offering the positive energy you generate in your practice to those who have helped you. Maybe it is someone who took care of things at home so you'd have more free time or someone who has been encouraging you in your practice. You can offer the energy, the positive force, the sense of possibility you've been generating to this person, so that the work you do within is for them as well. *May my practice be dedicated to your well-being.*

Maybe someone you know is hurting. The greater awareness, sensitivity, love, and kindness you're developing can be dedicated to their happiness as well. Or think of your family and the greater community. Every step we take toward peace and understanding affects everyone around us.

At the end of your meditation, say to yourself, *May the actions I take toward the good, toward understanding myself, toward being more peaceful, be of benefit to all beings everywhere.*

And when you feel ready, you can open your eyes.

Finding Your "Breathing Room": How to Create a Meditation Space

Thich Nhat Hanh

It doesn't need to be ornate, but arranging a dedicated place for your practice can make a difference. Zen master Thich Nhat Hanh explains the benefits of having a breathing room.

YOUR BREATHING ROOM is a sacred place. You don't need any furniture, maybe just a cushion or two, and perhaps an altar or a table with fresh flowers. If you want, you can have a bell to help you with the practice of stopping and mindful breathing.

Think about the setup of this room or corner carefully. How much we enjoy being in a certain place very much depends on the energy that is generated within it. A room can be well decorated but feel cold and unfriendly; another can lack color and furniture but can feel simple, spacious, and comfortable. If you live with other people, you should design and decorate this space together, perhaps with flowers, pebbles, or photographs. Don't put a lot in this area. The most important elements are a place to sit and a feeling of peace.

There needs to be an agreement in advance that everyone respects the breathing area. Once you're in it, no one can shout at you anymore. You have immunity. When you hear members of your family in the breathing room, you can support them by lowering your own voice, or you might want to join them. If you're very upset, you can restore your clarity by going to the breathing room.

When you feel uneasy, sad, or angry, you can go into the breathing room, close the door, sit down, invite the sound of the bell—in the Zen tradition, we don't say that we ring or strike the bell, instead we "invite" the bell with the "inviter" (usually a wooden stick)—and practice breathing mindfully. When you breathe like this for ten or fifteen minutes, you begin to feel better. Without such a room, you may not allow yourself to take a break, even in your own home. You may be restless, angry with others, or sad. If you spend even a few minutes in your breathing room, you can ease your suffering and better understand the source of your discomfort.

Whenever they need to, anyone in the household can go into the breathing room, invite the bell, and sit. This will help everyone in the house remember to breathe and to return to themselves.

If you live alone, you still need to have a breathing room. Otherwise, you'll have no separate place which facilitates coming home to yourself, and the house will be filled with your restlessness.

If you have a breathing room, you have a sanctuary, a place you can always go in your home to return to yourself and restore your sense of peace.

What's What

Ajahn Chah

The beginning meditator needs to let go of thinking and maintain relaxed attention on the breath, says Ajahn Chah. When the mind has been stabilized by mindfulness and self-awareness, supported by generosity, moral restraint, and loving-kindness, wisdom can arise.

WHY DO YOU PRACTICE MEDITATION? It is because your heart and mind do not understand what should be understood. In other words, you don't truly know how things are, or what is what. You don't know what is wrong and what is right, what it is that brings you suffering and causes you to doubt. The reason that you have come to want to develop calm and restraint is that your heart and mind are not at ease. They are swayed by doubting and agitation.

Although there may appear to be many ways to practice, really there is only one. As with fruit trees, it is possible to get fruit quickly by planting a cutting, but the tree will not be resilient and hardy. Another way is to cultivate a tree right from the seed, which produces a strong and resilient tree. Practice is the same.

When I first began to practice, I had problems understanding this. As long as I still didn't know what's what, sitting meditation was a real chore, even bringing me to tears on occasion. Sometimes I would be aiming too high, at other times not high enough, never finding the point of balance. To practice in a way that's peaceful means to place the mind neither too high nor too low, but at the point of balance.

Practicing in different ways with different teachers can be very confusing. One teacher says you must practice one way; another says you should practice another way. You wonder which method to use, unsure of the essence of the practice. The result is confusion, doubt, and uncertainty. Nobody knows how to harmonize their practice.

So you must try not to think too much. If you do think, then do so with awareness. First, you must make your mind calm. Where there is knowing, there is no need to think. Awareness will arise in its place, and this will in turn become wisdom. The ordinary kind of thinking is not wisdom, but simply the aimless and unaware wandering of the mind, which inevitably results in agitation.

So at this stage you don't need to think. It just stirs up the heart. Obsessive thinking can even bring you to tears. The Buddha was a very wise person: he learned how to stop thinking. To meditate, you have to resolve that now is the time for training the mind and nothing else. Don't let the mind shoot off to the left or to the right, to the front or behind, above or below. At that time our only duty is to practice mindfulness of breathing. Fix your attention at the crown of the head and move it down through the body to the tips of the feet, and then back up to the head. Pass your awareness down through the body, observing with wisdom. We do this to gain an initial understanding of the way the body is. Then begin the meditation, remembering that your sole duty is to observe the inhalations and exhalations. Don't force the breath to be any longer or shorter than normal, just allow it to continue easily. Let it flow evenly, letting go with each in-breath and out-breath.

Although you are letting go, there should still be awareness. You must maintain this awareness, allowing the breath to enter and leave comfortably. Maintain the resolve that at this time you have no other duties or responsibilities. Thoughts about what will happen or what you will see during a meditation may arise from time to time, but once they arise just let them cease by themselves; don't be unduly concerned with them.

During the meditation there is no need to pay attention to sense impressions. Whenever the mind is affected by sense contact, wherever there is a feeling or sensation in the mind, just let it go. Whether those sensations are good or bad is unimportant. Don't make something out of those sensations; just let them pass away and return your attention to the breath. Maintain the awareness of the breath entering and leaving. Don't create suffering over the breath being too long or too short, but simply observe it without trying to control or suppress it in any way. In other words, don't attach. As you continue, the mind will gradually lay things down and come to rest, the breath becoming lighter and lighter until it becomes so faint that it seems like it's not there at all. Both the body and the mind will feel light and energized. All that will remain will be a one-pointed knowing. The mind has reached a state of calm.

If the mind is agitated, set up mindfulness and inhale deeply till there is no space left for more air, then release it all completely until none remains. Follow this with another deep inhalation and exhalation. Do this two or three times, then reestablish concentration. The mind should be calmer. Each time sense impressions agitate the mind, repeat the process. It is similar with walking meditation. If, while walking, the mind becomes agitated, stop, calm the mind, reestablish the awareness with the meditation object, and then continue walking. Sitting and walking meditation are in essence the same, differing only in terms of the physical posture used.

Sometimes there may be doubt, so you must have *sati* (mindfulness; recollection). Be one who knows, who continually follows and examines the agitated mind in whatever form it takes. This is to have sati. Sati watches over and takes care of the mind. You must maintain this knowing and not be careless or wander astray, no matter what condition the mind takes on.

The trick is to have sati take control and supervise the mind. Once the mind is unified with sati, a new kind of awareness will emerge. The mind that has developed calm is held in check by that calm, just like a chicken held in a coop: The chicken is unable to wander outside, but it can still move around within the coop. Its walking to and fro doesn't get it into trouble because it is restrained by the coop. Likewise the awareness that takes place when the mind has sati and is calm does not cause trouble. None of the thinking or sensations that take place within the calm mind cause harm or disturbance.

Some people don't want to experience any thoughts or feelings at all, but this is going too far. Feelings arise within the state of calm. The mind is experiencing feelings and calm at the same time, without being disturbed. When there is calm like this, there are no harmful consequences. Problems occur when the chicken gets out of the coop. For instance, you may be watching the breath entering and leaving and then forget yourself, allowing the mind to wander away from the breath, back home, off to the shops, or to any number of different places. Perhaps even half an hour may pass before you suddenly realize you're supposed to be practicing meditation and reprimand yourself for your lack of sati. This is where you have to be really careful, because this is where the chicken gets out of the coop—the mind leaves its base of calm.

You must take care to maintain the awareness with sati and try to pull the mind back. Although I use the words "pull the mind back," in fact the mind doesn't really go anywhere; only the object of awareness has changed. You must make the mind stay right here and now. As long as there is sati there will be presence of mind. It seems like you are pulling the mind back, but really it hasn't gone anywhere; it has simply changed a little. When sati is regained, in a flash you are back with the mind, without it having to be brought from anywhere.

When there is total knowing, a continuous and unbroken awareness at each and every moment, this is called presence of mind. If your attention drifts from the breath to other places, then the knowing is broken. Whenever there is awareness of the breath, the mind is there.

There must be both sati and *sampajañña*. Sati is mindfulness and sampajañña is self-awareness. Right now you are clearly aware of the breath. This exercise of watching the breath helps sati and sampajañña develop together. They share the work. Having both sati and sampajañña is like having two workers to lift a heavy plank of wood. Suppose these two workers try to lift some heavy planks, but the weight is so great it's almost unendurable. Then a third worker, imbued with goodwill, sees them and rushes in to help. In the same way, when there is sati and sampajañña, then *paññā* (wisdom) will arise at the same place to help out. Then all three of them support one another.

With paññā there will be an understanding of sense objects. For instance, during meditation you may start to think of a friend, but then should immediately counter with "It doesn't matter," "Stop," or "Forget it." Or if there are thoughts about where you will go tomorrow, then the response of paññā will be, "I'm not interested, I don't want to concern myself with such things." If you start thinking about other people, you should think, "No, I don't want to get involved," "Just let go," or "It's all uncertain." This is how you should deal with sense objects in meditation, recognizing them as "not sure, not sure," and maintaining this kind of awareness.

You must give up all the thinking, the inner dialogue, and the doubting. Don't get caught up in these things during the meditation. In the end all that will remain in the mind in its purest form are sati, sampajañña, and paññā. Whenever these weaken, doubts will arise, but try to abandon those doubts immediately, leaving only sati, sampajañña, and paññā. Try to develop sati like this until it can be maintained at all times. Then you will understand sati, sampajañña, and paññā thoroughly.

Focusing the attention at this point you will see sati, sampajañña, *samadhi* (mental concentration), and paññā together. Whether you are attracted to or repelled by external sense objects, you will be able to tell yourself, "It's not sure." Either way they are just hindrances to be swept away till the mind is clean. All that should remain is sati, mindfulness; sampajañña, clear awareness; samadhi, the firm and unwavering mind; and pañña, or consummate wisdom.

Now about the tools or aids to meditation practice—there should be *metta* (goodwill) in your heart; in other words, the qualities of generosity, kindness, and helpfulness. These should be maintained as the foundation for mental purity. For example, begin doing away with *lobha*, or greed, through giving. When people are selfish they aren't happy. Selfishness leads to a sense of discontent, and yet people tend to be very selfish without realizing how it affects them.

You can experience this at any time, especially when you are hungry. Suppose you get some apples and you have the opportunity to share them with a friend; you think it over for a while, and, sure, the intention to give is there all right, but you want to give the smaller one. To give the big one would be . . . well, such a shame. It's hard to think straight. You tell them to go ahead and pick one, but then you say, "Take this one!" and give them the smaller apple! This is a form of selfishness that people usually don't notice.

You really have to go against the grain to give. Even though you may really only want to give the smaller apple, you must force yourself to give away the bigger one. Of course, once you have given it to your friend you feel good inside. Training the mind by going against the grain requires self-discipline—you must know how to give and how to give up, not allowing selfishness to stick. Once you learn how to give to others, your mind will be joyful. If you hesitate over which fruit to give, then while you deliberate you will be troubled, and even if you give a bigger one, there will still be a sense of reluctance. But as soon as you firmly decide to give the bigger one, the matter is over and done with. This is going against the grain in the right way.

Doing this, you win mastery over yourself. If you can't do it, you'll be a victim of yourself and continue to be selfish. All of us have been selfish—it's a defilement that has to be cut off. In the Pali scriptures, giving is called *dana*, which results in happiness for others and helps to cleanse the mind of defilement. You should reflect on this and develop it in your practice.

You may think that practicing like this involves hounding yourself, but it doesn't really. Actually it's hounding craving and the defilements. If defilements arise within you, you have to do something to remedy them. Defilements are like a stray cat. If you give it as much food as it wants, it will always be coming around looking for more; but if you stop feeding it, after a couple of days it'll stop coming around. It's the same with the defilements. If you stop feeding them, they won't come to disturb you; they'll leave your mind in peace. So rather than being afraid of defilements, make them afraid of you. You do that by seeing the dhamma within your mind.

Where does the dhamma arise? It arises with our knowing and understanding in this way. Everyone is able to know and understand the dhamma. It's not something that has to be researched in books or studied a lot. Just reflect right now, and you can see what I am talking about. Everybody has defilements, don't they? In the past you've pampered your defilements, but now you must know their nature and not allow them to bother you.

The next constituent of practice is moral restraint (*sila*). Sila watches over and nurtures the practice in the same way as parents look after their children. Maintaining moral restraint means not only to avoid harming others but also to help and encourage them. At the very least you should maintain the five precepts, which are:

1. Not only not killing or deliberately harming others, but also spreading goodwill toward all beings.

2. Being honest, refraining from infringing on the rights of others—in other words, not stealing.

3. Knowing moderation in sexual relations. A husband or wife should know each other's disposition, needs, and wishes, observe moderation, and know the proper bounds of sexual activity. Some people don't know the limits. Having a husband or wife isn't enough; they have to have a second or third

partner. The way I see it, you can't consume even one partner completely, so to have two or three is just plain indulgence. You must try to cleanse the mind and train it to know moderation. Knowing moderation is true purity. Without it there are no limits to your behavior. When eating delicious food don't dwell too much on how it tastes; think of your stomach and consider how much is appropriate to its needs. If you eat too much, there'll be trouble. Moderation is the best way. Just one partner is enough. Two or three is an indulgence and will only cause problems.

4. Being honest in speech. This is also a tool for eradicating defilements. You must be honest and straight, truthful and upright.

5. Refraining from taking intoxicants. You must know restraint and preferably give these things up altogether. People are already intoxicated enough with their families, relatives and friends, material possessions, wealth, and all the rest of it. That's quite enough already without making things worse by taking intoxicants as well. These things just create darkness in the mind. Those who take large amounts should try to gradually cut down and eventually give it up altogether. You need to know what is what. What are the things that are oppressing you in your everyday lives? What are the actions that cause this oppression? Good actions bring good results and bad actions bring bad results. These are the causes.

Once moral restraint is pure there will be a sense of honesty and kindness toward others. This will bring about contentment and freedom from worries and remorse. Freedom from remorse is a form of happiness. It's almost like a heavenly state. You eat and sleep in comfort with the happiness arising from moral restraint. This is a principle of dhamma practice—refraining from bad actions so that goodness can arise. If moral restraint is maintained in this way, evil will disappear and good will arise in its place.

But this isn't the end of the story. Once people have attained some happiness they tend to be heedless and not go any further in the practice. They get stuck on happiness. They don't want to progress any further; they prefer the happiness of "heaven." It's comfortable, but there's no real understanding. You must keep reflecting to avoid being deluded. Reflect again and again on the disadvantages of this happiness. It's transient; it doesn't last forever. Soon you are separated from it. It's not a sure thing. Once happiness disappears, suffering arises in its place and the tears come again. Even heavenly beings end up crying and suffering.

So the Buddha taught us that there is an unsatisfactory side to happiness. Usually when this kind of happiness is experienced, there is no real understanding of it. The peace that is truly certain and lasting is masked by this deceptive happiness. This happiness is a refined form of defilement to which we attach. Everybody likes to be happy. Happiness arises because of our liking for something. But as soon as that liking changes to dislike, suffering arises. We must reflect on this happiness to see its uncertainty and limitation. Once things change, suffering arises. This suffering is also uncertain; don't think that it is fixed or absolute. This kind of reflection is called *adinavakatha*, or reflection on the inadequacy and limitation of the conditioned world. This means to reflect on happiness rather than accepting it at face value. Seeing that it is uncertain, you shouldn't cling fast to it. You should take hold of it but then let it go, seeing both the benefit and the harm of happiness.

When you see that things are imperfect, your heart will come to understand *nekkhammakatha*, or reflection on renunciation. The mind will become disenchanted and seek for a way out. Disenchantment comes from having seen the way forms really are, the way tastes really are, the way love and hatred really are. By disenchantment we mean that there is no longer the desire to cling to or attach to things. There is a withdrawal from clinging, to a point where you can abide comfortably, observing with an equanimity that is free of attachment. This is the peace that arises from practice.

The Four Foundations
of Mindfulness

Chögyam Trungpa Rinpoche

According to the late Chögyam Trungpa Rinpoche, spirituality means relating with the working basis of one's existence, which is one's state of mind. The method for beginning to relate directly with mind is the practice of mindfulness.

FOR THE FOLLOWER of the buddhadharma, the teachings of Buddhism, there is a need for great emphasis on the practice of meditation. One must see the straightforward logic that mind is the cause of confusion and that by transcending confusion one attains the enlightened state. This can only take place through the practice of meditation. The Buddha himself experienced this, by working on his own mind, and what he learned has been handed down to us.

Mindfulness is a basic approach to the spiritual journey that is common to all traditions of Buddhism. But before we begin to look closely at that approach, we should have some idea of what is meant by spirituality itself.

Some say that spirituality is a way of attaining a better kind of happiness, transcendental happiness. Others see it as a benevolent way to develop power over others. Still others say the point of spirituality is to acquire magical powers so we can change our bad world into a good world or purify the world through miracles. It seems that all of these points of view are irrelevant to the Buddhist approach. According to the buddhadharma, spirituality means relating with the working basis of one's existence, which is one's state of mind.

There is a problem with one's basic life, one's basic being. This problem is that we are involved in a continual struggle to survive, to maintain our position. We are continually trying to grasp on to some solid image of ourselves. And then we have to defend that particular fixed conception. So there is warfare, there is confusion, and there is passion and aggression; there are all kinds of conflicts. From the Buddhist point of view, the development of true spirituality is cutting through our basic fixation, that clinging, that stronghold of something-or-other, which is known as ego.

In order to do that we have to find out what ego is. What is this all about? Who are we? We have to look into our already existing state of mind. And we have to understand what practical step we can take to do that. We are not involved here in a metaphysical discussion about the purpose of life and the meaning of spirituality on an abstract level. We are looking at this question from the point of view of a working situation. We need to find some simple thing we can do in order to embark on the spiritual path.

People have difficulty beginning a spiritual practice because they put a lot of energy into looking for the best and easiest way to get into it. We might have to change our attitude and give up looking for the best or the easiest way. Actually, there is no choice. Whatever approach we take, we will have to deal with what we are already. We have to look at who we are. According to the Buddhist tradition, the working basis of the path and the energy involved in the path is the mind—one's own mind, which is working in us all the time.

Spirituality is based on mind. In Buddhism, mind is what distinguishes sentient beings from rocks or trees or bodies of water. That which possesses discriminating awareness, that which possesses a sense of duality—which grasps or rejects something external—that is mind. Fundamentally, it is that which can associate with an "other"—with any "something" that is perceived as different from the perceiver. That is the definition of mind. The traditional Tibetan phrase defining mind means precisely that: "That which can think of the other, the projection, is mind."

So by mind we mean something very specific. It is not just something very vague and creepy inside our heads or hearts, something that just happens as part of the way the wind blows and the grass grows. Rather, it is something very concrete. It contains perception—perception that is very uncomplicated, very basic, very precise. Mind develops its particular nature as that perception begins to linger on something other than oneself. Mind makes the fact of perceiving something else stand for the existence of oneself.

That is the mental trick that constitutes mind. In fact, it should be the opposite. Since the perception starts from oneself, the logic should be: "I exist, therefore the other exists." But somehow the hypocrisy of mind is developed to such an extent that mind lingers on the other as a way of getting the feedback that it itself exists, which is a fundamentally erroneous belief. It is the fact that the existence of self is questionable that motivates the trick of duality.

This mind is our working basis for the practice of meditation and the development of awareness. But mind is something more than the process of confirming self by the dualistic lingering on the other. Mind also includes what are known as emotions, which are the highlights of mental states.

Mind cannot exist without emotions. Daydreaming and discursive thoughts are not enough. Those alone would be too boring. The dualistic trick would wear too thin. So we tend to create waves of emotion which go up and down: passion, aggression, ignorance, pride—all kinds of emotions. In the beginning we create them deliberately, as a game of trying to prove to ourselves that we exist. But eventually the game becomes a hassle; it becomes more than a game and forces us to challenge ourselves more than we intended.

So we have created a world that is bittersweet. Things are amusing but, at the same time, not so amusing. Sometimes things seem terribly funny but, on the other hand, terribly sad. Life has the quality of a game of ours that has trapped us. The setup of mind has created the whole thing. We might complain about the government or the economy of the country or the prime rate of interest, but those factors are secondary. The original process at the root of the problems is the competitiveness of seeing oneself only as a reflection of the other. Problematic situations arise automatically as expressions of that. They are our own production, our own neat work. And that is what is called mind.

According to the Buddhist tradition, there are eight types of consciousness and fifty-two types of conceptions and all kinds of other aspects of mind, about which we do not have to go into detail. All these aspects are based largely on the primeval dualistic approach. There are the spiritual aspects and the psychological aspects and all sorts of other aspects. All are bound up in the realm of duality, which is ego.

As far as meditation practice is concerned, in meditation we work on this thing, rather than on trying to sort out the problem from the outside. We work on the projector rather than the projection. We turn inward, instead of trying to sort out external problems of A, B, and C. We work on the creator of duality rather than the creation. That is beginning at the beginning.

A gigantic world of mind exists to which we are almost totally unexposed. This whole world is made by mind. Minds made this up, put these things together. Every bolt and nut was put in by somebody-or-other's mind. This whole world is mind's world, the product of mind. This is needless to say; I am sure everybody knows this. But we might remind ourselves of it so that we realize that meditation is not an exclusive activity that involves forgetting this world and getting into something else. By meditating, we are dealing with the very mind that devised our eyeglasses and put the lenses in the rims.

So this is a living world, mind's world. When we realize this, working with mind is no longer a remote or mysterious thing to do. It is no longer dealing with something that is hidden or somewhere else. Mind is right here. Mind is hanging out in the world. It is an open secret.

The method for beginning to relate directly with mind, which was taught by Lord Buddha and which has been in use for the past 2,500 years, is the practice of mindfulness. There are four aspects to this practice, traditionally known as the four foundations of mindfulness.

Mindfulness of Body

Mindfulness of body, the first foundation of mindfulness, is connected with the need for a sense of being, a sense of groundedness.

To begin with, there is some problem about what we understand by body. We sit on chairs or on the ground; we eat; we sleep; we wear clothes. But the body we relate with in going through these activities is questionable.

According to the tradition, the body we think we have is what is known as psychosomatic body. It is largely based on projections and concepts of body. This psychosomatic body contrasts with the enlightened person's sense of body, which might be called body-body. This sense of body is free from conceptualizations. It is just simple and straightforward. There is a direct relationship with the earth.

As for us, we do not actually have a relationship with the earth. We have some relationship with the body, but it is very uncertain and erratic. We flicker back and forth between body and something else—fantasies, ideas. That seems to be our basic situation. Even though the psychosomatic body is constituted by projections of body, it can be quite solid in terms of those projections. We have expectations concerning the existence of this body; therefore we have to refuel it, entertain it, wash it. Through this psychosomatic body we are able to experience a sense of being.

Mindfulness of body brings this all-pervasive mind-imitating-body activity into the practice of meditation. The practice of meditation has to take into account that mind continually shapes itself into body-like attitudes. Consequently, since the time of the Buddha, sitting meditation has been recommended and practiced, and it has proved to be the best way of dealing with this situation. The basic technique that goes with sitting meditation is working with the breath. You identify with the breath, particularly with the out-breath. The in-breath is just a gap, a space. During the in-breath you just wait. So you breathe out and then you dissolve and then there is a gap. Breathe out . . . dissolve . . . gap. An openness, an expansion, can take place constantly that way.

Mindfulness plays a very important role in this technique. In this case, mindfulness means that when you sit and meditate, you actually do sit. You actually do sit as far as the psychosomatic body is concerned. You feel the ground, body, breath, temperature. You don't try specifically to watch and keep track of what is going on. You don't try to formalize the sitting situation and make it into some special activity that you are performing. You just sit.

And then you begin to feel that there is some sense of groundedness. This is not particularly a product of being deliberate, but it is more the force of the actual fact of being there. So you sit. And you sit. And you breathe. And you sit and you breathe. Sometimes you think, but still you are thinking sitting thoughts. The psychosomatic body is sitting, so your thoughts have a flat bottom. Mindfulness of body is connected with the earth. It is an openness that has a base, a foundation. A quality of expansive awareness develops through mindfulness of body—a sense of being settled and of therefore being able to afford to open out.

Going along with this mindfulness requires a great deal of trust. Probably the beginning meditator will not be able simply to rest there, but will feel the need for a change. I remember someone who had just finished a retreat telling me how she had sat and felt her body and felt grounded. But then she had thought immediately how she should be doing something else. And she went on to tell me how the right book had "just jumped" into her lap, and she had started to read. At that point one doesn't have a solid base anymore. One's mind is beginning to grow little wings. Mindfulness of body has to do with trying to remain human, rather than becoming an animal or fly or etheric being. It means just trying to remain a human being, an ordinary human being.

The basic starting point for this is solidness, groundedness. When you sit, you actually sit. Even your floating thoughts begin to sit on their own bottoms. There are no particular problems. You have a sense of solidness and groundedness, and, at the same time, a sense of being.

Without this particular foundation of mindfulness, the rest of your meditation practice could be very airy-fairy—vacillating back and forth, trying this and trying that. You could be constantly tiptoeing on the surface of the universe, not actually getting a foothold anywhere. You could become an eternal hitchhiker. So with this first technique you develop some basic solidness. In mindfulness of body, there is a sense of finding some home ground.

Mindfulness of Life

The application of mindfulness has to be precise. If we cling to our practice, we create stagnation. Therefore, in our application of the techniques of mindfulness, we must be aware of the fundamental tendency to cling, to survive.

We come to this in the second foundation of mindfulness, which is mindfulness of life, or survival. Since we are dealing with the context of meditation, we encounter this tendency in the form of clinging to the meditative state. We experience the meditative state and it is momentarily tangible, but in that same moment it is also dissolving. Going along with this process means developing a sense of letting go of awareness as well as of contacting it. This basic technique of the second foundation of mindfulness could be described as touch-and-go. You are there—present, mindful—and then you let go.

A common misunderstanding is that the meditative state of mind has to be captured and then nursed and cherished. That is definitely the wrong approach. If you try to domesticate your mind through meditation—try to possess it by holding on to the meditative state—the clear result will be regression on the path, with a loss of freshness and spontaneity. If you try to hold on without lapse all the time, then maintaining your awareness will begin to become a domestic hassle. It will become like painfully going through housework. There will be an underlying sense of resentment, and the practice of meditation will become confusing. You will begin to develop a love-hate relationship toward your practice, in which your concept of it seems good, but, at the same time, the demand this rigid concept makes on you is too painful.

So the technique of the mindfulness of life is based on touch-and-go. You focus your attention on the object of awareness, but then, in the same moment, you disown that awareness and go on. What is needed here is some sense of confidence—confidence that you do not have to securely own your mind, but that you can tune in to its process spontaneously.

Mindfulness of life relates to the clinging tendency not only in connection with the meditative state, but, even more important, in connection with the level of raw anxiety about survival that manifests in us constantly, second by second, minute by minute. You breathe for survival; you lead your life for survival. The feeling is constantly present that you are trying to protect yourself from death.

For the practical purposes of the second foundation, instead of regarding this survival mentality as something negative, instead of relating to it as ego-clinging as is done in the abstract philosophical overview of Buddhism, this particular practice switches logic around. In the second foundation, the survival struggle is regarded as a stepping-stone in the practice of meditation. Whenever you have the sense of the survival instinct functioning, that can be transmuted into a sense of being, a sense of having already survived. Mindfulness becomes a basic acknowledgment of existing. This does not have the flavor of "Thank God, I have survived." Instead, it is more objective, impartial: "I am alive, I am here, so be it."

In this way, meditation becomes an actual part of life, rather than just a practice or exercise. It becomes inseparable from the instinct to live that accompanies all one's existence. That instinct to live can be seen as containing awareness, meditation, mindfulness. It constantly tunes us in to what is happening. So the life force that keeps us alive and that manifests itself continually in our stream of consciousness itself becomes the practice of mindfulness.

Such mindfulness brings clarity, skill, and intelligence. You are here; you are living; let it be that way—that is mindfulness. Your heart pulsates and you breathe. All kinds of things are happening in you at once. Let mindfulness work with that, let that be mindfulness, let every beat of your heart, every breath, be mindfulness itself. You do not have to breathe specially; your breath is an expression of mindfulness. If you approach meditation in this way, it becomes very personal and very direct.

But again it is necessary to say, once you have that experience of the presence of life, don't hang on to it. Just touch and go. Touch that presence of life being lived, then go. You do not have to ignore it. "Go" does not mean that we have to turn our backs on the experience and shut ourselves off from it; it means just being in it without further analysis and without further reinforcement.

Holding on to life, or trying to reassure oneself that it is so, has the sense of death rather than life. It is only because we have that sense of death that we want to make sure that we are alive. We would like to have an insurance policy. But if we feel that we are alive, that is good enough. We do not have to make sure that we actually do breathe, that we actually can be seen. We do not have to check to be sure we have a shadow. Just living is enough. If we don't stop to reassure ourselves, living becomes very clear-cut, very alive, and very precise.

Mindfulness of Effort

The next foundation of mindfulness is mindfulness of effort. The idea of effort is apparently problematical. Effort would seem to be at odds with the sense of being that arises from mindfulness of body.

Also, pushing of any kind does not have an obvious place in the touch-and-go technique of the mindfulness of life.

In either case, deliberate, heavy-handed effort would seem to endanger the open precision of the process of mindfulness. Still we cannot expect proper mindfulness to develop without some kind of exertion on our part. Effort is necessary. But the Buddhist notion of right effort is quite different from conventional definitions of effort.

The traditional Buddhist analogy for right effort is the walk of an elephant or tortoise. The elephant moves along surely, unstoppably, with great dignity. Like the worm, it is not excitable, but unlike the worm, it has a panoramic view of the ground it is treading on. Though it is serious and slow, because of the elephant's ability to survey the ground there is a sense of playfulness and intelligence in its movement.

In the case of meditation, trying to develop an inspiration that is based on wanting to forget one's pain and on trying to make one's practice thrive on a sense of continual accomplishment is quite immature. On the other hand, too much solemnity and dutifulness creates a lifeless and narrow outlook and a stale psychological environment. The style of right effort, as taught by the Buddha, is serious but not too serious. It takes advantage of the natural flow of instinct to bring the wandering mind constantly back to the mindfulness of breathing.

The crucial point in the bringing-back process is that it is not necessary to go through deliberate stages. It is not a question of forcing the mind back to some particular object, but of bringing it back down from the dream world into reality. We are breathing, we are sitting. That is what we are doing, and we should be doing it completely, fully, wholeheartedly.

There is a kind of technique, or trick, here that is extremely effective and useful, not only for sitting meditation, but also in daily life, or meditation-in-action. The way of coming back is through what we might call the abstract watcher. This watcher is just simple self-consciousness, without aim or goal.

When we encounter anything, the first flash that takes place is the bare sense of duality, of separateness. On that basis, we begin to evaluate, pick and choose, make decisions, execute our will. The abstract watcher is just the basic sense of separateness—the plain cognition of being there before any of the rest develops.

Instead of condemning this self-consciousness as dualistic, we take advantage of this tendency in our psychological system and use it as the basis of the mindfulness of effort. The experience is just a sudden flash of the watcher's being there. At that point we don't think, "I must get back to the breath" or "I must try and get away from these thoughts." We don't have to entertain a deliberate and logical movement of mind that repeats to itself the purpose of sitting practice. There is just suddenly a general sense that something is happening here and now, and we are brought back. Abruptly, immediately, without a name, without the application of any kind of concept, we have a quick glimpse of changing the tone. That is the core of the mindfulness of effort practice.

One of the reasons that ordinary effort becomes so dreary and stagnant is that our intention always develops a verbalization. Any kind of sense of duty we might have is always verbalized, though the speed of conceptual mind is so great that we may not even notice the verbalization. Still, the contents of the verbalization are clearly felt. This verbalization pins the effort to a fixed frame of reference, which makes it extremely tiresome.

In contrast, the abstract effort we are talking about flashes in a fraction of a second, without any name or any idea with it. It is just a jerk, a sudden change of course which does not define its destination. The rest of the effort is just like an elephant's walk—going slowly, step by step, observing the situation around us.

You could call this abstract self-consciousness leap if you like, or jerk, or sudden reminder; or you could call it amazement. Sometimes it could also be felt as panic, unconditioned panic, because of the change of course—something comes to us and changes our whole course. If we work with this sudden jerk, and do so with no effort in the effort, then effort becomes self-existing. It stands on its own two feet, so to speak, rather than needing another effort to trigger it off.

This kind of effort is extremely important. The sudden flash is a key to all Buddhist meditation, from the level of basic mindfulness to the highest levels of tantra. Such mindfulness of effort could definitely be considered the most important aspect of mindfulness practice. Mindfulness of body creates the general setting; it brings meditation into the psychosomatic setup of one's life. Mindfulness of life makes meditation practice personal and intimate. Mindfulness of effort makes meditation workable: it connects the foundations of mindfulness to the path, to the spiritual journey. It is like the wheel of a chariot, which makes the connection between the chariot and the road, or like the oar of a boat. Mindfulness of effort actualizes the practice; it makes it move, proceed.

But we have a problem here. Mindfulness of effort cannot be deliberately manufactured: on the other hand, it is not enough just to hope that a flash will come to us and we will be reminded. There must be a background of discipline which sets the tone of the sitting practice. Effort is important on this level also; it is the sense of not having the faintest indulgence toward any form of entertainment. We have to give something up. Unless we give up our reservations about taking the practice seriously, it is virtually impossible to have that kind of instantaneous effort dawn on us. So it is extremely important to have respect for the practice, a sense of appreciation, and a willingness to work hard.

Once we do have a sense of commitment to relating with things as they actually are, we have opened the way to the flash that reminds us: that, that, that. "That what?" does not apply anymore. Just that, which triggers an entirely new state of consciousness and brings us back automatically to mindfulness of breathing or a general sense of being.

We work hard at not being diverted into entertainment. Still, in some sense, we can enjoy the very boring situation of the practice of sitting meditation. We can actually appreciate not having lavish resources of entertainment available. Because of having already included our boredom and ennui, we have nothing to run away from and we feel completely secure and grounded.

This basic sense of appreciation is another aspect of the background that makes it possible for the spontaneous flash of the reminder to occur more easily. This is said to be like falling in love. When we are in love with someone, because our whole attitude is open toward that person somehow or other we get a sudden flash of that person not as a name or as a concept of what the person looks like; those are afterthoughts. We get an abstract flash of our lover as that. A flash of that comes into our mind first. Then we might ponder on that flash, elaborate on it, enjoy our daydreams about it. But all this happens afterward. The flash is primal.

Mindfulness of Mind

Often mindfulness is referred to as watchfulness. But that should not give the impression that mindfulness means watching something happening. Mindfulness means being watchful, rather than watching some thing. This implies a process of intelligent alertness, rather than the mechanical business of simply observing what happens.

Particularly the fourth foundation—mindfulness of mind—has qualities of an aroused intelligence operating. The intelligence of the fourth foundation is a sense of light-handedness. If you open the windows and doors of a room the right amount, you can maintain the interior feeling of roomness and, at the same time, have freshness from outside. Mindfulness of mind brings that same kind of intelligent balance.

Without mind and its conflicts, we could not meditate or develop balance, or develop anything at all, for that matter. Therefore, conflicts that arise from mind are regarded as a necessary part of the process of mindfulness. But at the same time, those conflicts have to be controlled enough so that we can come back to our mindfulness of breathing. A balance has to be maintained. There has to be a certain discipline so that we are neither totally lost in daydream nor missing the freshness and openness that come from not holding our attention too tightly. This balance is a state of wakefulness, mindfulness.

Mindfulness of mind means being with one's mind. When you sit and meditate, you are there: you are being with your body, with your sense of life or survival, with your sense of effort, and at the same time, you are being with your mind. You are being there. Mindfulness of mind suggests a sense of presence and a sense of accuracy in terms of being there. You are there, therefore you can't miss yourself. If you are not there, then you might miss yourself. But that also would be a double-take: if you realize you are not there, that means you are there. That brings you back to where you are—back to square one.

The whole process is very simple, actually. Unfortunately, explaining the simplicity takes a lot of vocabulary, a lot of grammar. However, it is a very simple matter. And that matter concerns you and your world. Nothing else. It does not particularly concern enlightenment, and it does not particularly concern metaphysical comprehension. In fact, this simple matter does not particularly concern the next minute, or the minute before this one. It only concerns the very small area where we are now.

Really we operate on a very small basis. We think we are great, broadly significant, and that we cover a whole large area. We see ourselves as having a history and a future, and here we are in our big-deal present. But if we look at ourselves clearly in this very moment, we see we are just grains of sand—just little people concerned only with this little dot which is called nowness.

We can only operate on one dot at a time, and mindfulness of mind approaches our experience in that way. We are there and we approach ourselves on the very simple basis of that. That does not particularly have many dimensions, many perspectives; it is just a simple thing. Relating directly to this little dot of nowness is the right understanding of austerity. And if we work on this basis, it is possible to begin to see the truth of the matter, so to speak—to begin to see what nowness really means.

This experience is very revealing in that it is very personal. It is not personal in the sense of petty and mean. The idea is that this experience is your experience. You might be tempted to share it with somebody else, but then it becomes their experience, rather than what you wished for: your/their experience, jumbled together. You can never achieve that. People have different experiences of reality, which cannot be jumbled together. Invaders and dictators of all kinds have tried to make others have their experience, to make a big concoction of minds controlled by one person. But that is impossible. Everyone who has tried to make that kind of spiritual pizza has failed. So you have to accept that your experience is personal. The personal experience of nowness is very much there and very obviously there. You cannot even throw it away!

In sitting practice, or in the awareness practice of everyday life, for that matter, you are not trying to solve a wide array of problems. You are looking at one situation that is very limited. It is so limited that there is not even room to be claustrophobic. If it is not there, it is not there. You missed it. If it is there, it is there. That is the pinpoint of mindfulness of mind, that simplicity of total up-to-dateness, total directness. Mind functions singly. Once. And once. One thing at a time.

The practice of mindfulness of mind is to be there with that one-shot perception, constantly. You get a complete picture from which nothing is missing: that is happening, now that is happening, now that is happening. There is no escape. Even if you focus yourself on escaping, that is also a one-shot movement of which you could be mindful. You can be mindful of your escape—of your sexual fantasy or your aggression fantasy.

Things always happen one at a time, in a direct, simple movement of mind. Therefore, in the technique of mindfulness of mind, it is traditionally recommended that you be aware of each single-shot perception of mind as thinking: "I am thinking I hear a sound." "I am thinking I smell a scent." "I am thinking I feel hot." "I am thinking I feel cold." Each one of these is a total approach to experience—very precise, very direct, one single movement of mind.

Things always happen in that direct way. That one-shot reality is all there is. Obviously we can make up an illusion. We can imagine that we are conquering the universe by multiplying ourselves into hundreds of aspects and personalities: the conquering and the conquered. But that is like the dream state of someone who is actually asleep. There is only the one shot; everything happens only once. There is just that. Therefore mindfulness of mind is applicable.

So meditation practice has to be approached in a very simple and very basic way. That seems to be the only way that it will apply to our experience of what we actually are. That way, we do not get into the illusion that we can function as a hundred people at once. When we lose the simplicity we begin to be concerned about ourselves: "While I'm doing this, such-and-such is going to happen. What shall I do?" Thinking that more than that is happening, we get involved in hope and fear in relation to all kinds of things that are not actually happening.

Really it does not work that way. While we are doing that, we are doing that. If something else happens, we are doing something else. But two things cannot happen at once; it is impossible. It is easy to imagine that two things are happening at once, because our journey back and forth between the two may be very speedy. But even then we are doing only one thing at a time.

It is necessary to take that logic all the way and realize that even to apply bare attention to what we are doing is impossible. If we try, we have two personalities: one personality is the bare attention; the other personality is doing things. Real bare attention is being there all at once. We do not apply bare attention to what we are doing; we are not mindful of what we are doing. That is impossible. Mindfulness is the act as well as the experience, happening at the same time.

Obviously, we could have a somewhat dualistic attitude at the beginning, before we get into real mindfulness, that we are willing to be mindful, willing to surrender, willing to discipline ourselves. But then we do the thing; we just do it. It is like the famous Zen saying "When I eat, I eat; when I sleep, I sleep." You just do it, with absolutely no implication behind what you are doing, not even of mindfulness.

PART TWO

Cultivating Calm and Insight (and More)

Rouse yourself. Train your own heart.
Start pondering your own in-and-out breath.
— AJAAN LEE DHAMMADHARO

WE HAVE BEEN INTRODUCED to the rudiments of meditation, with teachings on how to foster mindfulness in our body, our life, our effort, and our mind—and helpful guidelines for confidently bringing the best of ourselves to the meditation seat. Now we take what we've learned and see if we can go deeper, applying ourselves to creating a sense of calm and concentration and, in turn, the insight and wisdom that sustained awareness and attention can uncover.

We do this primarily through two meditation techniques that often work hand in glove: *shamatha*, or tranquillity meditation, and *vipassana*, known also as insight meditation. Together these two forms of meditation represent an overall meditative practice fittingly known as *shamatha-vipassana*.

You'll get the hang of these terms. The main thing is cultivating a sense of calm stability. First we calm our minds. Then, we can use the stability and clarity we've gained and set ourselves to the task of developing our wisdom. This is how the Buddha practiced, and it's at the heart of the meditation done by the later Buddhist schools, including Zen and Tibetan Buddhism.

This section also describes meditation and compassion practices associated with the oldest school of Buddhism and undertaken by all kinds of meditators, Buddhist or not.

How to Practice Shamatha Meditation

Gen Lamrimpa

This instruction in shamatha *meditation by Gen Lamrimpa, translated by B. Alan Wallace, is specially aimed at creating a calm, stable mind that leads to physical and mental pliancy. You'll see that the posture, as described here, can be used in other forms of meditation practice.*

IN GENERAL, it is said that the supreme posture for meditative quiescence is the full lotus posture. There are many auspicious ramifications of using it, but it is a difficult posture to maintain. If it is very uncomfortable, the half lotus will do, as will the ordinary cross-legged position (which is called the bodhisattva posture). Use the one you find most comfortable.

Place the hands in the lap, the left hand beneath the right and the thumbs touching lightly. When the meditation is going well, you might find that the thumbs will start pressing together with force, and this can cause some pain in the joints. If such pain arises, the mind is disturbed. In general, the hands should be very relaxed. You can help keep your thumbs touching lightly and your hands soft by placing something soft under them as a gentle support. A small pillow or even just a fold in your meditation blanket should be sufficient.

The spine should be perfectly straight and upright. Normally there is a slight curve in the upper back. In meditation we try to straighten that curve out. The proper position for the head is slightly tilted or inclined to the front with the chin tucked back toward the neck. As you straighten the curve in the back, it is important to keep the head from falling back. Conversely, when you tilt the head forward, the tendency is to let it fall all the way forward. That too is a problem.

The eyes should be slightly open. If the position of the head is correct, the eyes will then focus gently and unforced on the floor about three feet in front of you.

Keep the jaw and lips soft. Let the tongue rest gently against the palate just behind your teeth. This position helps keep the saliva in the mouth when the mind becomes rather stable and there is a tendency to drool.

There is an almost irresistible tendency to elevate the shoulders. Don't. Let them relax. Let them drop down.

It is important that your cushion be exactly level, not tilted to either side. If there is an incline to the left or right, to the front or the rear, it's going to cause problems. They may not be so evident during the beginning stages of the meditation. You may find yourself saying, "Ah, this hardly matters." After a while, as meditation becomes deeper, the only way you'll know the problem has arrived is when you start to keel over to one side. You can test the level of your cushion by placing a bowl of water on it, checking to see if the liquid tilts to one side or the other.

Don't let your posture become too tight. Let the body be very relaxed, very natural. If you get tight in certain areas, take a deep breath and then exhale the tension with the next out-breath. In the course of time, wherever there is too much tightness, tension will arise and you will feel pain and discomfort. That will act as an obstacle to your practice. If you develop bad habits in the first two or three months, it will take another two or three months to break them.

Be conscientious about maintaining good posture right from the beginning. When you feel even the slightest presence of tension, do whatever is necessary to correct the situation.

Pay special attention to the coccyx. There is a natural tendency to let it roll forward a bit. If that happens over a long period of time, it will cause problems all over the body. Tuck the pelvis forward and think of the coccyx as an arrow pointing into the earth. If you are having trouble keeping the pelvis tilted in the proper manner, keeping the arrow pointing down, find something to support it. You can use a small pillow, or even a folded towel will do. Don't sit on the support. Just nudge it right up there at the base of the spine. This will help you hold the bottom of the spine perfectly erect.

Sitting erect with a straight back creates the least stress on the body and one is able to sit for long periods of time without feelings of pain or exhaustion. Another advantage of the erect posture is that the channels within the body are not scrunched up. They're nice and straight, they are free, and the energies within them are free to flow more easily. Because of the very close relationship between the mind, the states of consciousness, and the *prana* (energy, or life force), a smooth, uninterrupted flow of prana enhances both the clarity as well as the stability of the mind. Slouching over yields laxity, mental sluggishness, drowsiness, and eventually sleep. The erect posture gives rise to vitality and enhanced awareness.

Erect posture is highly conducive to the arising of two forms of pliancy. Physical pliancy is a supple sensation one feels in the body, a very pleasurable tactile sensation associated with the movement of the subtle energies of prana within the body. Mental pliancy is an actual mental event which renders the body and mind "fit for action" or "serviceable."

The function of pliancy is the eradication of obscurations. Moreover, both mental and physical pliancy act as an antidote for *dysfunction*, which is the opposite of *serviceability*.

Pliancy is a direct antidote for dysfunction, as well as a remedy for what are sometimes called the five faults. Beyond that, pliancy acts as an antidote for both afflictive and cognitive obscurations.

As the body and mind become more and more stable, mental pliancy arises quite naturally, without any forceful effort. It is a *mental state* accompanied by immense joy. Physical pliancy follows quickly. The body is truly "serviceable"; it takes on a suppleness that enables one to assume any posture and sit for hours and hours without feeling the slightest fatigue.

Actually, all of us are endowed with both mental and physical pliancy, but it is not in a manifest state. When conditions are ripe and they actually do manifest, the joy that accompanies this blissful state increases to a peak and then tapers off. After this tapering-off there arises a more stable, nonfluctuating kind of subtle pliancy which is the most effective.

Sitting in the proper posture, one can engage in this introductory practice. Following the breath in and out, one may count up to seven or twenty-one. Most important is seeing how much of the conceptual mind has been quieted by this technique. If that mind is still rambunctious even after a series of twenty-one breaths, continue counting from one again. If the conceptual mind is quiet after just seven breaths, the introductory practice of counting breaths has served its function. There is no need to go on. This is pertinent to all shamatha techniques.

How to Practice Insight Meditation

Sayadaw U Pandita

Through his answers to fifty-two questions that arc through the stages and concerns of meditation practice, vipassana *master Sayadaw U Pandita tells us precisely what to do every step of the way, from how to place our legs to what to do with our attitude— invaluable guidance for the absolute beginner as well as the longtime meditator.*

1. *Which place is best for meditation?*

   The Buddha suggested that either a forest place under a tree or any other very quiet place is best for meditation.

2. *How should the meditator sit?*

   He said the meditator should sit quietly and peacefully with legs crossed.

3. *How should those with back troubles sit?*

   If sitting with crossed legs proves to be too difficult, other sitting postures may be used. For those with back trouble, a chair is quite acceptable. In any case, sit with your back erect, at a right angle to the ground, but not too stiff.

4. *Why should you sit straight?*

The reason for sitting straight is not difficult to see. An arched or crooked back will soon bring pain. Furthermore, the physical effort to remain upright without additional support energizes the meditation practice.

5. *Why is it important to choose a position?*

To achieve peace of mind, we must make sure our body is at peace. So it's important to choose a position that will be comfortable for a long period of time.

6. *After sitting down, what should you do?*

Close your eyes. Then place your attention at the belly, at the abdomen. Breathe normally—not forcing your breathing—neither slowing it down nor hastening it. Just a natural breath.

7. *What will you become aware of as you breathe in and breathe out?*

You will become aware of certain sensations as you breathe in and the abdomen rises, and as you breathe out and the abdomen falls.

8. *How should you sharpen your aim?*

Sharpen your aim by making sure that the mind is attentive to the entirety of each process. Be aware from the very beginning of all sensations involved in the rising. Maintain a steady attention through the middle and the end of the rising. Then be aware of the sensations of the falling movement of the abdomen from the beginning, through the middle, and to the very end of the falling.

Although we describe the rising and falling as having a beginning, middle, and end, this is only in order to show that your awareness should be continuous and thorough. We don't intend you to break these processes into three segments. You should try to be aware of each of these movements from beginning to end as one complete process, as a whole. Do not peer at the sensations with an over-focused mind, specifically looking to discover how the abdominal movement begins or ends.

9. *Why is it important in this meditation to have both effort and precise aim?*

It is very important to have both effort and precise aim so that the mind meets the sensation directly and powerfully.

10. *What is one way to aid precision and accuracy?*

One helpful aid to precision and accuracy is to make a soft, mental note of the object of awareness, naming the sensation by saying the word gently and silently in the mind, like "rising, rising . . . ," and "falling, falling. . . ."

11. *When the mind wanders off, what should you do?*

Watch the mind! Be aware that you are thinking.

12. *How can you clarify your awareness of thinking?*

Note the thought silently with the verbal label "thinking," and come back to the rising and falling.

13. *Is it possible to remain perfectly focused on the rising and falling of the abdomen all the time?*

Despite making an effort to do so, no one can remain perfectly focused on the rising and falling of the abdomen forever. Other objects inevitably arise and become predominant. Thus, the sphere of meditation encompasses all of our experiences: sights, sounds, smells, tastes, sensations in the body, and mental objects such as visions in the imagination or emotions. When any of these objects arises you should focus direct awareness on it, and silently use a gentle verbal label.

14. *During sitting meditation, what is the basic principle to follow? If another object impinges on the awareness and draws it away from the rising and falling, what should you do?*

During sitting meditation, if another object impinges strongly on the awareness so as to draw it away from the rising and falling of the abdomen, this object must be clearly noted. For example, if a loud sound arises during your meditation, consciously direct your attention toward that sound as soon as it arises. Be aware of the sound as a direct experience, and also identify it succinctly with the soft, internal, verbal label "hearing, hearing." When the sound fades and is no longer predominant, come back to the rising and falling. This is the basic principle to follow in sitting meditation.

15. *What is the best way to make the verbal label?*

There is no need for complex language. One simple word is best. For the eye, ear, and tongue doors we simply say, "seeing, seeing . . . ," or "hearing, hearing . . . ," or "tasting, tasting. . . ."

16. *What are some ways to note sensations in the body?*

For sensations in the body we may choose a slightly more descriptive term like "warmth," "pressure," "hardness," or "motion."

17. *How should you note mental objects?*

Mental objects seem to present a bewildering diversity, but actually they fall into just a few clear categories, such as "thinking," "imagining," "remembering," "planning," and "visualizing."

18. *What is the purpose of labeling?*

In using the labeling technique, your goal is not to gain verbal skills. Labeling helps us to perceive clearly the actual qualities of our experience, without getting immersed in the content. It develops mental power and focus.

19. *What kind of awareness do we seek in meditation, and why?*

    We seek a deep, clear, precise awareness of the mind and body. This direct awareness shows us the truth about our lives, the actual nature of mental and physical processes.

20. *After one hour of sitting, does our meditation come to an end?*

    Meditation need not come to an end after an hour of sitting. It can be carried out continuously through the day.

21. *How should you get up from sitting meditation?*

    When you get up from sitting, you must note carefully, beginning with the intention to open the eyes: "intending, intending"; "opening, opening." Experience the mental event of intending, and feel the sensations of opening the eyes. Continue to note carefully and precisely, with full observing power, through the whole transition of postures until the moment you have stood up, and when you begin to walk.

22. *Besides sitting and walking, what else should you be aware of throughout the day?*

    Throughout the day you should also be aware of—and mentally note—all other activities, such as stretching, bending your arm, taking a spoon, putting on clothes, brushing your teeth, closing the door, opening the door, closing your eyelids, eating, and so forth. All of these activities should be noted with careful awareness and a soft mental label.

23. *Is there any time during the day when you may relax your mindfulness?*

    Apart from the hours of sound sleep, you should try to maintain continuous mindfulness throughout your waking hours.

24. *It seems like a heavy task to maintain continuous mindfulness throughout the day.*

This is not a heavy task; it is just sitting and walking and simply observing whatever occurs.

25. *What is the usual schedule during a retreat?*

During a retreat it is usual to alternate periods of sitting meditation with periods of formal walking meditation of about the same duration, one after another throughout the day.

26. *How long should one walking period be?*

One hour is a standard period, but forty-five minutes can also be used.

27. *How long a pathway do retreatants choose for formal walking?*

For formal walking, retreatants choose a lane of about twenty steps, and then walk slowly back and forth along it.

28. *Is walking meditation helpful in daily life?*

Yes. A short period—say ten minutes of formal walking meditation before sitting—serves to focus the mind. Also, the awareness developed in walking meditation is useful to all of us as we move our bodies from place to place in the course of a normal day.

29. *What mental qualities are developed by walking meditation?*

Walking meditation develops balance and accuracy of awareness as well as durability of concentration.

30. *Can one observe profound aspects of the dhamma [dharma] while walking?*

One can observe very profound aspects of the dhamma while walking, and even get enlightened!

31. *If you don't do walking meditation before sitting, is there any disadvantage?*

    A yogi who does not do walking meditation before sitting is like a car with a run-down battery. He or she will have a difficult time starting the engine of mindfulness when sitting.

32. *During walking meditation, to what process do we give our attention?*

    Walking meditation consists of paying attention to the walking process.

33. *When walking rapidly, what should we note? Where should we place our awareness?*

    If you are moving fairly rapidly, make a mental note of the movement of the legs, "left, right, left, right," and use your awareness to follow the actual sensations throughout the leg area.

34. *When moving more slowly, what should we note?*

    If you are moving more slowly, note the lifting, moving, and placing of each foot.

35. *Whether walking slowly or rapidly, where should you try to keep your mind?*

    In each case you must try to keep your mind on just the sensations of walking.

36. *When you stop at the end of the walking lane, what should you do?*

    Notice what processes occur when you stop at the end of the lane, when you stand still, and when you turn and begin walking again.

37. *Should you watch your feet?*

    Do not watch your feet unless this becomes necessary due to some obstacle on the ground; it is unhelpful to hold the image of a foot in your mind while you are trying to be aware of sensations. You want to focus on the sensations themselves, and these are not visual.

38. *What can people discover when they focus on the sensations of walking?*

For many people it is a fascinating discovery when they are able to have a pure, bare perception of physical objects such as lightness, tingling, cold, and warmth.

39. *How is walking usually noted?*

Usually we divide walking into three distinct movements: lifting, moving, and placing the foot.

40. *How can we make our awareness precise?*

To support a precise awareness, we separate the movements clearly, making a soft mental label at the beginning of each movement, and making sure that our awareness follows it clearly and powerfully until it ends. One minor but important point is to begin noting the placing movement at the instant that the foot begins to move downward.

41. *Is our knowledge of conventional concepts important in meditation?*

Let us consider "lifting." We know its conventional name, but in meditation it is important to penetrate behind that conventional concept and to understand the true nature of the whole process of lifting, beginning with the intention to lift and continuing through the actual process, which involves many sensations.

42. *What happens if our effort to be aware of lifting is too strong, or alternatively, too weak?*

If our effort to be aware of lifting the foot is too strong it will overshoot the sensation. If our effort is too weak it will fall short of this target.

43. *What happens when effort is balanced?*

Precise and accurate mental aim helps balance our effort. When our effort is balanced and our aim is precise, mindfulness will firmly establish itself on the object of awareness.

44. *What mental factors must be present for concentration to develop?*

It is only in the presence of three factors—effort, accuracy, and mindfulness—that concentration develops.

45. *What is concentration?*

Concentration is collectedness of mind: one-pointedness. Its characteristic is to keep consciousness from becoming diffuse or dispersed.

46. *What will we see as we get closer and closer to the lifting process?*

As we get closer and closer to this lifting process, we will see that it is like a line of ants crawling across the road. From afar the line may appear to be static, but from closer up it begins to shimmer and vibrate.

47. *As we get even closer, what will we see?*

From even closer the line breaks up into individual ants, and we see that our notion of a line was just an illusion. We now accurately perceive the line of ants as one ant after another ant after another ant.

48. *What is "insight"?*

"Insight" is a mental factor. When we look accurately, for example, at the lifting process from beginning to end, the mental factor or quality of consciousness called "insight" comes nearer to the object of observation. The nearer insight comes, the clearer the true nature of the lifting process can be seen.

49. *What is the progress of insight?*

It is an amazing fact about the human mind that when insight arises and deepens through vipassana, or insight meditation practice, particular aspects of the truth about existence tend to be revealed in a definite order. This order is known as the progress of insight.

50. *What is the first insight that meditators commonly experience?*

Meditators comprehend, not intellectually or by reasoning but quite intuitively, that a process such as lifting is composed of distinct mental and material phenomena occurring together, as a pair. The physical sensations, which are material, are linked with, but different from, the awareness, which is mental.

51. *What is the second insight in the classical progress of insight?*

We begin to see a whole succession of mental events and physical sensations, and to appreciate the conditionality that relates mind and matter. We see with the greatest freshness and immediacy that mind causes matter, as when our intention to lift the foot initiates the physical sensations of movement, and we see that matter causes mind, as when a physical sensation of strong heat generates a wish to move our walking meditation into a shady spot. The insight into cause and effect can take a great variety of forms. When it arises, though, our life seems far more simple to us than ever before. Our life is no more than a chain of mental and physical causes and effects. This is the second insight in the classical progress of insight.

52. *What is the next level of insight?*

As we develop concentration, we see even more deeply that these phenomena of the lifting process are impermanent and impersonal, appearing and disappearing one by one at fantastic speed. This is the next level of insight, the next aspect of existence that concentrated awareness becomes capable of seeing directly. There is no one behind what is happening; the phenomena arise and pass away as an empty process, according to the law of cause and effect. This illusion of movement and solidity is like a movie. To ordinary perception it seems full of characters and objects, all the semblances of a world. But if we slow the movie down we will see that it is actually composed of separate, static frames of film.

Who Will Tame the Tamer?

Tsoknyi Rinpoche

The Tibetan master Tsoknyi Rinpoche illustrates how the meditative approaches of shamatha *and* vipashyana *work together to tame our minds and dissolve the duality of the watcher and the watched.*

IMAGINE THAT A WILD ELEPHANT is to be tamed by an elephant tamer, but the elephant tamer is also a little wild and also needs to be tamed. In fact, you need to be a little wild to even want to deal with a wild elephant, or you may get stepped on and squashed. But what happens if this wild, slightly too energetic elephant tamer gets into your home and starts to move things around? Maybe he'll smash things; maybe he will rob you or beat you up. He needs some taming as well. *Shamatha* is the method of taming the conceptual mind; it is the elephant tamer. But who will tame the elephant tamer?

That method is called *vipashyana,* egoless vipashyana.

The wild elephant is our rampant emotions, our tendency to get attached, get angry, get closed-minded. The elephant tamer is our ability to be mindful and alert, to tell ourselves, "I'm not going to get involved in these strong emotions. I'm going to be quiet and calm; I will stay collected; I'm going to be mindful; I'm going to be alert. Now I'm quiet; now I'm peaceful; now I'm at ease." That is the tamer.

But this tamer himself also needs to be tamed. What can do that? The elephant tamer continues thinking in a dualistic way: "I must remain mindful; I shouldn't be distracted. Who knows, maybe the elephant will get wild again. I'd better watch out. I must be mindful, I must be alert," and so on. If this attentiveness of the elephant tamer is not allowed to be naturally liberated, dissolved, then one is still stuck in that dualistic way. The watcher has not dissolved. He is still watching.

A Mind Like Sky

Jack Kornfield

Is there an optimal way to pay attention? Jack Kornfield instructs on how to let our wise attention, or mindfulness, open into awareness as vast and boundless as space.

MEDITATION COMES ALIVE through a growing capacity to release our habitual entanglement in the stories and plans, conflicts and worries that make up the small sense of self, and to rest in awareness. In meditation we do this simply by acknowledging the moment-to-moment changing conditions—the pleasure and pain, the praise and blame, the litany of ideas and expectations that arise. Without identifying with them, we can rest in the awareness itself, beyond conditions, and experience what my teacher Ajahn Chah called *jai pongsai*, our natural lightness of heart. Developing this capacity to rest in awareness nourishes *samadhi* (concentration), which stabilizes and clarifies the mind, and *prajna* (wisdom), which sees things as they are.

We can employ this awareness or wise attention from the very start. When we first sit down to meditate, the best strategy is to simply notice whatever state of our body and mind is present. To establish the foundation of mindfulness, the Buddha instructs his followers "to observe whether the body and mind are distracted or steady, angry or peaceful, excited or worried, contracted or released, bound or free." Observing what is so, we can take a few deep breaths and relax, making space for whatever situation we find.

From this ground of acceptance we can learn to use the transformative power of attention in a flexible and malleable way. Wise attention—mindfulness—can function like a zoom lens. Often it is most helpful to steady our practice with close-up attention. In this, we bring a careful attention and a very close focus to our breath or a sensation, or to the precise movement of feeling or thought. Over time we can eventually become so absorbed that subject and object disappear. We become the breath, we become the tingling in our foot, we become the sadness or joy. In this we sense ourselves being born and dying with each breath, each experience. Entanglement in our ordinary sense of self dissolves; our troubles and fears drop away. Our entire experience of the world shows itself to be impermanent, ungraspable, and selfless. Wisdom is born.

But sometimes in meditation such close focus of attention can create an unnecessary sense of tightness and struggle. So we must find a more open way to pay attention. Or perhaps when we are mindfully walking down the street we realize it is not helpful to focus only on our breath or our feet. We will miss the traffic signals, the morning light, and the faces of the passersby. So we open the lens of awareness to a middle range. When we do this as we sit, instead of focusing on the breath alone, we can feel the energy of our whole body. As we walk we can feel the rhythm of our whole movement and the circumstances through which we move. From this perspective it is almost as if awareness "sits on our shoulder" and respectfully acknowledges a breath, a pain in our legs, a thought about dinner, a feeling of sadness, a shop window we pass. Here wise attention has a gracious witnessing quality, acknowledging each event—whether boredom or jealousy, plans or excitement, gain or loss, pleasure or pain—with a slight bow. Moment by moment we release the illusion of getting "somewhere" and rest in the timeless present, witnessing with easy awareness all that passes by.

As we let go, our innate freedom and wisdom manifest. Nothing to have, nothing to be. Ajahn Chah called this "resting in the One Who Knows."

Yet at times this middle level of attention does not serve our practice best. We may find ourselves caught in the grip of some repetitive thought pattern or painful situation, or lost in great physical or emotional suffering. Perhaps there is chaos and noise around us. We sit and our heart is tight, our body and mind are neither relaxed nor gracious, and even the witnessing can seem tedious, forced, effortful.

In this circumstance we can open the lens of attention to its widest angle and let our awareness become like space or the sky. As the Buddha instructs in the *Majjhima Nikaya*, "Develop a mind that is vast like space, where experiences both pleasant and unpleasant can appear and disappear without conflict, struggle, or harm. Rest in a mind like vast sky."

From this broad perspective, when we sit or walk in meditation, we open our attention like space, letting experiences arise without any boundaries, without inside or outside. Instead of the ordinary orientation where our mind is felt to be inside our head, we can let go and experience the mind's awareness as open, boundless, and vast. We allow awareness to experience consciousness that is not entangled in the particular conditions of sight, sound, and feelings, but consciousness that is independent of changing conditions—the unconditioned. Ajahn Jumnien, a Thai forest elder, speaks of this form of practice as *Maha Vipassana*, resting in pure awareness itself, timeless and unborn. For the meditator, this is not an ideal or a distant experience. It is always immediate, ever present, liberating; it becomes the resting place of the wise heart.

Fully absorbed, graciously witnessing, or open and spacious— which of these lenses is the best way to practice awareness? Is there an optimal way to pay attention? The answer is "all of the above." Awareness is infinitely malleable, and it is important not to fixate on any one form as best. Mistakenly, some traditions teach that losing the self and dissolving into a breath or absorbing into an experience is the optimal form of attention. Other traditions erroneously believe that resting in the widest angle, the open consciousness of space, is the highest teaching. Still others say that the middle ground—an ordinary, free, and relaxed awareness of whatever arises here and now, "nothing special"—is the highest attainment. Yet in its true nature awareness cannot be limited. Consciousness itself is both large and small, particular and universal. At different times our practice will require that we embrace all these perspectives.

Every form of genuine awareness is liberating. Each moment we release entanglement and identification is selfless and free. But remember too that every practice of awareness can create a shadow when we mistakenly cling to it. A misuse of space can easily lead us to become spaced-out and unfocused. A misuse of absorption can lead to denial, the ignoring of other experiences, and a misuse of ordinary awareness can create a false sense of "self" as a witness. These shadows are subtle veils of meditative clinging. See them for what they are and let them go. And learn to work with all the lenses of awareness to serve your wise attention.

The more you experience the power of wise attention, the more your trust in the ground of awareness itself will grow. You will learn to relax and let go. In any moment of being caught, awareness will step in, a presence without judging or resisting. Close-in or vast, near or far, awareness illuminates the ungraspable nature of the universe. It returns the heart and mind to its birthright, naturally luminous and free.

To amplify and deepen an understanding of how to practice with awareness as space, the following instructions can be helpful. One of the most accessible ways to open to spacious awareness is through the ear door, listening to the sounds of the universe around us. Because the river of sound comes and goes so naturally, and is so obviously out of our control, listening brings the mind to a naturally balanced state of openness and attention. I learned this particular practice of sound as a gateway to space from my colleague

Joseph Goldstein more than twenty-five years ago and have used it ever since. Awareness of sound in space can be an excellent way to begin practice because it initiates the sitting period with the flavor of wakeful ease and spacious letting go. Or it can be used after a period of focused attention.

Whenever you begin, sit comfortably and at ease. Let your body be at rest and your breathing be natural. Close your eyes. Take several full breaths and let each release gently. Allow yourself to be still.

Now shift awareness away from the breath. Begin to listen to the play of sounds around you. Notice those that are loud and soft, far and near. Just listen. Notice how all sounds arise and vanish, leaving no trace. Listen for a time in a relaxed, open way.

As you listen, let yourself sense or imagine that your mind is not limited to your head. Sense that your mind is expanding to be like the sky—open, clear, vast like space. There is no inside or outside. Let the awareness of your mind extend in every direction like the sky.

Now the sounds you hear will arise and pass away in the open space of your own mind. Relax in this openness and just listen. Let the sounds that come and go, whether far or near, be like clouds in the vast sky of your own awareness. The play of sounds moves through the sky, appearing and disappearing without resistance.

As you rest in this open awareness, notice how thoughts and images also arise and vanish like sounds. Let the thoughts and images come and go without struggle or resistance. Pleasant and unpleasant thoughts, pictures, words, and feelings move unrestricted in the space of mind. Problems, possibilities, joys, and sorrows come and go like clouds in the clear sky of mind.

After a time, let this spacious awareness notice the body. Become aware of how the sensations of breath and body float and change in the same open sky of awareness. The breath breathes itself; it moves like a breeze. The body is not solid. It is felt as areas of hardness and softness, pressure and tingling, warm and cool sensation, all floating in the space of the mind's awareness.

Let the breath move like a breeze. Rest in this openness. Let sensations float and change. Allow all thoughts and images, feelings and sounds to come and go like clouds in the clear open space of awareness.

Finally, pay attention to the awareness itself. Notice how the open space of awareness is naturally clear, transparent, timeless, and without conflict—allowing all things, but not limited by them.

The Buddha said, "O Nobly Born, remember the pure open sky of your own true nature. Return to it. Trust it. It is home."

May the blessings of these practices awaken your own inner wisdom and inspire your compassion. And through the blessing of your heart may the world find peace.

Working with "Method 2"

Ajaan Lee Dhammadharo

In his vivid and concise meditation manual Keeping the Breath in Mind, *Thai meditation master Ajaan Lee Dhammadharo presents a method to help us dive right into meditation, bringing our full body and mind to the practice. "Method 2," as it's called, is introduced here by translator Thanissaro Bhikkhu. If you sometimes have a tough time keeping your attention on your breath, this method can really help.*

THE TEACHINGS HERE are drawn from the works of Ajaan Lee Dhammadharo (1906–61), one of Thailand's most renowned teachers of Buddhist meditation. Ajaan Lee was a forest monk—one who prefers to live in the seclusion of the forest and makes meditation the central theme of his practice—so his teachings grow out of personal, practical experience, although he also makes a point of relating them to standard Buddhist doctrine.

If you want to begin your practice of meditation immediately and fill in the details later, turn to Method 2. Read over the seven basic steps until you have them firmly in mind and then start meditating. Take care, especially at the beginning, not to clutter your mind with extraneous ideas or information. Otherwise, you might spend too much time looking for things in your meditation and not see what is actually there.

There are seven basic steps to Ajaan Lee's Method 2:

1. Start out with three or seven long in-and-out breaths, thinking *bud-* with the in-breath, and *dho* with the out. Keep the meditation syllable as long as the breath.

2. Be clearly aware of each in-and-out breath.

3. Observe the breath as it goes in and out, noticing whether it's comfortable or uncomfortable, broad or narrow, obstructed or free-flowing, fast or slow, short or long, warm or cool. If the breath doesn't feel comfortable, adjust it until it does. For instance, if breathing in long and out long is uncomfortable, try breathing in short and out short.

   As soon as you find that your breathing feels comfortable, let this comfortable breath sensation spread to the different parts of the body. To begin with, inhale the breath sensation at the base of the skull and let it flow all the way down the spine. Then, if you are male, let it spread down your right leg to the sole of your foot, to the ends of your toes, and out into the air. Inhale the breath sensation at the base of the skull again and let it spread down your spine, down your left leg to the ends of your toes, and out into the air. (If you are female, begin with the left side first, because the male and female nervous systems are different.)

   Then let the breath from the base of the skull spread down over both shoulders, past your elbows and wrists, to the tips of your fingers, and out into the air.

   Let the breath at the base of the throat spread down the central nerve at the front of the body, past the lungs and liver, all the way down to the bladder and colon.

   Inhale the breath right at the middle of the chest and let it go all the way down to your intestines.

   Let all these breath sensations spread so that they connect and flow together, and you'll feel a greatly improved sense of well-being.

4. Learn four ways of adjusting the breath:

   a. in long and out long
   b. in long and out short
   c. in short and out long
   d. in short and out short

   Breathe whichever way is most comfortable for you. Or, better yet, learn to breathe comfortably all four ways, because your physical condition and your breath are always changing.

5. Become acquainted with the bases or focal points for the mind—the resting spots of the breath—and center your awareness on whichever one seems most comfortable. A few of these bases are:

   a. the tip of the nose,
   b. the middle of the head,
   c. the palate,
   d. the base of the throat,
   e. the breastbone (the tip of the sternum), and
   f. the navel (or a point just above it).

   If you suffer from frequent headaches or nervous problems, don't focus on any spot above the base of the throat. And don't try to force the breath or put yourself into a trance. Breathe freely and naturally. Let the mind be at ease with the breath—but not to the point where it slips away.

6. Spread your awareness—your sense of conscious feeling—throughout the entire body.

7. Unite the breath sensations throughout the body, letting them flow together comfortably, keeping your awareness as broad as possible. Once you're fully aware of the aspects of the breath you already know in your body, you'll come to know all sorts of other aspects as well. The breath, by its

nature, has many facets: breath sensations flowing in the nerves, those flowing around and about the nerves, those spreading from the nerves to every pore. Beneficial breath sensations and harmful ones are mixed together by their very nature.

To summarize: (a) for the sake of improving the energy already existing in every part of your body, so that you can contend with such things as disease and pain; and (b) for the sake of clarifying the knowledge already within you, so that it can become a basis for the skills leading to release and purity of heart—you should always bear these seven steps in mind, because they are absolutely basic to every aspect of breath meditation. When you've mastered them, you will have cut a main road. As for the side roads—the incidentals of breath meditation—there are plenty of them, but they aren't really important. You'll be perfectly safe if you stick to these seven steps and practice them as much as possible.

Developing Insight

Sylvia Boorstein

We suffer, according to the Buddha's teachings, not because there's anything inherently wrong with us but simply because we misunderstand the nature of reality. Sylvia Boorstein talks about developing insight into the way things really are.

I WAS WALKING through the airport terminal when my eyes met those of a baby approaching me, strapped into a carrier on his mother's chest, and I *knew* that baby was me. A thrill went through me. I knew in that moment it did not matter that I was aging because that baby—*me*, in a newer, fresher guise—was on his way up in life.

I recall laughing, maybe even out loud, as the baby and mother passed by. I knew that the others around me were all me too, and the mother and baby and each other as well, coming and going in this airline terminal and in life. I felt happy and said to myself, "Thinking about interconnection is one thing, but these moments of direct understanding are great." I sat in the boarding lounge feeling tremendous affection for my fellow travelers.

Such an understanding of interconnection comes, in Buddhist practice, from awareness of the three characteristics of experience, also known as the three marks of existence. The first is *imperma-*

nence, or as one teacher put it to me, the idea that "last year's Super Bowl is in the same past as the Revolutionary War." The second is *suffering*, which he described as the result of "the mind unable to accommodate its experience."

These two characteristics, or insights, are fairly easy to make sense of, and when I first began my Buddhist practice, I found I had a basic grasp of them. I thought, "Who doesn't know these things?" But the third characteristic, *emptiness*—the insight that there is no enduring self that separates anything from anything else—seemed more elusive to me, and not particularly relevant to my life. I liked the rest of what I was learning and practicing, so I figured I would just let that one alone for now. The insight about impermanence was, in my early years of practice, what seemed most dramatically evident—although not in a comfortable way. There were periods, especially on retreat, in which it seemed to me that all I could see was the passing away of everything. I saw, as I hadn't ever before, that sunsets followed every dawn and that the beautiful full moon immediately waned. As I came upon a flower that was newly opening I simultaneously envisioned the wilted look it would have three days hence. I remember tearfully reporting to my teacher, Joseph Goldstein, "It's so sad! Everything is dying!" He responded, "It's not sad, Sylvia. It's just true." I found that calming at the time, but I would say it differently now. I would say, "It's not sad. But it *is* poignant."

Everything has a life cycle, with beauty in every part of it, and the passing of any part of it evokes a response, either of relief or nostalgia. Eighteen-year-olds are usually glad to be finished with adolescence and off to whatever they'll do next. A woman in a class I was teaching recently said her daughter, at that point anticipating her marriage a week hence, was sad that all the excitement of planning and imagining would soon be over forever. An elderly man who once took a seniors' yoga class I was teaching thanked me after the class but said he would not be coming back. "It is too hard for me," he said. "But I would like to tell you that I was a member of the 1918 Olympic rowing team."

I find now that time seems to be speeding up. I've become seventy-five years old in what feels like a brief time. The woman I see when I look in the mirror is my Aunt Miriam. It still startles me, but it also inspires me. Knowing that I have limited time left inspires me not to mortgage any time to negative mind states. I am determined not to miss any day waiting for a better one. "Carpe diem!" has never seemed like a more important injunction.

An immediately helpful aspect of my earliest insights into impermanence was the increased tolerance and courage I experienced in difficult situations. However much I had known intellectually that things pass, more and more I knew it in the marrow of my bones. I responded better to difficult news. Hearing that my father had been diagnosed with an incurable cancer, I felt both deeply saddened and uncharacteristically confident. I thought, "We'll manage this together. We've run 10K races together. We'll do this too." On a more mundane level, I noticed that I was more relaxed about ordinary unpleasantness. "This painful procedure at the dentist is taking very long, but in another hour I'll be out of here."

From the beginning of my practice, the insight about suffering, especially the extra mental tension that compounds the pain of life's inevitable losses, made sense to me. A melancholy boyfriend I had when I was in high school enjoyed reciting Dylan Thomas poetry to me. I found it romantic, in a Brontë kind of way, but also depressing. I definitely thought it would be wrong to "Rage, rage against the dying of the light," and I knew I didn't want to do that. When, years later, I learned about Buddhism's four noble truths, I was particularly inspired by the promise of the fourth noble truth, the path of practice that I thought would assure me of a mind that did not rage.

When I first began to teach, I would explain the four truths this way:

Life is challenging because everything is always changing and we continually need to adjust to new circumstances.

Adding struggle to challenge creates suffering. Pain is inevitable but suffering is optional.

Peace is possible. In the middle of a complicated life, the mind can remain at ease.

The path for developing this kind of mind involves attention to ethical behavior, to disciplining the habits of mind through meditation, and to ardent intention.

I loved the third noble truth, the truth that liberation is possible. I felt that after hearing about the ubiquitous ways that we are challenged—and how heedlessly and habitually we respond to the challenges in unwise ways—it was a great relief to hear, "Peace is possible!" I said it with great conviction and I believed it then and I believe it now. What I've started to add now, out of my own experience, is that however much I know that struggling makes things worse, I still suffer. If I am pained enough, or disappointed enough, or anxious enough, I still suffer.

Some life experiences bring us to our knees. Someone in a class I was once teaching, after I had talked about the intensity of even terrible experiences modulating with time because "everything passes," said, "In my case I think I am going to pass before the horror of this passes." I was humbled by the anguish I heard in what that person said, and it has kept me more real and more honest.

For a while, in an attempt to be honest but lighthearted, I added what I called the third-and-a-half noble truth: that the intention to "surrender to the experience" doesn't necessarily cause it to happen. These days even light-heartedness seems glib to me, so I don't do it anymore. I say, "When the mind is able to surrender to the truth, grieving happens and suffering lessens." But there is no timetable for that to happen, and the only possible response I can have is compassion for myself and for other people. Maybe *that* truth—that we suffer in spite of knowing that peace is possible, and sense it is true for everyone—contributes to our sense of kinship, the sense of feeling like I'm accompanied that I sometimes experience in a crowd of strangers.

The idea of no separate, enduring self—emptiness—*is* a peculiar idea until we have a direct experience of it. It certainly feels that there is a little "Me" living in our bodies that decides what to do, that sees out of our eyes, that realizes it has woken up in the morning. The "Me" has thought patterns that are habitual associated with it, so it feels enduring. If I woke up one morning thinking other people's thoughts it would be deeply disturbing.

So it was a complete surprise to me, some years into my retreat practice, to be practicing walking meditation, sensing physical movements and sights and smells and heat and cool, and realizing that everything was happening all by itself. No one was taking that walk: "I" wasn't there. I *was* there a few seconds later, recovering my balance after the "uh-oh" feeling of "if no one is here, who is holding me up?" I thought, "This is wild! There really *isn't* anyone in here directing the show. It is all just happening." I understood that the arising of intention causes things to happen, and that intention arises as a result of circumstances such as hearing the instruction, "Do walking meditation." Hearing the instruction was the proximal cause of walking happening. The habit of following instructions, developed since birth, was another cause.

In years since, the understanding that everything anyone does is a result of karma—of causes and effects—has helped to keep me from labeling people as good or bad. Circumstances and behavior can change, of course, but at any given time no one can be other than the sum of all of their contingent causes. A student in a class discussion about this topic once said, "When people ask me, 'How are you?' I always answer, 'I couldn't be better. Because, I couldn't!'" It's true. We couldn't, any of us, be better. In our most out-of-sorts days, we couldn't be better. If we could, we would. Suffering happens, but no "one" decides to suffer.

As a beginning student, I wondered whether hearing about the three characteristics of experience, rather than discovering them for myself, would diminish their impact—that thinking about them wouldn't count as much as discovering them directly. Today, I know that thinking, pondering, and reflecting on them count as well as direct moments of experience. Everything counts.

Meditation: Interconnectedness

Here's a practice that directly evokes the truth that there is no separate and enduring self, meditated on in the context of interconnectedness.

Read these instructions and then sit up or lie down with your spine straight and your body relaxed so that breath can flow easily in and out of your body. Close your eyes. Don't do anything at all to manipulate or regulate your breathing. Let your experience be like wide-awake sleeping, with breath coming and going at its own rate.

Probably you'll be aware of your diaphragm moving up and down as your chest expands and contracts. Of course you cannot feel that the exhaling air is rich in carbon dioxide and the inhaling air is rich in oxygen, but you probably know that. You also probably know that the green life in the world—the trees and vines and shrubs and grasses—are breathing in carbon dioxide and releasing oxygen back into the environment. The green world and your lungs, as long as they both are viable, are keeping each other alive.

Without any volition on your part, your body is part of the world happening, and the world is part of your body continuing. Nothing is separate. Your life is part of all life. Where is the self?

Getting Grounded through Walking Meditation

Thich Nhat Hanh

The practice of mindful walking, says Thich Nhat Hanh, is a profound and pleasurable way to deepen the connection between our body and the earth. We breathe, take a mindful step, and come back to our true home.

MANY OF US WALK for the sole purpose of getting from one place to another. Now suppose we are walking to a sacred place. We would walk quietly and take each gentle step with reverence. I propose that we walk this way every time we walk on the earth. The earth is sacred and we touch her with each step. We should be very respectful, because we are walking on our mother. If we walk like that, then every step will be grounding, every step will be nourishing.

We can train ourselves to walk with reverence. Wherever we walk, whether it's to the railway station or the supermarket, we are walking on the earth and so we are in a holy sanctuary. If we remember to walk like that, we can be nourished and find solidity with each step.

To walk in this way, we have to notice each step. Each step made in mindfulness can bring us back to the here and the now. Go slowly. Mindfulness lights our way. We don't rush. With each breath we may take just one step. We may have run all our life, but now we don't have to run anymore. This is the time to stop running. To be grounded in the earth is to feel its solidity with each step and know that we are right where we are supposed to be.

Each mindful breath, each mindful step, reminds us that we are alive on this beautiful planet. We don't need anything else. It is wonderful enough just to be alive, to breathe in, and to make one step. We have arrived at where real life is available—the present moment. If we breathe and walk in this way, we become as solid as a mountain.

There are those of us who have a comfortable house, but we don't feel that we are home. We don't want for anything, and yet we don't feel home. All of us are looking for our solid ground, our true home. The earth is our true home and it is always there, beneath us and around us. Breathe, take a mindful step, and arrive. We are already at home.

Uniting Body and Mind

We can't be grounded in our body if our mind is somewhere else. We each have a body that has been given us by the earth. This body is a wonder. In our daily lives, we may spend many hours forgetting the body. We get lost in our computer or in our worries, fear, or busyness. Walking meditation makes us whole again. Only when we are connected with our body are we truly alive. Healing is not possible without that connection. So walk and breathe in such a way that you can connect with your body deeply.

Walking meditation unites our body and our mind. We combine our breathing with our steps. When we breathe in, we may take two or three steps. When we breathe out, we may take three, four, or five steps. We pay attention to what is comfortable for our body.

Our breathing has the function of helping our body and mind to calm down. As we walk, we can say, *Breathing in, I calm my body. Breathing out, I bring peace into my body.* Calming the breath calms the body and reduces any pain and tension.

When we walk like this, with our breath, we bring our body and our mind back together. Our body and our mind are two aspects of the same reality. If we remove our mind from our body, our body is dead. If we take our body out of our mind, our mind is dead. Don't think that one can be if the other is not.

Walking meditation is first and foremost a practice to bring body and mind together peacefully. No matter what we do, the place to start is to calm down, because when our mind and our body have calmed down, we see more clearly. When we see our anger or sadness clearly, it dissipates. We begin to feel more compassion for ourselves and others. We can only feel this when body and mind are united.

Walking meditation should not be work. It is very pleasant, especially in the early morning when the air is still very fresh. When we walk mindfully, we see the beauty and the wonder of the earth around us, and we wake up. We see that we are living a very wonderful moment. If our mind is caught and preoccupied with our worries and suffering, we miss these things. We can value each step we take, and each step brings us happiness. When we look again at the earth and the sky, we see that the earth is a wonderful reality.

We Are Not Separate from the Earth

We think that the earth is the earth and we are something outside of the earth. But in fact we are inside of the earth. Imagine that the earth is the tree and we are a leaf. The earth is not the environment, something outside of us that we need to care for. The earth is us. Just as your parents, ancestors, and teachers are inside you, the earth is in you. Taking care of the earth, we take care of ourselves.

When we see that the earth is not just the environment, that the earth is in us, at that moment we can have real communion with the earth. But if we see the earth as only the environment, with ourselves in the center, then we only want to do something for the earth in order for us to survive. But it is not enough to take care of the earth. That is a dualistic way of seeing.

We have to practice looking at our planet not just as matter, but as a living and sentient being. The universe, the sun, and the stars have contributed many elements to the earth, and when we look into the earth we see that it's a very beautiful flower containing the presence of the whole universe. When we look into our own bodily formation, we are made of the same elements as the planet. It has made us. The earth and the universe are inside of us.

When we take mindful steps on the earth, our body and mind unite, and we unite with the earth. The earth gave birth to us and the earth will receive us again. Nothing is lost. Nothing is born. Nothing dies. We don't need to wait until after our body has disintegrated to go back to Mother Earth. We are going back to Mother Earth at every moment. Whenever we breathe, whenever we step, we are returning to the earth. Even when we scratch ourselves, skin cells will fall and return to the earth.

Earth includes the life sphere and the atmosphere. So you don't have to wait until you die to go back to Mother Earth, because you are *already* in Mother Earth. We have to return to take refuge in our beautiful planet. I know that earth is my home. I don't need to die in order to go back to Mother Earth. I am in Mother Earth right now, and Mother Earth is in me.

You may like to try this exercise while you walk: *Breathing in, I know Mother Earth is in me. Breathing out, I know Mother Earth is in me.*

Paul Tillich, the German theologian, said, "God is not a person but not less than a person." This is true of the earth as well. It is more than a person. It has given birth to millions of species, including human beings. Many ancient cultures believed there was a deity that inhabited the sun, and they worshiped the sun. But when I do walking meditation and touching the earth, I do not have that kind of dualistic view. I am not worshiping the earth as a separate deity outside of myself.

I think of the earth as a bodhisattva, a great and compassionate being. A bodhisattva is a being who has awakening, understanding, and love. Any living being who has awakening, peace,

understanding, and love can be called a bodhisattva, but a bodhisattva doesn't have to be a human being. When we look into a
tree, we see the tree is fresh, it nourishes life, and it offers shade
and beauty. It's a place of refuge for so many birds and other crea-
tures. A bodhisattva is not something that is up in the clouds far
away from us. Bodhisattvas are all around us. A young person who
has love, who has freshness, who has understanding, who offers us
a lot of happiness, is a bodhisattva. The pine standing in the garden gives us joy, offers us oxygen, and makes life more beautiful.

When we say that earth is a beautiful bodhisattva, this is not
our imagination. It is a fact that the earth is giving life and she is
very beautiful. The bodhisattva is not a separate spirit inhabiting
the earth; we should transcend that idea. There are not two separate
things—the earth, which is a material thing, and the spirit of the
earth, a nonmaterial thing that inhabits the earth.

Our planet earth is itself a true, great bodhisattva. It embodies
so many great virtues. The earth is solid—it can carry so many
things. It is patient—it takes its time moving glaciers and carving
rocks. The earth doesn't discriminate. We can throw fragrant flowers on the earth, or we can throw urine and excrement on the earth,
and the earth purifies it. The earth has a great capacity to endure,
and it offers so much to nourish us—water, shelter, food, and air
to breathe.

When we recognize the virtues, the talent, the beauty of the
earth bodhisattva, love is born. You love the earth and the earth
loves you. You would do anything for the well-being of the earth.
And the earth will do anything for your well-being. That is the natural outcome of the real loving relationship. The earth is not just
your environment, to be taken care of or worshiped; you are each
other. Every mindful step can manifest that love.

Part of love is responsibility. In Buddhism, we speak of meditation as an act of awakening. To awaken is to be awake to *something*.
We need to be awake to the fact that the earth is in danger and living species on earth are also in danger. When we walk mindfully,
each step reminds us of our responsibility. We have to protect the

earth with the same commitment we have to protect our family and ourselves. The earth can nourish and heal us but it suffers as well. With each step the earth heals us, and with each step we heal the earth.

When we walk mindfully on the face of the earth, we are grounded in her generosity and we cannot help but be grateful. All of the earth's qualities of patience, stability, creativity, love, and nondiscrimination are available to us when we walk reverently, aware of our connection.

Let the Buddha Walk

I have a student named Sister Tri Hai who spent a long time in prison. She was a peace activist I knew since she was in middle school. She came to the United States to study English literature before going back to Vietnam and becoming a nun. When she was out in the streets advocating for peaceful change, she was arrested and put in prison.

During the day, the prison guards didn't like her to sit in meditation. When they see someone sitting in a prison cell solidly and stably, it feels a bit threatening. So she waited until the lights had gone out, and she would sit like a person who has freedom. In outer appearance she was caught in the prison. But inside she was completely free. When you sit like that, the walls are not there. You're in touch with the whole universe. You have more freedom than people outside who are imprisoning themselves in their agitation.

Sister Tri Hai also practiced walking meditation in her prison cell. It was very small—after seven steps she had to turn around and come back. Sitting and walking mindfully gave her space inside. She taught other prisoners in her cell how to sit and how to breathe so they would suffer less. They were in a cold cell, but through their walking meditation, they were grounded in the solid beauty of the earth.

Those of us who can walk on the earth, who can walk in freedom, should do it. If we rush from one place to another, without practicing walking meditation, it is such a waste. What is walking for? Walking is for nothing. It's just for walking. That is our ultimate aim—walking in the spring breeze. We have to walk so that we have happiness, so that we can be a free person. We have to let go of everything, and not seek or long or search for anything. There is enough for us to be happy.

All the Buddhist stories tell us that the Buddha had a lot of happiness when he sat, when he walked, when he ate. We have some experience of this. We know there are moments when we're walking or sitting that we are so happy. We also know that there are times, because of illness or physical disability or because our mind is caught elsewhere, when we cannot walk freely like the Buddha. There are those of us who do not have the use of our legs. There are those of us who are in prison, like Sister Tri Hai, and only have a few feet of space. But we can all invite the Buddha to walk for us. When we have difficulty, we can leave that difficulty behind and let the Buddha walk for us. In a while the solidity of the earth can help us return to ourselves.

We are made of body and mind. Our body can radiate the energy of peace and compassion. Our mind also has energy. The energy of the mind can be powerful. If the energy of the mind is filled with fear and anger, it can be very destructive. But if we sit mindfully, if we walk mindfully and reverently on the earth, we will generate the energies of mindfulness, of peace, and of compassion in both body and mind. This kind of energy can heal and transform.

If you walk reverently on the earth with two other people, soaking in the earth's solidity, you will all three radiate and benefit from the energy of peace and compassion. If three hundred people sit or walk like this, each one generates the energy of mindfulness, peace, and compassion, and everyone in the group receives that healing energy. The energy of peace and mindfulness does not come from elsewhere. It comes from us. It comes from our capacity to breathe, to walk, to sit mindfully and recognize the wonders of life.

When you walk reverently and solidly on this earth and I do the same, we send out waves of compassion and peace. It is this compassion that will heal ourselves, each other, and this beautiful green earth.

Meditation: Walking on the Earth

Walk slowly, in a relaxed way. When you practice this way, your steps are those of the most secure person on earth. Feel the gravity that makes every step attach to the earth. With each step, you are grounded on the earth.

One way to practice walking meditation is to breathe in and take one step, and focus all your attention on the sole of your foot. If you have not arrived fully, 100 percent in the here and the now, don't take the next step. I'm sure you can take a step like that because there is buddha nature in you. Buddha nature is the capacity of being aware of what is going on. It is what allows you to recognize what you are doing in the current moment and to say to yourself, I am alive, I am taking a step. Anyone can do this. There is a buddha in every one of us, and we should allow the buddha to walk.

While walking, practice conscious breathing by counting steps. Notice each breath and the number of steps you take as you breathe in and as you breathe out. Don't try to control your breathing. Allow your lungs as much time and air as they need, and simply notice how many steps you take as your lungs fill up and how many you take as they empty, mindful of both your breath and your steps. The link is the counting.

When you walk uphill or downhill, the number of steps per breath will change. Always follow the needs of your lungs. You may notice that your exhalation is longer than your inhalation. You might find that you take three steps during your in-breath and four steps during your out-breath, or two steps, then three steps. If this is comfortable for you, please enjoy practicing this way. You can also try making the in-breath and the out-breath the same length, so that you take three steps with your in-breath and three with your out-breath. Keep walking and you will find the natural connection between your breath and your steps.

Don't forget to practice smiling. Your half-smile will bring calm and delight to your steps and your breath, and help sustain your attention. After practicing for half an hour or an hour, you will find that your breath, your steps, your counting, and your half-smile all blend together in a marvelous balance of mindfulness. Each step grounds us in the solidity of the earth. With each step we fully arrive in the present moment.

Walking-Meditation Poem

> I take refuge in Mother Earth.
> Every breath, every step
>   manifests our love.
> Every breath brings happiness.
> Every step brings happiness.
> I see the whole cosmos in the earth.

Compassion and Loving-Kindness Meditation

Noah Levine

Noah Levine teaches two practices for fostering a sense of caring and goodwill toward ourselves and our world.

Compassion Meditation

Find a comfortable place to sit, and allow your attention to settle into the present-time experience of the body. Ten to twenty minutes is a good amount of time to start with for your formal meditation, but eventually you will want to increase that to thirty to forty-five minutes at a time.

Relax any physical tension that is being held in the body by softening the belly; relax the eyes and jaw and allow your shoulders to naturally fall away from the head.

After a short period of settling into present-time awareness, begin to reflect on your own deepest desire for happiness or freedom from suffering. Allow your heart's truest longing for truth and well-being to come into consciousness. With each breath, breathe into the heart's center the acknowledgment of your wish to be free from harm, safe, and protected and to experience compassion for all beings.

Slowly begin to offer yourself compassionate phrases with the intention to uncover the heart's sometimes-hidden caring and friendly response. Your phrases can be as simple as the following:

"May I learn to care about suffering and confusion."
"May I respond with mercy and empathy to pain."
"May I be filled with compassion."

If those phrases do not mean anything to you, create your own words to meditate upon. Find a few simple phrases that have a compassionate and merciful intention, and slowly begin to offer these well wishes to yourself.

As you sit in meditation repeating these phrases in your mind, the attention will be drawn back, as in mindfulness meditation, into thinking about other things or resisting and judging the practice or your own capacity for compassion. It takes a gentle and persistent effort to return to the next phrase each time the attention wanders:

"May I learn to care about suffering and confusion." Feel the breath and the body's response to each phrase.
"May I respond with mercy and empathy to pain." Notice where the mind goes with each phrase.
"May I be filled with compassion." Allow the mind and body to relax into the reverberations of each phrase.

Simply repeat these phrases over and over to yourself like a kind of mantra or statement of positive intention. But don't expect to instantly feel compassionate through this practice. Sometimes all we see is our lack of compassion and the judging mind's resistance. Simply acknowledge what is happening and continue to repeat the phrases, being as friendly and merciful with yourself as possible in the process.

After a few minutes of sending these compassionate phrases to yourself, bring the attention back to the breath and body, again relaxing into the posture

Then bring someone to mind who has been beneficial for you to know or know of, someone who has inspired you or shown you great compassion. Recognizing that just as you wish to be cared for and understood, and that your benefactor too shares the universal desire to be met with compassion, begin offering him or her the caring phrases. Slowly repeat each phrase with that person in mind as the object of your well wishing:

> "Just as I wish to learn to care about suffering and confusion, to respond with mercy and empathy to pain, and to be filled with compassion, may you learn to care about suffering and confusion."
> "May you respond with mercy and empathy to pain."
> "May you be filled with compassion."

Continue offering these phrases from your heart to your benefactor's, developing the feeling of compassion in relationship to the pain of others. When the mind gets lost in a story, memory, or fantasy, simply return to the practice. Begin again offering mercy and care to the benefactor.

After a few minutes of sending compassion to the benefactor, let him or her go and return to your own direct experience of the breath and body. Pay extra attention to your heart or emotional experience.

Then bring to mind someone whom you do not know well, someone who is neutral. Someone you neither love nor hate—perhaps someone you don't know at all, a person you saw during your day, walking down the street or in line at the market. With the understanding that the desire for freedom from suffering is universal, begin offering that neutral person the compassionate phrases:

> "May you learn to care about suffering and confusion."
> "May you respond with mercy and empathy to pain."
> "May you be filled with compassion."

After a few minutes of sending compassion to the neutral person, bring attention back to your own breath and body.

Then expand the practice to include family and friends toward whom your feelings may be mixed, both loving and judgmental.

"May you all learn to care about suffering and confusion."
"May you all respond with mercy and empathy to pain."
"May you all be filled with compassion."

After a few minutes of sending compassion to the mixed category, bring attention back to your own breath and body. Then expand the practice to include the difficult people in your life and in the world. (By *difficult* I mean those whom you have put out of your heart, those toward whom you hold resentment.)

With even the most basic understanding of human nature, it will become clear that all beings wish to be met with compassion; all beings—even the annoying, unskillful, violent, confused, and unkind—wish to be free from suffering. With this in mind, and with the intention to free yourself from hatred, fear, and ill will, allow someone who is a source of difficulty in your mind or heart to be the object of your compassion meditation, meeting that person with the same phrases and paying close attention to your heart-mind's response:

"May you learn to care about suffering and confusion."
"May you respond with mercy and empathy to pain."
"May you be filled with compassion."

After a few minutes of practice in the direction of difficult people, begin to expand the field of compassion to all those who are in your immediate vicinity. Start by sending compassionate phrases to anyone in your home or building at the time of practice. Then gradually expand to those in your town or city, allowing your positive intention for meeting everyone with compassion to spread out in all directions.

Imagine covering the whole world with these positive thoughts. Send compassion to the north and south, east and west, radiate an open heart and fearless mind to all beings in existence—those above and below, the seen and the unseen, those being born and those who are dying. With a boundless and friendly intention, begin to repeat the phrases:

"May all beings learn to care about suffering and confusion."
"May all beings respond with mercy and empathy to pain."
"May all beings be filled with compassion."

After a few minutes of sending compassion to all beings every-where, simply let go of the phrases and bring your attention back to the breath and body, investigating the sensations and emotions that are present now. Then, whenever you are ready, allow your eyes to open and your attention to come back to your surroundings.

Loving-Kindness Meditation

Find a comfortable place to sit, and allow your attention to settle in the present-time experience of the body. Relax any physical tension that is being held in the body by softening the belly; relax the eyes and jaw and allow your shoulders to naturally fall away from the head.

After a short period of settling into present-time awareness, begin to reflect on your own deepest desire for happiness and free-dom from suffering. Allow your heart's sincere longing for truth and well-being to come into consciousness. With each breath, breathe into the heart's center the acknowledgment of your wish to be free from harm, safe, and protected, and to experience love and kindness.

Slowly begin to offer yourself kind and friendly phrases with the intention to uncover the heart's sometimes-hidden loving and kind response. Your phrases can be as simple as the following:

"May I be happy."
"May I be at peace."
"May I be free from suffering."

If those phrases do not mean anything to you, create your own words to meditate upon. Find a few simple phrases that have a kind and loving intention, and slowly begin to offer these well wishes to yourself.

As you sit in meditation repeating these phrases in your mind, the attention will be drawn back, as in mindfulness meditation, into thinking about other things or resisting and judging the practice or your own capacity for love. It takes a gentle and persistent effort to return to the next phrase each time the attention wanders:

"May I be happy." Feel the breath and the body's response to each phrase.
"May I be at peace." Notice where the mind goes with each phrase.
"May I be free from suffering." Allow the mind and body to relax into the reverberations of each phrase.

Simply repeat these phrases over and over to yourself like a kind of mantra or statement of positive intention. But don't expect to instantly feel loving or kind as result of this practice. Sometimes all we see is our lack of kindness and the judging mind's resistance. Simply acknowledge what is happening and continue to repeat the phrases, being as friendly and merciful with yourself as possible in the process.

After a few minutes of sending these loving and kind phrases to yourself, bring attention back to the breath and body, again relaxing into the posture.

Then bring someone to mind who has been beneficial for you to know or know of, someone who has inspired you or shown you great kindness. Recognizing that just as you wish to be happy and at peace, and that benefactor too shares the universal desire for well-being and love, begin offering him or her the loving and kind phrases. Slowly repeat each phrase with that person in mind as the object of your well wishing:

"Just as I wish to be happy, peaceful, and free, may you too be happy."
"May you be at peace."
"May you be free from suffering."

Continue offering these phrases from your heart to your benefactor's, developing the feeling of kindness and response of love to others. When the mind gets lost in a story, memory, or fantasy, simply return to the practice. Begin again offering loving-kindness to the benefactor.

After a few minutes of sending loving-kindness to the benefactor, let him or her go and return to your own direct experience of the breath and body. Pay extra attention to your heart or emotional experience.

Then bring to mind someone whom you do not know well, someone who is neutral. Someone you neither love nor hate—perhaps someone you don't know at all, a person you saw during your day, walking down the street or in line at the market. With the understanding that the desire for happiness and love is universal, begin offering that neutral person your loving-kindness phrases:

"May you be happy."
"May you be at peace."
"May you be free from suffering."

After a few minutes of sending loving-kindness to the neutral person, bring attention back to your own breath and body. Then expand the practice to include family and friends toward whom your feelings may be mixed, both loving and judgmental:

"May you be happy."
"May you be at peace."
"May you be free from suffering."

After a few minutes of sending loving-kindness to the mixed category, bring attention back to your own breath and body. Then expand the practice to include the difficult people in your life and in the world. (By difficult I mean those whom you have put out of your heart, those toward whom you hold resentment.)

With even the most basic understanding of human nature, it will become clear that all beings wish to be met with love and kindness; all beings—even the annoying, unskillful, violent, confused, and unkind—wish to be happy. With this in mind and with the intention to free yourself from hatred, fear, and ill will, allow someone who is a source of difficulty in your mind or heart to be the object of your loving-kindness meditation.

Meeting that person with the same phrases, pay close attention to your heart-mind's response:

"May you be happy."
"May you be at peace."
"May you be free from suffering."

After a few minutes of practice in the direction of difficult people, begin to expand the field of loving-kindness to all those who are in your immediate vicinity. Start by sending phrases of loving-kindness to anyone in your home or building at the time of practice. Then gradually expand to those in your town or city, allowing your positive intention for meeting everyone with love and kindness to spread out in all directions.

Imagine covering the whole world with these positive thoughts. Send loving-kindness to the north and south, east and west. Radiate an open heart and fearless mind to all beings in existence—those above and below, the seen and the unseen, those being born and those who are dying. With a boundless and friendly intention, begin to repeat the phrases:

"May all beings be happy."
"May all beings be at peace."
"May all beings be free from suffering."

After a few minutes of sending loving-kindness to all beings everywhere, simply let go of the phrases and bring your attention back to the breath and body, investigating the sensations and emotions that are present now. Then, whenever you are ready, allow your eyes to open and your attention to come back to your surroundings.

PART THREE

A Taste of Zazen

> To study the Buddha Way is to study the self. To study the self is
> to forget the self. To forget the self is to be actualized by myriad
> things. When actualized by myriad things, your body and mind
> as well as the bodies and minds of others drop away. No trace of
> enlightenment remains, and this no-trace continues endlessly.
>
> —EIHEI DOGEN

WHILE ZEN IS, of course, a distinct school of Buddhism with its
own techniques and lineage of teachings, the practice of meditation
as prescribed by the Buddha is at its heart. Indeed, the name *Zen*
derives from *Ch'an*—the Chinese forebear of Zen—and both of
these derive from the Sanskrit word *dhyana*, which means "meditation" or "absorption." In fact, the word *zazen*, referring to Zen meditation, literally means "sitting meditation."

So it comes as no surprise that Zen emphasizes meditation,
building upon all that came before it. Zazen, in its form known as
shikantaza, or "just sitting," echoes the choiceless awareness that
vipassana, or insight meditation, fosters. But there is more to Zen
practice than just sitting. Practitioners might also take up koan introspection, a powerful but largely misunderstood discipline. You
may have, for example, encountered the koan "What is the sound of
one hand clapping?" This and other koans are commonly explained

as paradoxes or riddles. But such simplistic definitions miss the point and certainly don't hint at koans' capacity to develop our practice.

Here we'll get a deeper sense of how shikantaza and koans work, learn the nuances of meditation as taught in the Zen tradition, and receive inspiration and guidance from Zen masters of our time.

This Life Which Is Wonderful and Evanescent

Blanche Hartman

Zazen, says former San Francisco Zen Center abbess Blanche Hartman, is really about living in the present so that we can manifest this precious life in a way that feels right, a way that is consonant with the truth.

IF YOU THINK ABOUT IT, it's awesomely, amazingly wonderful just to be alive! It's a wonderful gift. But it took me several years of meditation practice and a heart attack before I really got it that just to be alive is awesome. As I was walking out of the hospital I thought, "Wow! I could be dead. The rest of my life is just a gift." And then I thought, "Well, it always has been a gift from the very beginning, and I never noticed it until it was almost gone."

I think it is true of many of us that we don't notice what a gift it is just to be alive. How could we not notice? Well, we sort of take it for granted. But this gift is not without its problems. One of these problems is actually the very thing that made me realize how awesome life is, what a gift it is, and how much I appreciate it. That is the fact that life is evanescent, impermanent. It is precious because we can't just take it for granted. When we realize this, we may wonder, "Well, if my life is a gift, how shall I use it, how shall I give it back, how shall I express my appreciation for it, or completely live this life which is wonderful and evanescent?"

In *Zen Mind, Beginner's Mind*, Suzuki Roshi tells the story of the four horses. One of the horses starts to run just seeing the shadow of the whip, before it even touches him. The next one starts to run just having the whip touch the hair of its skin. The third horse starts to run when it really feels the pain of the whip on its skin. And the fourth horse doesn't really get going until it feels the whip in the marrow of its bones.

What is this whip? This whip is just that evanescence of life, just that teaching of impermanence. One of the Buddha's most significant teachings is to hold up impermanence for us to see, but actually it is just how things are—anything, anytime, anywhere. There is a Pali chant which expresses this:

All things are impermanent.
They arise and they pass away.
To live in harmony with this truth
Brings great happiness.

If you see how things are, "things-as-it-is" as Suzuki Roshi used to say, you see that they arise and they pass away. The trick is to live in harmony with the way things actually are; our suffering comes from wanting things to be different than they are.

I don't know why those of you who came today for the first time came. Why come to meditate? Why is anyone here? Why I'm here is that I began to notice that all things are impermanent, including myself. I came to practice the first time I almost died. The second time I almost died, I really came to recognize what a joy it is to be alive.

Maybe that's like the fourth horse. I didn't get it until it really got to the marrow. But maybe it's not so bad to be the fourth horse, because when it gets to the marrow, you've got it through and through. You don't think, "Well, maybe just some things are impermanent, maybe, but not me. Maybe I'll live forever, or maybe whatever I love will live forever, or maybe impermanence is not really the truth."

So we may try to bargain with impermanence or get into denial about it. But somehow, if we're lucky, we do come to understand "things-as-it-is" and that this is actually the life we are living. Then the question of how we live it becomes really urgent for us. It's not going to last forever; I just have a limited amount of time to live in a way that feels satisfying to me, that feels right, that feels in consonance with the way things are. "To live in harmony with this truth brings great happiness," the Pali chant says.

When I first came to Zen Center I heard Suzuki Roshi say, "Just to be alive is enough." That went right past me and it may be going right past you. I just put it out there so you can take a look at it and decide what it means to you. But I do think that we become curious about Zen practice or any kind of religious discipline when we begin to run into some of the difficulties of life, and the question of how to live with those difficulties becomes a direct issue for us. Or we may notice that how we are living doesn't feel quite right. Or that the familiar fixed ideas we have don't seem to hold up on closer examination.

The chant that we do at the beginning of lectures says:

An unsurpassed, penetrating, and perfect dharma
Is rarely met with even in a hundred thousand million kalpas.
Having it to see and listen to, to remember and accept,
I vow to taste the truth of the Tathagata's words.

Notice that it doesn't say that an unsurpassed, penetrating, and perfect dharma is rare. That is just the truth of things-as-it-is and it is always in front of you every moment of your life. It is right here, nowhere else.

The chant ends, "I vow to taste the truth of the Tathagata's words." This is a vow to taste the truth of how things really are, a vow to see directly. Taste is a very intimate sense—you get it right on your tongue, right here in your body. That is what my heart attack did for me; I got it right up close and personal. And each of us has some experience in our own life where the way things are is tasted directly, personally, right here. And that changes our life. We look at our life and we say, "This life is not in harmony with the way things are. That's why I'm always uncomfortable. So how do I bring myself into harmony with the actuality of this life?"

The Zen teacher Kobun Chino once said in a *sesshin* talk that when you realize how precious your life is, and that it is completely your responsibility how you manifest it and how you live it, that is such a big responsibility that "such a person sits down for a while"! He continued, "It is not an intended action, it is a natural action."

Some of you came here today for meditation instruction, for zazen instruction, for instruction in how to just sit. Now, why do you need instruction in how to just sit?

There was a wonderful young Danish man who came to Tassajara in the early days. He arrived at the gate and he said, "I want to come in and be a Zen monk." The person he was speaking to asked him, "Have you ever sat?" English was not his native language so he kind of took the question in and considered it for a bit, looking perplexed. Finally he drew himself up to his full height and he said, "All men have sat!"

So, why would you need to have instruction in just sitting? Well, just sitting doesn't mean merely sitting. It means completely sitting; not doing anything else, just sitting. You may have noticed that when you sit down intending to just sit, there is a lot going on! We don't really notice how active our mind is until we sit still with the intention of not deliberately thinking. Even though we are not deliberately thinking, a lot of thinking is going on! I had no idea how completely, incessantly busily active my mind was until I sat down with the intention of just being still and just being quiet and not grasping the thoughts that came along.

So one of the reasons we need instruction in how to just sit is that we need to know what might support us in letting some of that busyness just go along, without grabbing on to it. Something like paying attention to posture and paying attention to breath. Paying attention to what's happening right here and right now, which is this physical body, whatever sensations there might be, and breathing.

Most of the stuff that is going on in our mind is not about what is happening right here and right now. Check it out sometime and see: most of the stuff that is going on in your mind is either chasing after the past or chasing after the future. Or worrying about the future and regretting or chewing over the past incessantly. And figuring out who to blame for all our difficulties. It takes a long time to realize that there is no one to blame and to be willing just to be here.

I was invited recently to participate in a spirituality discussion group. My friend said the group was going to be giving attention to what we do in situations where there has been some real loss, where things are never going to be the same again. Someone you know and love has died; you have had a serious illness or an accident. Something has occurred that feels like a terrible loss that can't be recovered. How do you work with those circumstances?

Some of the people there had experienced losses which they could relate to the question, but the discussion was really about how our lives were going now and about how to arrive at a sense of ease or a feeling of composure in our lives. One person said, "Things are going pretty well for me now, but I just noticed today that even though everything is fine I have this kind of worried uneasiness, not about anything in particular, and it seems strange when everything is going fine."

The teaching that there is suffering in the midst of joy was right there in what he was saying—the worried uneasiness that although everything is fine now, something might happen and it won't be fine. Have you ever had that kind of experience? It is a very common human experience.

We have all kinds of ways of imagining the future that distract us from actually living in the present. What just sitting, what zazen, is really about is living in the present so that we can actually manifest this precious life in a way that feels right, a way that is consonant with our inner understanding of the dharma, of the truth.

Shortly before he died, William Butler Yeats said, "If I had to put it in a single phrase, I would say that one can live the truth but one can really not know the truth, and I must express the truth with the remainder of my life." I can live the truth but cannot know it, and I must express it with the remainder of my life.

Dogen Zenji, the Japanese founder of this particular stream of Zen, said this about the precept "I vow not to disparage the Three Treasures (Buddha, Dharma, Sangha)": "To expound the dharma with this body is foremost. Its virtue returns to the ocean of reality. It is unfathomable. We just accept it with respect and gratitude." It is unfathomable. We cannot know it. The inconceivable really is inconceivable! But we still try to find a way to grab on to it.

In his lecture in the San Francisco Zen Center's "Buddhism at the Millennium's Edge" series, Stephen Batchelor was talking about a willingness to live in perplexity, a willingness to live in the realm of not knowing. This is quite difficult. We can expound the dharma with this body, we can live the truth; we just can't grasp it. We can feel in our body when we are out of line with it. That is why Kobun Chino says it is such a big responsibility that naturally a person sits down for a while. We want to attune ourselves carefully to our body and mind so that we can notice when we are out of line with our deepest intention. We want to cultivate that intimate knowing without words and ideas—an intimacy with ourselves—so that we can tell if we are living our life the way we really want to or whether it is just a little off.

We can do this by just tuning in with ourselves, with our fundamental human nature, which is sometimes in Buddhism called buddha nature. Suzuki Roshi says a human being practicing true human nature is our zazen. Buddha nature is not something mysterious or arcane. Buddha just means awake; one who is awake. We find out how to be awake and to align ourselves with our true intention, with our true being, with the wisdom and compassion that is already inherent in each being, including ourselves. No one is the one single exception to the fact that all beings are Buddha. We are not that special!

Sitting Zen

John Daishin Buksbazen

How should I sit? Where should I look? What should I do with my hands, my breath, my mind? John Daishin Buksbazen provides a practical checklist of Zen meditation basics.

When your body is in position for sitting, run down this checklist to make sure everything is arranged properly (at first, it may even help to sit in front of a mirror so you can visually check your posture):

1. Sit on the forward third of your *zafu* cushion.

2. Arrange your legs in the position you can do best.

3. Sway in decreasing arcs to center your spine.

4. Straighten your spine and align your head by doing the ceiling-pushing-up exercise: Imagine that the ceiling is resting on the crown of your head at a point directly over your spine. Now imagine that you are a tire jack and that your spine is going to push the ceiling up a little bit. The action here is all in your spine, so be careful not to tense your shoulders or move your head. Just let your spine begin to extend itself, from the base of the spine upward toward the head, carrying the head with it as it straightens. Now let the energy flow upward, and as you do so, lift that ceiling a half inch. Don't tilt

your head, though. Let your spine do the lifting. Push harder, and harder still. Then, relax your effort.

5. Lower your eyes and allow them to go out of focus.

6. Close your mouth and position your tongue.

7. Place your hands in the cosmic mudra: Place your right hand, palm up, so that the blade of the hand (the part you would strike with in a karate chop) rests against your lower belly. Then place the left hand, palm upward also, on top of the right, so that the middle knuckles overlap and the thumb tips lightly touch, forming a nice oval frame. (If your attention wanders, you'll find that the thumbs move apart; and if your sitting becomes dull and drowsy, you'll usually find that the thumbs sag in the middle, revealing the loss of alertness. So the thumbs can serve you well as a built-in biofeedback device, continuously reflecting the state of your mind.)

8. Make sure your whole body is arranged properly and comfortably before you begin zazen.

Always remember this rule of thumb: Except for the normal discomfort always associated with a new kind of physical activity, zazen should be comfortable, not agonizing! All of these instructions are intended primarily to help you get and stay comfortable in your sitting. Don't get involved in a competition with yourself (or anyone else) just to see how much pain or how difficult a posture you can take. Be strong and be calm, and pay close attention to what you are doing. Little else is as important as the attitude you bring to sitting.

Your first job in regulating your mind is to get your mind to sit along with your body and breath. In the beginning of Zen practice, you do this by counting your breaths.

First, seat yourself properly and allow your breathing to become regular and calm.

As you start to exhale, count that exhalation as the number one.

Then, when you inhale, count that inhalation as two. Then as you exhale again, count that as three, and the following inhalation as four, and so on until you reach ten. Then start all over again on the very next breath with the number one, and repeat the counting from one through ten, over and over again. Keep doing this steadily until you can do it with full attention, not losing count, getting bored, daydreaming, or in any way interrupting your concentration. (When you reach that point in your practice, it is time to move on to a slightly different practice of counting only the exhalations or just following the breath without counting it.)

Counting the breath is a very simple thing to do, but it's not easy. One thing most people have trouble with when starting out is that they keep thinking thoughts, and find this distressing. To put this in perspective, let's take a look at the two kinds of thinking that concern us.

First of all, since the nature of the human brain is to generate thoughts continuously, nobody need feel upset when this occurs.

Anyone who is not unconscious or brain damaged will produce one thought after another. This is quite normal.

These innocent flashes of mental activity, random thoughts, are not a problem in sitting; they are simply the natural action of a healthy brain. If you tried to stop those random thoughts you would have a very hard time and might go into a trance-like state that is not at all what zazen is about. In zazen, you are not trying to stop all thoughts from occurring.

On the other hand, there is a kind of thinking that is precisely what you must let go of when you sit, for otherwise it will dominate your mind as it has all your life. That form of thought is called discursive thought, or sequential thought; it is thought with a story line, a continuing theme, for it consists of a progression of ideas arising originally from a spontaneous and random thought and gradually turning into an elaborate theatrical or philosophical production that takes you quite effectively out of your concentration and stirs up the surface of the water of the mind.

But to deal with either random thoughts or discursive thoughts, the procedure is the same. As soon as you realize what is happening, stop, go back to one, and start counting again with renewed vigor. If you only have random thoughts from time to time, you can just keep on going and ignore them. But if the random thoughts start turning into stream-of-consciousness soliloquies, then you will find it most useful to simply return to one and start your counting again. The principle involved is basically quite simple: nobody can really concentrate on two things at once. If this seems to be happening, in reality neither thought-object is getting your full attention. And conversely, if you really turn your attention wholly onto one focal point, there's no attention left over for such thoughts as distraction, boredom, or self-criticism.

Don't be fooled by the simplicity of this practice. It may take quite a bit of hard work until you can count from one to six, let alone ten. But there's nothing magical about the number ten! If you don't get that far but only reach two or three, that could be highly effective sitting practice too, as long as you keep returning to your counting. What is important is the consistency of attention and intention. The counting from one to ten is not an end in itself, but simply a temporary structure to help develop single-pointed attention. If "getting to ten" becomes the goal, that too can become a distraction. The numbers are only markers, not objectives. When we count, we just count. If we have to start over by the time we reach five, or even two, we just start over, without comment, without judgment. That way, you'll soon develop strong concentration, and the results will encourage you to go further. This aspect of mental training is like lifting weights. Even if you're weak when you start, regular workouts will soon produce results.

In practice, body, breath, and mind are inseparable. The better your posture, the more well-aligned you can make your spine, the easier your breathing will become, and the quieter your mind will be. And on the other hand, the clearer your mind and the stronger your concentration, the less difficulty you will have keeping your back straight or sitting through your discomforts without fidgeting or changing position.

With this in mind, don't be discouraged if one aspect of your practice comes along more slowly than another. Each person's practice develops differently, and usually the three aspects of sitting will mature at different rates. In dealing with discouragement, it may be helpful to think of tuning a guitar; if the strings are tightened too much or too little, the proper pitch cannot be achieved. Similarly, in sitting, we are not trying to see how tightly we can wind the strings of our body, breath, and mind; rather, we are trying to achieve the proper pitch of stillness. We need to recognize that each moment is a fresh moment that has never existed before. Naturally experiences in our mind and body come and go. Fatigue, excitement, depression, discomfort, scattered attention, preoccupations—these are natural events, like changes in the weather. Sometimes it's hot, sometimes cold. Sometimes it's bright, sometimes cloudy. But it's always just weather. In sitting, it is just our lives, moment by moment, unfolding. Even discouragement itself is just another moment of being, not to be clung to or dreaded. Take each moment as it comes, and go on to the next unique, new moment. This is sitting.

Nonetheless, as you practice sitting sincerely and energetically, you are likely to encounter questions that are important to resolve. Here again, we see the need for a personal teacher-student relationship. Just as an athlete can be coached to regard her difficulties as guideposts to improvement, so too a sitter can be taught. But just as an athlete must train even when not under the guidance of a coach, so too the sitter must practice even in the absence of a teacher. Although a teacher is essential, also understand that sitting practice is itself a wonderful teacher. Sitting alone or in a group of peers is always valuable; it is better to practice this way than not to practice simply because you may not have easy access to a teacher.

Even so, it is worth emphasizing again that sooner or later it is crucial to practice with a qualified teacher you can trust and with whom you can honestly discuss your practice. No amount of reading could ever deal effectively with all the possible experiences, since these always arise intimately out of the depths of who you are.

The Practices of Zen

James Ishmael Ford

James Ishmael Ford examines the history and the fundamentals of the two core practices of Zen—shikantaza and koan introspection—and explains how they complement each other.

FROM ITS FIRST EMERGENCE as an independent school, Zen has focused on the arts of meditation. Meditation has always been central to Buddhist practice. Traditionally, there are three main styles of meditation practice: *shamatha*, *metta*, and *vipashyana*. Shamatha is a practice of concentration and calmness. Metta is the discipline of reorienting consciousness into a realm of persisting loving-kindness. And vipashyana is the Buddha's Way of insight.

All Zen practices are based in what might be seen as *shamatha-vipashyana*, the blending of shamatha with vipashyana, a practice of concentration and an opening to the insights that arise amid it. But in their transmission through China, these disciplines take on the specific flavors of Zen's formative personalities. Echoing the two dominant perspectives of Zen, one practice emphasizes shikantaza, "just sitting," or the way of silent illumination, while the other follows the sudden insight that deep introspection with koans can reveal.

There is constant tension between these two great streams and their dominant practices, and there are examples, in the literature of various eras, of advocates of one denigrating the other. But each of these disciplines can take us successfully on our journey to depth and wisdom. Personally, I follow a tradition that sees how these two approaches complement each other. Though in no way new, this view seems to be becoming increasingly common, especially among Western Zen teachers and practitioners.

It's impossible to understand Zen without some perspective, ideally firsthand, on its great spiritual disciplines. So let us look briefly at the two core meditation practices of shikantaza and koan introspection.

Shikantaza means quite simply "just sitting." Some trace the root of this word to the Japanese pronunciation of the Sanskrit *vipashyana*, though this is far from certain. Vipashyana practice attends to various details such as labeling thoughts or noting shifts in sensation. However, even this brief description is complicated by the fact many meditation teachers, including Zen meditation teachers, offer shamatha-vipashyana. Shamatha is a practice of "stopping" or "settling," through the cultivation of concentration, which is joined with and supports the practice of insight.

The term *shikantaza* describes a practice that happens not only as we sit but also as we stand, walk, and engage in all of our waking activities. It sometimes even infuses our sleep, becoming the content of our dreams. This practice is sometimes called "silent illumination" or "serene contemplation." While "just sitting" is really just a simple way of saying "being present," people often have trouble grasping what that really means. Shikantaza reveals the ancient nature of our human minds.

The rhetoric of shikantaza can sometimes be challenging, however. Consider the following words of the great master Yaoshan Weiyan, who lived from the first half of the eighth century through the first quarter of the ninth century. When asked what he thought while sitting in meditation, he replied, "I think of not-thinking." When asked how he did that, he replied, "Beyond-thinking." Sometimes simple doesn't seem simple!

I recall many years back, I was guiding a small sitting group in

Berkeley, California. Someone who had been sitting for several years with another Zen group had begun sitting with us. After a month or two she said she was going back to her old center. I asked if there was anything I should know. She said there was: Whereas our group sat for twenty-five-minute periods before moving into *kinhin*, a simple form of walking meditation, the other group sat for forty-minute periods. And she explained she could only experience "theta waves" after a half hour of continuous sitting.

This kind of misunderstanding of the practices of Zen is not that uncommon. Western Zen teachers often refer to such people as "*samadhi* junkies," and there have been quite a few meditators who have left my own sitting groups for organizations that offer longer meditation periods or more of them, seeking opportunities for deeper states of samadhi.

Samadhi is a Sanskrit term, literally meaning "to make (one's concentration)," and it refers to deep experiences of unity that arise in meditation, particularly in longer sitting periods or meditation retreats. No doubt, experiences of samadhi can be powerful and compelling. But samadhi is not itself the end of the Zen path. Without a good guide, people can and often do get stuck (in a psychological sense, of course, not a literal one) in their samadhi experiences.

The Platform Sutra itself teaches the identity of samadhi and *prajna*, or deepest wisdom. But one-sided attention to samadhi quickly becomes problematic. People who've experienced these states of deep oneness without understanding those states' connection to wisdom can easily miss the real purpose of Zen—finding an authentic way of being present to everything that is—and instead trade that "what is" for a deep but passing sensation of peace.

"Just sitting" shouldn't be understood as mere quietism, nor is it a way to dwell in states of bliss, suppress our thoughts, or cultivate any kind of blankness. Shikantaza invites us to intimately be within the spaciousness that includes thought, as well as the space outside the thoughts and the very thoughts themselves. We are invited to simply experience the natural expansiveness of our mind and whatever it may reveal—even if what it reveals is an experience of contraction!

Because shikantaza is such a simple practice, there often isn't a lot of instruction in Zen meditation. While rooted in the practices of vipashyana, shikantaza lets go of the minute and detailed focus of the traditional vipashyana discipline. Often in traditional settings—both ancient and modern—the sum total of zazen instruction really amounts to little more than to "sit down and hold still."

Many contemporary Japanese teachers report that this "sit down and hold still" was all they were told as young novices. But for most of us in our culture, such limited instruction is not very helpful.

In formal meditation posture, we may soon discover that the spaciousness of our mind is elusive. Instead of just being present, we're fretting about the past, scheming about the future, worrying, resenting, fearing, hating, grasping, desiring—anything but experiencing spaciousness.

So today in the West most Zen teachers offer some form of meditation technique to help us get to spaciousness. Most commonly this involves using a form of breath-counting or breath-awareness as an anchor for the wandering mind.

Hongzhi, Dogen, and Shikantaza

Hongzhi Zhengjue, who lived from the end of the eleventh century through the middle of the twelfth, was the first great theorist of the way of "silent illumination," and this is the term most often associated with his teaching. At the beginning of his classic treatise translated in Taigen Dan Leighton's *Cultivating the Empty Field,* Hongzhi declares: "The practice of true reality is simply to sit in silent introspection." Hongzhi describes a dynamic experience, one that avoids the seductions of inner bliss states as well as the wandering roads of ideas—thus pushing us to engage actively in finding our essential spaciousness, our nondual reality.

The principal exponent of the practice of shikantaza per se was the great thirteenth-century master Eihei Dogen. The term *shikantaza* appears to have been coined by his teacher Tiantong Rujing, but it was Dogen who carried it forward, explaining and expanding what it can mean for us as a living practice. In his *Fukanzazengi*, or "Universal Recommendations for Zazen" (which can be found in the collection translated as *Dogen's Extensive Record*), Dogen explains the practice.

He suggests finding a clean, dry place, if possible cool in summer and warm in winter. He goes on to describe the use of the *zafu*, the small round pillow one sits upon, and the *zabuton*, the larger square, flat cushion under the zafu, which supports the ankles and knees. He then describes the basic posture—sitting erect, with hands in the lap, eyes cast downward—as "the method used by all Buddha ancestors for zazen."

"Therefore," Dogen continues, "put aside the intellectual practice of investigating words and chasing phrases, and learn to take the backward step that turns the light and shines it inward. Body and mind of themselves will drop away, and your original face will manifest." He concludes by echoing that famous dialogue with Yaoshan: "Think of not-thinking. How do you think of not-thinking? Beyond-thinking."

Just sitting is the universal solvent. It is the way to confirm all the teachings presented in all of Zen literature, the way to confirm our original awakening, our true nature, and the way to heal this world.

Dahui, Hakuin, and Koan Introspection

No one knows the precise origin of koan introspection, though some trace it to the Taoist tradition of "pure conversation." Rinzai Zen priest and scholar Victor Sogen Hori, the premier writer on koan introspection in the English language, advances a compelling argument that the distant ancestor of koan study can be found in the

Chinese tradition of literary games. Whatever its origins, two teachers in particular gave koan study the shape that most Western Zen practitioners will encounter: the Chinese monk Dahui Zonggao and the Japanese monk Hakuin Ekaku.

Dahui, a twelfth-century Linji-lineage master, is often identified as one of the first teachers to exclusively emphasize koan study. Having read the *Record of Yunmen* as a young man, he was inspired to undertake the Zen way. His first teacher, Zhan Tangshun, pointed out that the young monk's inability to achieve awakening was due to his pride and intellectual acumen. Dahui's understanding of the outside prevented him from entering the inside.

On his deathbed, Dahui's teacher directed him to go to master Yuanwu Keqin—the master who would be remembered as the compiler of *The Blue Cliff Record*, one of the most important collections of koans. Eventually, Yuanwu gave his dharma transmission to Dahui, who in 1137 would become abbot of Nengren Temple. While there he began to collect a multivolume anthology of koans and became a strong advocate of using the koan known as "Zhaozhou's Dog." In Dahui's teachings it is possible to see the beginnings of the approach that would flower with the eighteenth-century Japanese master Hakuin.

In the ensuing years, war and famine plagued the country, and more than half the hundred monks in Dahui's monastery died. In 1158 he became abbot at Mount Jing near Hangzhou, and it was during these years that Dahui began to publicly criticize the over-emphasis on silent illumination and to hold up the possibilities inherent in koan introspection. While he was personally quite close to Hongzhi—who would, in fact, request Dahui be his executor following his death—the great division between koan introspection and shikantaza began at the temples of these two great teachers.

Personally, I find it wonderfully compelling that the masters of these monasteries were in fact friends, each respecting the other while at the same time criticizing a too-one-sided clinging to this practice or that. I find this a powerful model for us as we engage our various Zen practices today. Sadly, however, in the ensuing centuries, this division would continue to exist, with sectarian narrow-mindedness raging strong.

Over time, koan introspection would gradually ossify, losing its dynamism and becoming more an exercise in formalism, mere study, though surely there were some who continued to find insight through studying koans. The next major development in koan introspection came in the eighteenth century, with Japanese master Hakuin Ekaku. For our purposes here, suffice it to say that Hakuin is of particular importance for his systematization of the practice of koan introspection, helping forge it into a reliable tool of training that, when wielded by a master, could serve to awaken students and bring powerful nondual insights. Dahui and Hakuin gave koan introspection its unique shape and placed it as a clearly distinct practice within the Zen schools.

What Koan Introspection Is and What It's Not

What, in fact, is koan introspection? What does it mean to engage in it? These are important questions worth exploring, as koans and koan study are some of the most perennially misunderstood elements of Zen. Indeed, the practice at the heart of koan introspection is unique to the Zen school and has no significant corollary anywhere else.

Unfortunately, most of what has been published in the English language clouds the matter. This is partially the fault of the Zen tradition itself, which tends to guard the koan way as an esoteric treasure. And it is partially the fault of some European and American commentators, who frequently misunderstand both Zen and koan study.

The various scholars who have taken up the subject of koan introspection often seem like the blind men described by the Buddha: exploring the elephant and interpreting the leg, tail, or trunk as the whole. As Sogen Hori writes, these scholars explore Zen's "nondual epistemology, its ritual and performance, its language, [or] its politics," and indeed, some such perspectives can help clarify how the koan can be engaged at different levels; some point to the shortcomings of Zen institutions; some examine how koan study can be and in fact is abused or misused: all speak to one truth or another. But none of these considerations captures the essence of koan introspection.

It should be said that koans are also engaged by some Soto Zen teachers, though usually in a discursive way, as objects of conversation among practitioners. These conversations are guided by mature practitioners who often have great insight but little or no formal training in koan introspection, in wielding the tools of Master Hakuin's refined system. Without a doubt, contemporary Soto practitioners can profit from this engagement, as can we all. We and they may find moments of startling clarity or gentle prodding toward greater depth in our practice. In fact this dialogistic approach is one (among several) of the "orthodox" uses of koans.

The Linji/Hakuin legacy of koan practice, however, is more dramatic and intimate than the critical engagement of a spiritual literary tradition, even when it is grounded in shikantaza. To distinguish these disciplines, let us consider the emerging use of the term "koan introspection" for the Linji/Hakuin style. Traditional Linji koan introspection is about our possible awakening, our turning in a heartbeat from delusion to awakening. To achieve this, Zen practice requires three things: great doubt, great faith, and great determination. These become particularly obvious through koan introspection.

The idea of great doubt might seem startling in this context. Matters of religion often seem to be about faith and sometimes, sadly, even about the crushing of doubters. In Zen, however, great doubt must be turned onto ourselves. And as such, this "great doubt" must not be confused with a merely dismissive variety of skeptical doubt. We can see one of the true meanings of great doubt in a reply from Robert Aitken, one of the elders of Western Zen, when asked what he thought about contemporary deconstruction-ist philosophy: it could be valuable so long as it includes the neces-sary step of deconstructing itself. Turning doubt on ourselves, we strive to manifest the truth behind that delightful bumper sticker: DON'T BELIEVE EVERYTHING YOU THINK.

Koans cultivate and make use of this great doubt. Contrary to what some might say on the subject, koans are not meaningless phrases meant to break through to a transrational consciousness (whatever we may imagine that means). Rather they are a direct pointing to reality, an invitation for us to "taste water" and to know for ourselves whether it is cool or warm.

While there is an aspect beyond discursive thought, koan in-trospection very much includes our experiences of judging and as-sessing. One of my koan teachers suggested that shikantaza is a mature practice for mature people, but that for more difficult cases such as the likes of me, koans could shake us up and put us on the right path. I had spent the first ten or so years of my practice en-gaged in shikantaza, and today it is again my baseline practice. But it wasn't until I found the koan way that I found myself opened up, my heart broken and restored, and my place in the world revealing itself.

In koan introspection, doubt and faith travel together. It is our relentless presence to doubt and faith that takes us to the gate of nondual insight. Indeed both the path to the gate and the gate itself are discovered within that relentlessness.

From an instrumentalist view of koan introspection, words like *Mu* (employed in the aforementioned Zhaozhou's Dog) or phrases like "What is the sound of the single hand clapping?" or "What is your original face from before your parents were born?" are often mistakenly assumed to be meaningless: it is assumed that the "point" of such koans is to simply startle the discursive mind into some kind of transrational state. But this understanding of koans simply posits a new dualism: a lower discursive consciousness and a higher nondiscursive state. That is not what koan introspection is about.

Rather, as we push through any koan—experiencing great doubt, great faith, and great determination—we find the exact identity between our ordinary consciousness and fundamental openness. Nondual reality includes subject and object, each itself and freely transposing with the other; first this, now that, sometimes one drops away, sometimes the other, sometimes both drop away, sometimes one emerges from the other, sometimes both emerge together—but we rest nowhere. Resting nowhere and moving fluidly among these perspectives is the true practice of koan introspection.

Let us return for a moment to the question of what koans actually are and explore the ways they are used in training. The word *koan* is believed to be derived from the Chinese *kung* and *an*. *Kung* means "public" and *an* means "case"—like a legal document. A koan can be a single word, a short phrase, a bit of traditional poetry, or a story. Most commonly it is an anecdote about an encounter between a student and teacher.

In China and Korea the primary form of koan engagement is through a *huatou* (in Chinese; *wato* in Japanese), which literally means "word head." In this practice, we are given one single koan for a lifetime. This koan becomes a touchstone of our practice: it is a place to put our doubt, to cultivate great doubt, to allow the revelation of great faith, and to focus our great energy.

But in Japan and the Japanese-derived koan lineages in the West, koan study has taken on a new dimension. By the eighteenth century, various Japanese Rinzai teachers began introducing koan "curricula." These were programs of koan study through which a student might "pass" after many years. While there is some dispute over who actually developed this system, it is usually believed to have culminated in the work of the great master Hakuin Ekaku and his principal students or, at least, in that of teachers who followed them. This program is used by orthodox Japanese Rinzai to this day. And it is the source for the single modern reform used in some Soto schools: the so-called Harada-Yasutani curriculum.

This form of koan study begins with a step reminiscent of the

Chinese original: the new student is given a "breakthrough" koan, a case specifically meant to elicit an initial experience of nonduality. The Japanese term for this koan is *shokan*, or "first barrier." A student might spend years struggling with it; only rarely does someone pass through the breakthrough koan quickly.

A breakthrough koan might be "What is your original face from before your parents were born?" or Hakuin's own question "What is the sound of the single hand clapping?" But most commonly it is Zhaozhou's Dog. This simple koan is the gateway to all koan practice, without which additional explorations cannot begin.

Zhaozhou Congshen was a ninth-century Ch'an master and dharma heir of Nanquan. Although he had thirteen dharma successors of his own, his particular line eventually died out. But he continues to live as a Zen teacher through his record and the numerous citations of his encounters with students in the various koan collections.

Zhaozhou is best known for the following koan, offered here in its entirety: A monk asked Zhaozhou, "Does a dog have buddha nature?" Zhaozhou said, "No." (This koan is also known in shorthand by the Japanese translation of Zhaozhuo's answer, *Mu*.) Let me take just a little time to explore this.

Now, assuming that the questioner knew that the "theologically correct" response is that all things have buddha nature—or, more properly, are buddha nature—we can also assume that the student's question is hinting at a deeper concern: perhaps he is expressing doubts in his own ability to awaken, for instance.

With or without explanation, however, the koan student is advised to throw away the setup and simply engage that single word, *Mu*. As my own teacher John Tarrant observes, whether the word is *Mu* or *No* or the Chinese variant *Wu* (which some observers point out is somewhat echoic of a dog's bark), one is, of necessity, given insufficient instructions—basically, "Just deal with it."

So we throw ourselves into the great matter, allowing the doubt to arise. At some point we may try critical analysis; at another point, the word may become a mantra—chanted, breathed, whispered, yelled. And each time we think we gain some insight, we take it into the interview room where, most probably, our teacher will reject our response.

My own teacher once told me that awakening is always an accident, and I tell my own students this today. There is no obvious causal relationship between nondual insight and anything we might do or not do. But if awakening is an accident, certain practices can help us become accident-prone. Koan practice is effective at this.

If we open ourselves to this great adventure—with due diligence along with our doubt, faith, and energy—eventually it will happen: We are hit by a bus and everything changes. Or, perhaps the bus just grazes us as it passes by. This is the point of most koans. They give us an opportunity to break out of what we thought the world had been all about for us and encounter it anew.

The teacher trained in koan introspection may go on to ask "checking questions," which reveal how nuanced our insight is. In the case of a breakthrough koan, there might be dozens of checking questions—with some teachers, a hundred. As we move through the breakthrough koan into other cases, there are usually several checking questions for each case beyond the central question.

There are a few books to be found that purport to give "answers" to koans. Occasionally, for reasons that completely elude me, people will take other students' answers and present them to their teacher in the interview room, as if some formal or official "passing" of a koan were somehow the important thing, and not our own liberation from our own suffering. But it doesn't take too many checking questions to reveal the true quality of a student's insight.

There are a number of ways to categorize koans, and over the years various systems developed to help clarify how one may engage them. Hakuin's system is the most commonly represented in contemporary Western koan studies, although even it has variations. Hakuin suggested there are five types of koan, the Japanese terms for which are *hoshin*, *kikan*, *gonsen*, *nanto*, and *goi jujukin*.

Hoshin means *dharmakaya* (*kaya* is the Sanskrit word for "body"). These koans are concerned with our fundamental insight into nonduality. Kikan ("dynamic action") koans reveal the activity of emptiness. Gonsen ("explication of words") koans are often quite long and involved. Traditionally one is expected to memorize these koans and recite them in front of the teacher before actually engaging in their points.

Nanto koans are "difficult to pass through"—or at least they seem to have been for old Master Hakuin, who alluded to eight such cases. It isn't precisely clear what this designation really means. Sogen Hori quotes one roshi who remarked bluntly that "the nanto koans have no significance beyond the fact that Hakuin found them difficult to pass through." In my notes from teachers in my lineage, there are occasional references to one koan or another being "particularly difficult." However, they were not all the ones that I'd found problematic. I've come to suspect that we who walk this path each find our own nanto koans.

Goi jujukin koans are actually comprised of two sets of koans. In orthodox Japanese Rinzai, the koans one first completes are the ten grave precepts of moral and ethical action. One also usually includes the Three Refuges of Buddha, Dharma, and Sangha and the three pure precepts of ceasing from evil, practicing good, and actualizing good for others. Together with the ten grave precepts, these crown the formal study of koans. There can be hundreds of questions derived from the precepts. One then finishes with the five ranks, an ancient system of categorizations that recapitulate all that one has encountered over years of koan study. In the Harada-Yasutani curriculum, the order is reversed, culminating in an investigation of the precepts as koans.

In Japan a student of koan Zen also engages a practice of *jakugo*, or "capping phrases." These are literary tags drawn from the range of East Asian cultures and compiled in various books. Having completed the checking questions, one must then find the appropriate phrase to "cap" the case. Capping phrases are largely eliminated in the Harada-Yasutani curriculum. In the few instances where they are retained, the student is usually asked to compose his or her own verse of appreciation. Most of the orthodox Rinzai teachers in the West also drop the use of capping phrases.

The koan curricula of the Harada-Yasutani system (which ultimately derives from Hakuin's disciple Takuju) might be described like this: After encountering a breakthrough koan and up to a hundred checking questions, we would pass through a collection of brief cases that set the form for future practice. These are "in-house" koans, meaning they are unpublished and not for the general public. After this, we'd work through several classic collections, normally *The Gateless Gate*, *The Blue Cliff Record*, *The Book of Equanimity*, and *The Record of Transmitting the Light*.

The first two collections are associated with the historic Linji/Rinzai tradition; the last two are traditional Soto collections and represent the reformist inclinations of the Harada-Yasutani curriculum. While the varying traditions may use slightly different collections, the arc remains the same.

In Japanese Rinzai, according to Sogen Hori, two curricula are associated with the two principal heirs of Hakuin. In the Takuju school, after the breakthrough students begin *The Gateless Gate* (*Mumonkan*), and move on *The Blue Cliff Record* (*Hekigan-roku*). The third collection, *The Shumon Kattoshu*, is only recently available in English under the title *Entangling Vines*. Their last formal collection is *Chin'u-shu*, "The Collection of Wings of the Poison Blackbird," which is not to my knowledge currently available in English.

The other principal line of Hakuin's Zen, through his disciple Inzan, uses its own internally generated list of koans, rather than those found in traditional collections. This school's style is considered more direct and immediate, if somewhat "rougher" in approach than within the Takuju style.

The two schools have minor stylistic differences. As I've suggested, the Inzan school is said to be a bit more dynamic, while the Takuju school is said to be a bit more gentle and meticulous. Nevertheless, we can find teachers of either temperament in either tradition. And each school easily recognizes in the work of the other that they're practicing within the same spiritual system.

In Japan, someone who "completes" formal koan study might have been practicing for thirty years or more. Without the capping phrases, the Harada-Yasutani curriculum is often completed in as little as ten years from the passing of the breakthrough koan, although usually it takes considerably longer. It appears that the Western Rinzai koan curricula can be passed through in about the same amount of time.

But most people who take up koan study never complete the formal curriculum—and this isn't seen as a problem. Koans are really just invitations to practice. We do koans to deepen and clarify our zazen, to engage the matter of life and death. Truthfully, we never "complete" our koan work. In schools that use a koan introspection curriculum, however, completion of the formal curriculum is often a necessary condition—if not a sufficient one—for becoming a teacher.

Going Nowhere

Lewis Richmond

The Zen practice of shikantaza, *just sitting, says Lewis Richmond, doesn't help us to reach our destination. It allows us to stop having one. But how do you "go" nowhere?*

THE PRACTICE OF "just-awareness" is the essence of Zen meditation. The Japanese word for this, *shikantaza*, is usually translated as "just sitting," but Dogen, the founder of the Soto school of Zen, specifically taught that zazen is "beyond sitting or lying down." Shikantaza is more than the mere physical posture of sitting, although it certainly includes that. Fundamentally it is the practice of just being here, being present—except that we are not rocks or stones, but aware beings—so I think "just-awareness" more fully captures the essence of the term. But awareness of what? That is the first question.

Most people new to zazen think that it's a skill that can be learned, like tai chi. We come to zazen instruction and are told to sit a certain way, hold the hands just so, keep the eyes open, and pay attention to the breath. It seems rather easy; we look forward to becoming more accomplished in it. But Dogen admonishes us, "Zazen is not learning to do concentration." He seems to be implying that our ambitions to improve are not quite on the mark.

We can be forgiven for thinking that if we do the same thing over and over, we will improve. But is "just being here" a skill to be learned? Do we ever get better at that? I don't think so. From the first moment of life to the last, we're always just here. Our pure awareness doesn't develop, doesn't change, doesn't grow up, and doesn't grow old. I was recently talking to a 105-year-old woman, and she said, "Well, I don't feel 105. It's just me." She felt the same as she did when she was a young girl. So, from that point of view, none of us exactly grows old. Something grows old—the body perhaps, or our memories—but does our "being here" grow old? No. How could it?

This gives us a clue to the kind of practice we're talking about. It's not some kind of yogic concentration practice, such as Gautama Buddha himself practiced early in his spiritual career. When he was young, Gautama went around to various yoga teachers and learned how to develop trance states and psychic powers. He became very accomplished at these; he "improved." But in the end he felt that all these practices missed the fundamental point. No matter how good we get at something, eventually we grow old, become sick, and die; all our powers come to naught. Gautama's conclusion was that all of these concentration practices really didn't work, because in the end they're just states of consciousness to go into and come out of; they don't really address the ground of being or the cause of human suffering.

Leaving all those practices behind, Gautama recalled a time when, as a child, he sat under a tree and spontaneously felt ease and joy. Remembering this moment, Gautama sat down under a tree again—the Bodhi Tree—and reentered the natural childlike state of pure awareness. And that was the practice that led to his enlightenment. The traditional life stories of the Buddha always include this moment of returning to a child's experience. A young child doesn't think much about gaining something, about being different or better. The child just rests in her immediate experience. That's the point of another of Dogen's zazen instructions: "Do not desire to become a buddha." Don't try to get somewhere, to do something. Instead, be like a little child—naturally joyous, naturally aware.

But what does this really mean—naturally aware? In early Chinese Zen, many people thought it meant to clear the mind of all thinking. The Sixth Ancestor of Zen tried to correct this mistake, saying, "Emptying the mind and dwelling in emptiness is not Zen." So stopping one's thinking is not the goal, though many meditators . may think that.

Once someone asked my teacher Suzuki Roshi, "What do I do about all my thinking in zazen?"

"What's wrong with thinking?" Suzuki replied.

Dogen's own instruction on this point is the famous injunction, "Think not-thinking." Probably most people who hear that think it means we're not supposed to think, that thoughts are somehow a hindrance, and that the goal is a completely thought-free mind. But Dogen doesn't say, "Don't think." He says, "Think"; he uses a verb. We're being asked to think something, to make some kind of effort. But think what? How do we think not-thinking?

Suzuki Roshi used a beautiful phrase in explaining this point; he said that "think not-thinking" was "real thinking." This is an awareness that tracks exactly what's going on. So when you watch a plum blossom, he would say, you exactly track the flowering of the blossom—no more, no less. That isn't like our usual thinking. Usually we're thinking about some big problem in our life, or what we did yesterday, or are going to do tomorrow.

Dogen means that we're not trying to stop our thinking, but we're also not paying particular attention to it or trying to do anything with it. Instead there's a kind of deep acceptance or tolerance about everything. Thus we come to rest not in the track of our thinking, but in that which thinks. But who or what is that? We are back to some deep ineffable question at the root of our existence, our just-awareness. This means that in the midst of our childlike ease and joy, there is also some unusual and subtle effort—an inquiry that is beyond ratiocination or cogitation.

Without that effort—that deep questioning that drove Gautama to leave the comfort of his princely position and wander the world as a homeless monk—zazen can quickly devolve into a boring, enervated plopping down on a cushion. One Japanese Zen teacher liked to call this kind of too-passive sitting "shikan-nothing." Shikan-nothing isn't quite it either.

So what is "it"?

The best and most sincere answer is that we actually cannot say. There is something inexplicable about it—not because it is secret, but because our human condition itself is inexplicable. And that's all right. All of us naturally want a spiritual practice we can understand or conceive of, and most of conventional religious practice is like that—prayer, ritual, chanting, visualization, and so on. These are all practices that can be conceived of and understood. Zazen is a different sort of practice—mysterious and yet as simple and familiar as our own hand.

Our hand, though, has two sides: a front and a back.

Our ordinary life, our personality and conventional mental activity, are like the front of the hand. There's nothing wrong with the front of our hand, but if that's all we know—if we don't accept that our hand has two sides—then it's not really a hand. It's some kind of one-dimensional shadow of a hand. If we say, "I just want the front of my hand," that doesn't make sense.

It is equally true that zazen is not just the back of the hand, because then we'd be falling into the trap of "emptying the mind and dwelling in emptiness." Saying "I just want the back of my hand" is something like an idea or concept of emptiness; asking for just the back of the hand doesn't make sense either. That would simply be another kind of one-dimensional shadow. A hand has two sides; that is its nature. We lift it up and immediately both sides are there. So we might say that zazen practice is the practice of the whole hand.

There is some way in which, going beyond all of that, we all find ourselves swimming in the same sea, lifting up the same hand. In the fullness of the hand, front and back, we are all buddhas. To sit in the fullness of the whole hand has great power; it shakes the earth. They say that when Buddha was enlightened the earth shook. For a long time I didn't pay too much attention to such metaphors, but now I have a better appreciation of them. There's only one awareness that's deep enough and broad enough to encompass all of us, and that is the awareness of just-awareness, just being here. That is the awareness that can transform us all into beings of inexhaustible and intrinsic compassion.

Buddhist life is sometimes thought of as rather passive: sitting quietly, not saying or expressing anything, not celebrating things, not dancing, not playing music, not going to the movies. That understanding is a little too much back-of-the-hand. Zazen is not to reject one side of the hand or the other, but to equalize both sides so that the basis of our life has some deep compassionate support, some backdrop. We're not trying to suck the joy out of our experience and live a drab, black-robed life, but to round out our life so it can become deeply and authentically compassionate and joyous. This includes everything—joy, sorrow, birth, death, delusion, enlightenment.

Jack Kornfield's teacher said to him once, "You can't help anybody if you're afraid to die." My teacher once said something similar. He said, "Practice zazen like you're just about to die." At first blush, that sounds kind of grim. But actually, what he said is very practical and true. I remember him smiling when he said it. When we're about to die, there are a lot of things we don't have to worry about. Maybe there's a lot of sadness, or regret, but at least you don't have to wonder who's going to put the garbage out anymore. Whoever it is, it isn't going to be you; you're dying. So a lot drops away.

Dying is actually always here, throughout life. All human life is shadowed by the fact that we are mortal, that we are going to disappear. And our practice of zazen is to say, All right, fine, let's bring that in and get familiar with it so it doesn't frighten us anymore. Then we can be free of it, and fully embrace the compassionate mind that is our natural birthright.

In the last few years neurologists have been wiring up Zen meditators, and they've been discovering that the electrical patterns of the meditating brain look rather different from those of the normal waking mind. What does this mean? We might say that zazen is a different way to be awake. This difference may rest not so much in the cortex—the part that does thinking and logical tasks—but in the older parts of the brain, those having to do with emotion, spatial perception, and the faculty that defines the boundary of self and other.

This emerging neurological understanding may help us understand "think not-thinking" as a state where the higher brain functions are all operative and alert but not purposefully active. We don't shut down ordinary consciousness, as we would in states of deep concentration or trance. But we don't apply our mind to anything in particular, either. Instead, we just rest in awareness itself, consciousness itself.

Could this possibly be all there is to it? Is the essence of Buddhist practice really this simple? Well, yes and no. Thrangu Rinpoche, an eminent teacher of Tibetan Mahamudra (which has many similarities to Zen) once said, "It may be difficult to trust the fact that something so relatively simple could actually bring one all the way to awakening." On the other hand, the oral and written teachings of Buddhism are vast. The books of the Tibetan canon alone would fill a good-sized room, floor to ceiling, and that is just one tradition.

Yes, the essence practice of Buddhism—which is what zazen is—really is simple. It is we human beings who are complicated. It takes us a long time to trust the practice fully, as Thrangu Rinpoche implied. Consequently Buddhism offers us a great variety of other transformative practices—such as bowing, chanting, visualizing, or the meditations on compassion—to encourage us on the path while we cultivate this trust.

Many, many people, through countless generations, have cultivated and refined these practices. We are the inheritors and beneficiaries of their lifetimes of effort. In this difficult world of ours, where there seems to be so much confusion, strife, suffering, and terror, we must remember that Gautama Buddha lived in just such a world and confronted the very same imponderables as we—the same wonderment, hopefulness, confusion, and despair. He got through it, and so can we. He was not a god, not a superman, but a human being with the same mind, body, and faculties we have. At the moment of his enlightenment he exclaimed, "All beings are just like this—all of them are intrinsically buddhas!"

May it be so. May all beings immediately recognize their intrinsic nature as buddhas and become fully liberated!

The Power of Koan Practice

John Tarrant

John Tarrant explains how the seemingly absurd little stories called koans cut through conceptual mind.

THOSE WHO HAVE USED koans have described them as a poetic technology for bringing about awakening, a painful but effective gate into the consciousness of the Buddha, an easy method of integrating awakening into everyday life, the most frustrating thing they have ever done, an appalling waste of time, a tyranny perpetrated by Zen masters. . . . Well, you get the idea—about koans, opinions differ.

If it turns out that koans suit you or—to put it in more koan-like language—if koans choose you, then they are a help in living with less fear and more happiness in a quite individual way. Koans are a fairly old form and, coming through East Asia with its reverence for tradition, have been taught in a fashion that hasn't changed much since the twelfth century. There is nothing wrong with this in itself; however, I have been interested in other modes in which to describe and use them, modes that are true to the koan's original, innovative spirit and also available to our culture now. This is a report on a thirty-year experiment in that direction.

Although koans have made it into popular culture as riddles and wisecracks, they aren't all mystery and strangeness; they are intended to have an outcome, to work, to be effective in relieving unhappiness, and, just as important, to be amusing. Though they have heroic moments, koans encourage the notion that the comic is truer and more pleasant to live inside than the epic.

Koans seem true to life because they rely on uncertainty, surprise, and the imagination. They depend on the inconceivable, which is the largest part of life. At the same time, if koans leap, they take off from a specific place; they depend on the everyday world of the kitchen and the garden and on precise language. In this way they are like art; they encourage you to move beyond your self-imposed limits by offering a fresh view of things you have already seen or think you have already seen. Through the koans you find freedom by entering life more fully. As Suzuki Roshi said of koans:

> From the Buddha's time to our age, human nature has been nearly the same. We live in the world of time and space, and our life does not go beyond this limit. To live in the world of time and space is like putting a big snake into a small can. The snake will suffer in the small can. It does not know what is going on outside of the can. Because it is in the can, it is so dark he cannot see anything, but he will struggle in the small can. That is what we are doing. The more we struggle, the greater the suffering will be. That kind of practice will not work. Putting yourself in a small can and sitting day after day in a cross-legged position is worse than a waste of time. Do you understand? Sometimes our practice is something like this. We don't know how much our understanding is limited. That is why you have to study koans. Koans will open up your mind. If you understand your way of life more objectively, you will understand what you are doing.

The teachers made a few unusual decisions that kept the process interesting. First of all, they liked doubt and encouraged questions. This is rare in religion and an example of the Zen way of treating what is usually thought of as a problem—in this case, doubt—as a strength. The teachers also decided they would treat all questions as if they were worthwhile, no matter what their content. "Why is my boyfriend leaving?" would be treated as having the same spiritual value as "What happens when I die?" There was a trust in whatever forces had brought the student to the point of asking, and any question was treated as being about enlightenment, whether the student was aware of it or not. This is a generous view, but it didn't always have comforting results, because the teachers made yet a third decision. Instead of giving kind advice or step-by-step instructions, the teachers responded to the students as if they were capable of coming to a complete understanding in that moment. A teacher's words often made no rational sense yet possessed a compelling quality. Sometimes a student who had been stuck and unhappy would be suddenly full of joy. More often, the words would work away in the mind, drawing the student out of a limiting view he or she held.

Some exchanges became famous and were written down. They came to be known as koans—the word means "public case"—and there was a mania for collecting them. One well-known teacher forbade his students to write down what he said because he thought they were recording his comments as a substitute for the more necessary and dangerous task of letting them work on the mind. One student adapted by wearing paper clothing to lectures, and the notes he jotted down secretly on his sleeves were passed around.

Soldiers, housewives, farmers, and merchants used koans to find freedom within the often difficult conditions of their times. The method was simply to immerse yourself in the saying and see how it changed your view of reality; to let it teach you by interacting with the immediate circumstances of your life and your mind.

In one instance, when Genghis Khan's troops swept through China in the twelfth century, provincial governors went to the Khan and became senior ministers. They lived out on the steppes with him, hoping to persuade him to rule the cities rather than burning them and converting them into horse pasture. It would be hard not to feel unprepared for, and perhaps terrified of, such a task, and one of the ministers asked his teacher for advice. The most helpful thing the teacher could think of was to make a collection of koans and poems that he called *The Book of Serenity*. When this book arrived on the steppes, the story goes, the ministers sat up together all night in a yurt, reading the koans aloud.

I took up koan practice when I was meditating outdoors in the rain-forests and hills in Queensland, Australia, about thirty years ago. Koans seemed to fit my mind the way it was, as opposed to the way I wished it were. Most meditation instructions employ an engineer-ing metaphor, and my mind was not very efficient at being an en-gine. In the engineering model, everything is nicely laid out in stages. Meditation instructions were intended to be a map of escape routes from the mind's prison, but I knew that I was often reading that map with an inmate's consciousness. I might think I was taking down the prison walls, when I was really just doing interior design to make my cell more comfy. Some sort of leap was needed. "Hmm," I thought, "traditional meditation training makes sense, the steps follow—one, two, three, four—it is rational, it's serious, it knows where it wants to go. Obviously it won't work for me."

A koan, though, seemed to be a brief art form that, regardless of your opinions about it, rearranged the world. In the koan universe a creative leap isn't "one, two, three, four, six"; it is more like "one, two, three, four, rhinoceros." It doesn't allow the insanity defense and doesn't discriminate against those with attention deficit.

Somewhere I had read that it was bad to take up koans without a teacher at hand. But if you followed that advice in Australia you would have been limited to playing cricket in the bush with the kangaroos. There were no teachers to be found. So I chose a koan and started to keep it company. Since I didn't know how to work with it, I just spent about six years with it day and night. There was no instruction manual, I didn't know what I was doing, didn't know what the outcome would look like, and there was no one to ask. There was a nakedness about this approach that seemed right. My meditation wasn't contaminated by my prejudices. A year or so ago, when I visited him in hospice, the Zen poet Philip Whalen told me, "They want me to die in stages. I can't be bothered with that." It seemed to me that he thought the same thing about his journey into the deep dark: why take your opinions with you?

With koans, whatever you thought, the koan would take it away. "What is Buddha?" someone asked. "Three pounds of flax," said the teacher. Another teacher said, "This very heart and mind is Buddha." Someone checked his answer by asking him again, "What is Buddha?" and he answered, "Not mind, not Buddha." The koans took away what you believed, but they didn't put something else in its place. "What is Buddha?" asked yet another student, and the teacher said, "Dried shit stick." This teacher had gained enlightenment when his leg was caught and broken in an iron gate, so perhaps this wasn't shock therapy after all, but just an attempt to broaden the student's range of appreciation of life's offerings.

The theory, if there is one, that underlies koans is based on classical Buddhism but extends it. From the misty beginnings of the way, the Buddhist idea about transformation is that suffering comes from your own thinking. As Montaigne said, "No one is injured but by himself." So far, so good. If you want to be free from suffering, it follows, you have to remove your delusions. Original Buddhism was essentially mind training. "Stay calm, don't panic, no need to go shopping, keep away from influences that might trouble the mind" was the idea. Yogic concentration techniques were taught: "Pay attention to your breathing, and if your mind wanders bring it back to your breathing, no matter what, no matter if you feel happy or sad or go out of your mind with boredom" is a good example. Concentration methods are still the foundation practice. Anyone who has ever spent an hour in silence can find that such concentration is refreshing and healing.

There were also traditional prescriptions to induce detachment. They contained helpful suggestions along the lines of, "Imagine your girlfriend is ugly and repulsive." One would have thought this would pose a marketing problem. But times are usually hard, and if you have had enough civil war and poverty, it's amazing what you will be willing to try. From the koan point of view, though, the difficulty here wasn't marketing; it was accuracy and effectiveness. If you don't perceive your girl as ugly, that's not a problem, and to make it one feels like straining.

With the koan, you get to listen to the mind's conversation before trying to change it. Even without adding evaluations of beauty, the internal conversation is always happening and it defines the world you live in and who you are. And when you do listen, it's hard not to be amused, because, while the conversation has an immense variety, it has only one real interest, which is, "What about Little Me?"

"Little Me" is like an employee you hired to take care of the garden. Then he began to do a little bookkeeping, and then he decided whom you should marry and what job you should take. This out-of-control employee also took on the job of spiritual practice, turning it toward his own ends. The koan's job is to interrupt the conversation in such a way as to allow you to see through it, even to enjoy it. The less you believe your internal conversation, though, the less you need your employee, Little Me. You will still exist and eat and think and so on, but life will be very much expanded. If your girlfriend looks beautiful to you, she's just beautiful and that's all there is to it. It's not in the realm of right and wrong.

The first Buddhist stories were very grand. They went along the lines of: "Something terrible happened to me. My children were eaten by tigers and I went mad. Then I met the Buddha and he said come along with me and I did: I practiced meditation until suddenly one day the lamp of wanting and fearing blew out. That was it. No more being born and wanting stuff. I couldn't be more thrilled."

The imagination has a soft spot for such epic stories, but they all have the same ending, which is the part I never quite believe. It's not that I disbelieve the freedom or that there can be a heroic and demanding quality to the quest for enlightenment. It's just that such a story pushes the texture of life out of the way, and the texture is the field in which we experience freedom. The end of the story—

when the main character sees the light—is not actually the high moment. Such moments are not the story; they are just what allows the story to happen. At the end of the story people get married and have children or get divorced or the children go to college—it's the heaven of the ordinary which goes on and on until death stops it. It has its own beauty, but it is not grand.

The koans certainly touch on the epic, but they also offer an alternative that is at least as helpful: the comic. They undercut their otherwise similar stories by introducing a sense of the ridiculous. People get enlightened in the bathroom, or when a pot breaks in the kitchen, or in a brothel, or for no good reason. The seriousness of the epic consciousness requires a lot of the "What about poor Little Me?" attitude, and the koans offer compassion, not by taking you away from pain but by taking you through pain to freedom and even amusement, as the following dialogue shows.

"What if it's a disaster?" asked a student plaintively.
"That's it too," said the teacher.

How you work with a koan is largely up to you, though it doesn't hurt to know how other people have done it. As an example, a koan consisting of the single, common word *no* was introduced about 1,200 years ago. Enough people found it helpful that it became, hands down, the most often used—the gate through which almost everyone could pass. *No* has the advantage of being simple, portable, and enduring. It's easy to remember. It can't be burned or lost; it can't be stolen or thrown away. You have to come to terms with it, to be able to hear it and say it with relish, in order to hear and say *yes*. This koan is embedded in a brief dialogue.

Someone asked a teacher, "Does a dog have buddha nature?"
And the teacher said, "No."

It isn't always clear what a question means, or what sort of answer would satisfy it, but that is often true of someone else's burning issue. When you ask a question, you are usually looking for an answer about what color to paint your cell walls. What makes your question a koan is when it takes you farther than you intended, beyond the walls, beyond the range of what is already known, to the edge of the unknown. If you refuse the answers made up of what you can already conceive of, your question just might lead you all the way home.

In this koan, the answer, No, was a surprise—something to make you look twice and find out for yourself. When I worked on this koan, I just took the question as summing up all my own uncertainties and doubts—whatever incomprehension about life's difficulties gave me pain. I concentrated on the response, the No.

It can be painful to say No, as if you are refusing an offer from the universe. No can also come with a thrill of freedom. Both are still in the realm of yes and no, the realm of things you already understand. On the other hand, the koan No begins an initiation passage into the place beyond the known.

In my own practice, I just made up how to work with this koan, but that's always true of art and life. At first I tried to use the koan to stabilize the world, to get away from the world, to make things calm. This was another form of the prison-wall-painting project; that Little Me bloke was fond of calm and control. This approach didn't work—I found that the koan ignored interior decoration in favor of demolition.

A koan defeats the interior decoration project by bringing up the painful condition that project is trying to address. If competition, envy, and the mind of comparison are large in your makeup, the koan won't point this out gently; instead you will feel it in every bone of your body. You will be in an agony of comparison and even despair. Until, gradually, you won't. And it is the same for all issues—grief, paranoia, whatever you have in your heart. It is as if the koan were saying, "Look, this is how you deal with things; do you like to do it this way?" Yet the koan is impartial—it doesn't mind; it just shows you how you operate. It doesn't shirk or judge the darkness of being human. At the same time it opens for you another possibility: what it would be like, and who you would be, if you didn't operate that way. This is why the koan can be so freeing.

In the end I stopped trying to achieve calm and even enlightenment in favor of discovering the world through the koan. I just let the koan into whatever was happening. As I dropped the idea that what was happening was unworthy of the koan or that the koan wouldn't fit a secular context, I found that the koan made no distinction between secular and sacred, or calm mind and agitation, or even between my life and the life of the forest.

Here is an example of how someone else—a student I interviewed for a book I'm writing—worked with the same koan. In Japanese the koan is Mu, and she actually used it in that form, because in those days we didn't think that you could get enlightened in English. I've retranslated back into No.

No was an incredible process for me. It took a year and a half. I kept a journal and had major dreams. Over and over again I came to my teacher and said, "It's this," or, "It's that." For a long time the teacher rejected my answers and this made me confident, since I didn't really believe them myself. No pushed other thoughts away. Familiar places looked like I had never seen them before. This happened in flashes at first, and then became more consistent. I found that I could survive frustration and the continual, tormenting "I don't know."

I hit a dry place. "Why continue?" I thought. "I'm no good at this anyway. Why did I ever think that I could be included in this?" It was an important thing to go through the dry place, and it helped that I was encouraged to sit through it and value it. I realized that if I would just pay attention, little things would open up, little snatches. I was sorting seeds, as in the fairy tale.

Then, in a retreat, we did walking meditation out into the parking lot. I said to myself, "This is a regal procession." I noticed the guy in front had a black silk shirt on; it had a dull finish. Redwood branches parted in front of my eyes and then there was that thing that's hard to describe, the nothingness, that wham of past, present, future gone—no separation be-tween past and present. There is no self, absolutely none. The redwoods parted and it was whitish and granular, particulate, like seeing between the atoms. Who knows how long it lasted, but I found myself still walking when I arrived back, and my immediate thought was, "Wait, I have to be left with some word," and it was like, OK, if you insist on going back to this small world and having a word, even after everything has been shown to you, this is what you get: "No other."

Later, still working with No, I was at a retreat in the red-woods again and walked into a first-floor bathroom. Though it was cleaned regularly, that bathroom always had the fragrance of pee. No became that whole fragrance and essence of pee. I wasn't drawn or repelled; there was just nothing else in the whole world. I didn't have to live with the fragrance of pee but did have to live with that discovery—no attraction, no repul-sion, not doing, not picking and choosing. I used the tools at hand, in this case the pee. "What other tools," I thought, "would I use?" After that I could answer the teacher's questions.

So this narrative includes an account of a moment of light. If your mind clears at an identifiable point the way this woman's did, that's fine. As a very old teacher said to me once, "Don't worry, you couldn't help it." It's not an end to the story, though perhaps it's a kind of beginning.

Through the koans I stopped trying to improve myself. The koan had made me more interested in my actual life, and less inter-ested in an ideal or spiritual life. There's a sense of staying with things, and of commitment, as in my marriage, but at the same time there's not that fear of what would happen if something didn't work. And if I'm thinking something is not working it's probably not working. When I rest in what I don't know, I stick up for myself.

The koan universe is not normative or prescriptive. It's not fun-damentalist. Since all of the stories you tell about life, even ones about enlightenment, are just stories, there is no doctrine, just method, which is judged by effectiveness and, perhaps, by beauty. The method trusts the basic, loving possibility in humans as well as the uncertainty that everything rests on.

> Two teachers are on a picnic. One of them points to the ground and says, "This is the top of the mountain of heaven."
> The other says, "True, but a pity."

Other places are heaven too. And isn't it just as interesting if it's not heaven? The koans don't tell us to feel kind, but when the delusions are no longer running the show, it's easy to love. Then the kindness of life naturally extends into places where you wouldn't expect it.

> A student asked, "Where will you go when you die?"
> "I'll go straight to hell," said the teacher.
> "A good enlightened teacher like you, Master, how could that be?"
> "If I don't, who will teach you?"

When I stop laughing at a koan, I can be struck by wonder.

> "What is the blown hair sword?" asked a teacher, referring to the sword that cuts delusion, so sharp that a hair blown across it falls in two.
> Then he answered his own set-up line:
> "Each branch of coral holds up the moon."

I find this koan almost dangerously beautiful. It's true, but a pity.

Study Yourself

Shunryu Suzuki Roshi

What is the purpose of practice? "To have some deep feeling about Buddhism is not the point," wrote Zen pioneer Shunryu Suzuki Roshi in this teaching from his classic Zen Mind, Beginner's Mind. *"We just do what we should do, like eating supper and going to bed. This is Buddhism."*

THE PURPOSE OF STUDYING Buddhism is not to study Buddhism, but to study ourselves. It is impossible to study ourselves without some teaching. If you want to know what water is you need science, and the scientist needs a laboratory. In the laboratory there are various ways in which to study what water is. Thus it is possible to know what kind of elements water has, the various forms it takes, and its nature. But it is impossible thereby to know water in itself. It is the same thing with us. We need some teaching, but just by studying the teaching alone, it is impossible to know what "I" in myself am. Through the teaching we may understand our human nature. But the teaching is not we ourselves; it is some explanation of ourselves. So if you are attached to the teaching, or to the teacher, that is a big mistake. The moment you meet a teacher, you should leave the teacher, and you should be independent. You need a teacher so that you can become independent. If you are not attached to him, the teacher will show you the way to yourself. You have a teacher for yourself, not for the teacher.

Rinzai, an early Chinese Zen master, analyzed how to teach his disciples in four ways. Sometimes he talked about the disciple himself; sometimes he talked about the teaching itself; sometimes he gave an interpretation of the disciple or the teaching; and finally, sometimes he did not give any instruction at all to his disciples. He knew that even without being given any instruction, a student is a student. Strictly speaking, there is no need to teach the student, because the student himself is Buddha, even though he may not be aware of it. And even though he is aware of his true nature, if he is attached to this awareness, that is already wrong. When he is not aware of it, he has everything, but when he becomes aware of it he thinks that what he is aware of is himself, which is a big mistake.

When you do not hear anything from the teacher, but just sit, this is called teaching without teaching. But sometimes this is not sufficient, so we listen to lectures and have discussions. But we should remember that the purpose of practice in a particular place is to study ourselves. To be independent, we study. Like the scientist, we have to have some means by which to study. We need a teacher because it is impossible to study ourselves by ourselves. But you should not make a mistake. You should not take what you have learned with a teacher for you yourself. The study you make with your teacher is a part of your everyday life, a part of your incessant activity. In this sense there is no difference between the practice and the activity you have in everyday life. So to find the meaning of your life in the zendo is to end the meaning of your everyday activity. To be aware of the meaning of your life, you practice zazen.

When I was at Eiheiji monastery in Japan, everyone was just doing what he should do. That is all. It is the same as waking up in the morning; we have to get up. At Eiheiji monastery, when we had to sit, we sat; when we had to bow to Buddha, we bowed to Buddha. That is all. And when we were practicing, we did not feel anything special. We did not even feel that we were leading a monastic life. For us, the monastic life was the usual life, and the people who came from the city were unusual people. When we saw them we felt, "Oh, some unusual people have come!"

But once I had left Eiheiji and been away for some time, coming back was different. I heard the various sounds of practice—the bells and the monks reciting the sutra—and I had a deep feeling. There were tears flowing out of my eyes, nose, and mouth! It is the people who are outside of the monastery who feel its atmosphere. Those who are practicing actually do not feel anything. I think this is true for everything. When we hear the sound of the pine trees on a windy day, perhaps the wind is just blowing, and the pine tree is just standing in the wind. That is all that they are doing. But the people who listen to the wind in the tree will write a poem, or will feel something unusual. That is, I think, the way everything is.

So to feel something about Buddhism is not the main point. Whether that feeling is good or bad is out of the question. We do not mind, whatever it is. Buddhism is not good or bad. We are doing what we should do. That is Buddhism. Of course some encouragement is necessary, but that encouragement is just encouragement. It is not the true purpose of practice. It is just medicine. When we become discouraged we want some medicine. When we are in good spirits we do not need any medicine. You should not mistake medicine for food. Sometimes medicine is necessary, but it should not become our food.

So, of Rinzai's four ways of practice, the perfect one is not to give a student any interpretation of himself, nor to give him any encouragement. If we think of ourselves as our bodies, the teaching then may be our clothing. Sometimes we talk about our clothing; sometimes we talk about our body. But neither body nor clothing is actually we ourselves. We ourselves are the big activity. We are just expressing the smallest particle of the big activity, that is all. So it is all right to talk about ourselves, but actually there is no need to do so. Before we open our mouths, we are already expressing the big existence, including ourselves. So the purpose of talking about ourselves is to correct the misunderstanding we have when we are attached to any particular temporal form or color of the big activity.

It is necessary to talk about what our body is and what our activity is so that we may not make any mistake about them. So to talk about ourselves is actually to forget about ourselves.

Dogen Zenji said, "To study Buddhism is to study ourselves. To study ourselves is to forget ourselves." When you become attached to a temporal expression of your true nature, it is necessary to talk about Buddhism, or else you will think the temporal expression is it. But this particular expression of it is not it. And yet at the same time it *is* it! For a while this is it; for the smallest particle of time, this is it. But it is not always so: the very next instant it is not so, thus this is not it. So that you will realize this fact, it is necessary to study Buddhism. But the purpose of studying Buddhism is to study ourselves and to forget ourselves. When we forget ourselves, we actually are the true activity of the big existence, or reality itself. When we realize this fact, there is no problem whatsoever in this world, and we can enjoy our life without feeling any difficulties. The purpose of our practice is to be aware of this fact.

PART FOUR

Indo-Tibetan Innovations

We can all learn together to some degree, but the transformation of the world must begin within ourselves. Compassion and wisdom need to function together, combined with skillfulness, tolerance, and patience. If we give ourselves the time and space to really observe our own thoughts and actions, good can come about. We give ourselves and others a lot of space in which to function properly; rather than act selfishly, we act selflessly.

—VENERABLE KHANDRO RINPOCHE

AS THE DHARMA SPREAD through Asia over the centuries that followed the Buddha's passing, new approaches to the teachings were innovated. Among these were practices developed chiefly in India and Tibet for cultivating wisdom and compassion and generating the motivation to benefit all beings that is a mark of Mahayana Buddhism, which encompasses the Zen tradition as well as the Buddhism of Tibet. In this section we'll learn how to do some of these practices and get a taste of two approaches that are key to the Tibetan tradition: Mahamudra and Dzogchen.

What the Practice Can Do

John Powers

John Powers describes how the meditative practices of Tibetan Buddhism can be used to counteract anger and desire.

TIBETAN BUDDHISM has many different schools and lineages, with a variety of practices and goals. All schools of Tibetan Buddhism agree, however, that the final goal of Mahayana practice is the attainment of buddhahood for the benefit of all other sentient beings. The key factor of this process is meditation, a general term that encompasses a wide range of practices and goals. Some of these aim at pacifying the mind and quieting the mental confusion that afflicts ordinary beings. Other meditative practices are concerned with developing clear understanding of Buddhist tenets such as the four noble truths, impermanence, no-self, and so on, or with cultivating direct perception of the true nature of reality.

Most meditative practices aim at some form of cognitive restructuring. Since dissatisfaction arises from wrong ideas, the solution to the problem of suffering lies in changing these ideas, and this is accomplished through meditation. Suffering is linked to actions based on afflictive mental states such as desire, ignorance, hatred, and so on, and many of the techniques of Tibetan meditation are designed to serve as counteragents to afflictions. For instance, a meditator who is particularly prone to anger might be instructed to cultivate feelings of love and compassion. Love and compassion are incompatible with anger, and so the more one trains in the former attitudes, the more one's tendency toward anger diminishes.

A person with strong desire might be instructed to consider the impermanence of all the phenomena of cyclic existence. No matter how much money or power one accumulates, one must eventually lose them, either sooner or later. Even the richest people cannot know with certainty that they will still have their money in a week, a month, or a year. And no amount of wealth can forestall death, which is the final end of the ambitions, desires, and concerns of the present life. Through contemplating these truths, one should experience a diminution of mundane desires and a corresponding interest in pursuing their practice, which can lead to ultimate and lasting happiness.

Relaxing with the Truth

Pema Chödrön

It is only when we begin to relax with ourselves as we are, says Pema Chödrön, that meditation becomes a transformative process. The pith instruction is: Stay . . . stay . . . just stay.

As a species, we should never underestimate our low tolerance for discomfort. To be encouraged to stay with our vulnerability is news that we definitely can use. Sitting meditation is our support for learning how to do this. Sitting meditation, also known as mindfulness-awareness practice, is the foundation of *bodhichitta* training. It is the home ground of the warrior bodhisattva.

Sitting meditation cultivates loving-kindness and compassion, the relative qualities of bodhichitta, which could be defined as completely awakened heart and mind. It gives us a way to move closer to our thoughts and emotions and to get in touch with our bodies. It is a method of cultivating unconditional friendliness toward ourselves and for parting the curtain of indifference that distances us from the suffering of others. It is our vehicle for learning to be a truly loving person.

Gradually, through meditation, we begin to notice that there are gaps in our internal dialogue. In the midst of continually talking to ourselves, we experience a pause, as if awakening from a dream. We recognize our capacity to relax with the clarity, the space, the open-ended awareness that already exists in our minds. We experience moments of being right here that feel simple, direct, and uncluttered.

This coming back to the immediacy of our experience is training in unconditional bodhichitta. By simply staying here, we relax more and more into the open dimension of our being. It feels like stepping out of a fantasy and relaxing with the truth.

Yet there is no guarantee that sitting meditation will be of benefit. We can practice for years without it penetrating our hearts and minds. We can use meditation to reinforce our false beliefs: it will protect us from discomfort; it will fix us; it will fulfill our hopes and remove our fears. This happens because we don't properly understand why we are practicing.

Why *do* we meditate? This is a question we'd be wise to ask. Why would we even bother to spend time alone with ourselves?

First of all, it is helpful to understand that meditation is not just about feeling good. To think that this is why we meditate is to set ourselves up for failure. We'll assume we are doing it wrong almost every time we sit down: even the most settled meditator experiences psychological and physical pain. Meditation takes us just as we are, with our confusion and our sanity. This complete acceptance of ourselves as we are is called *maitri,* a simple, direct relationship with our being.

Trying to fix ourselves is not helpful. It implies struggle and self-denigration. Denigrating ourselves is probably the major way that we cover over bodhichitta.

Does not trying to change mean we have to remain angry and addicted until the day we die? This is a reasonable question. Trying to change ourselves doesn't work in the long run because we're resisting our own energy. Self-improvement can have temporary results, but lasting transformation occurs only when we honor ourselves as the source of wisdom and compassion. We are, as the eighth-century Buddhist master Shantideva pointed out, very much like a blind person who finds a jewel buried in a heap of garbage. It is right here in our smelliest of stuff that we discover the awakened heart of basic clarity and goodness, the completely open mind of bodhichitta.

It is only when we begin to relax with ourselves as we are that meditation becomes a transformative process. When we relate with ourselves without moralizing, without harshness, without deception, we finally let go of harmful patterns. Without maitri, renunciation of old habits becomes abusive. This is an important point.

There are four main qualities that are cultivated when we meditate: steadfastness, clear seeing, experiencing our emotional distress, and attention to the present moment. These four factors not only apply to sitting meditation, but are essential to all the bodhichitta practices and for relating with difficult situations in our daily lives.

Steadfastness

When we practice meditation we are strengthening our ability to be steadfast with ourselves. No matter what comes up—aching bones, boredom, falling asleep, or the wildest thoughts and emotions—we develop a loyalty to our experience. Although plenty of meditators consider it, we don't run screaming out of the room. Instead we acknowledge that impulse as thinking, without labeling it right or wrong. This is no small task. Never underestimate our inclination to bolt when we hurt.

We're encouraged to meditate every day, even for a short time, in order to cultivate this steadfastness with ourselves. We sit under all kinds of circumstances—whether we are feeling healthy or sick, whether we're in a good mood or depressed, whether we feel our meditation is going well or is completely falling apart. As we continue to sit we see that meditation isn't about getting it right or attaining some ideal state. It's about being able to stay present with ourselves. It becomes increasingly clear that we won't be free of self-destructive patterns unless we develop a compassionate understanding of what they are.

One aspect of steadfastness is simply being in your body. Because meditation emphasizes working with your mind, it's easy to forget that you even have a body.

When you sit down it's important to relax into your body and to get in touch with what is going on. Starting with the top of your head, you can spend a few minutes bringing awareness to every part of your body. When you come to places that are hurting or tense you can breathe in and out three or four times, keeping your awareness on that area. When you get to the soles of your feet you can stop or, if you feel like it, you can repeat this body sweep by going from bottom to top. Then at any time during your meditation period, you can quickly tune back in to the overall sense of being in your body. For a moment you can bring your awareness directly back to being right here. You are sitting. There are sounds, smells, sights, aches; you are breathing in and out. You can reconnect with your body like this when it occurs to you—maybe once or twice during a sitting session. Then return to the technique.

In meditation we discover our inherent restlessness. Sometimes we get up and leave. Sometimes we sit there but our bodies wiggle and squirm and our minds go far away. This can be so uncomfortable that we feel it's impossible to stay. Yet this feeling can teach us not just about ourselves but also about what it is to be human. All of us derive security and comfort from the imaginary world of memories and fantasies and plans. We really don't want to stay with the nakedness of our present experience. It goes against the grain to stay present. There are the times when only gentleness and a sense of humor can give us the strength to settle down.

The pith instruction is: Stay . . . stay . . . just stay. Learning to stay with ourselves in meditation is like training a dog. If we train a dog by beating it, we'll end up with an obedient but very inflexible and rather terrified dog. The dog may obey when we say, "Stay!" "Come!" "Roll over!" and "Sit up!" but he will also be neurotic and confused. By contrast, training with kindness results in someone who is flexible and confident, who doesn't become upset when situations are unpredictable and insecure.

So whenever we wander off, we gently encourage ourselves to "stay" and settle down. Are we experiencing restlessness? Stay! Discursive mind? Stay! Are fear and loathing out of control? Stay! Aching knees and throbbing back? Stay! What's for lunch? Stay! What am I doing here? Stay! I can't stand this another minute! Stay! That is how to cultivate steadfastness.

Clear Seeing

After we've been meditating for a while, it's common to feel that we are regressing rather than waking up. "Until I started meditating, I was quite settled; now it feels like I'm always restless." "I never used to feel anger; now it comes up all the time." We might complain that meditation is ruining our life, but in fact such experiences are a sign that we're starting to see more clearly. Through the process of practicing the technique day in and out, year after year, we begin to be very honest with ourselves. Clear seeing is another way of saying that we have less self-deception.

The Beat poet Jack Kerouac, feeling primed for a spiritual breakthrough, wrote to a friend before he retreated into the wilderness, "If I don't get a vision on Desolation Peak, then my name ain't William Blake." But later he wrote that he found it hard to face the naked truth. "I'd thought, in June when I get to the top—and everybody leaves—I will come face to face with God or Tathagata (Buddha) and find out once and for all what is the meaning of all this existence and suffering—but instead I'd come face to face with myself, no liquor, no drugs, no chance of faking it, but face to face with ole Hateful . . . Me."

Meditation requires patience and maitri. If this process of clear seeing isn't based on self-compassion it will become a process of self-aggression. We need self-compassion to stabilize our minds. We need it to work with our emotions. We need it in order to stay.

When we learn to meditate, we are instructed to sit in a certain position on a cushion or chair. We're instructed to just be in the present moment, aware of our breath as it goes out. We're instructed that when our mind has wandered off, without any harshness or judgmental quality, we should acknowledge that as "thinking" and return to the out-breath. We train in coming back to this moment of being here. In the process of doing this, our fogginess, our bewilderment, our ignorance begin to transform into clear seeing. "Thinking" becomes a code word for seeing "just what is"—both our clarity and our confusion. We are not trying to get rid of thoughts. Rather we are clearly seeing our defense mechanisms, our negative beliefs about ourselves, our desires, and our expectations. We also see our kindness, our bravery, our wisdom.

Through the process of practicing the mindfulness-awareness technique on a regular basis, we can no longer hide from ourselves. We clearly see the barriers we set up to shield us from naked experience. Although we still associate the walls we've erected with safety and comfort, we also begin to feel them as a restriction. This claustrophobic situation is important for a warrior. It marks the beginning of longing for an alternative to our small, familiar world. We begin to look for ventilation. We want to dissolve the barriers between ourselves and others.

Experiencing Our Emotional Distress

Many people, including longtime practitioners, use meditation as a means of escaping difficult emotions. It is possible to misuse the label "thinking" as a way of pushing negativity away. No matter how many times we've been instructed to stay open to whatever arises, we still can use meditation as repression. Transformation occurs only when we remember, breath by breath, year after year, to move toward our emotional distress without condemning or justifying our experience.

Trungpa Rinpoche describes emotion as a combination of self-existing energy and thoughts. Emotion can't proliferate without our internal conversations. If we're angry when we sit to meditate, we are instructed to label the thoughts "thinking" and let them go. Yet below the thoughts something remains—a vital, pulsating energy. There is nothing wrong, nothing harmful about that underlying energy. Our practice is to stay with it, to experience it, to leave it as it is, without proliferating.

There are certain advanced techniques in which you intentionally churn up emotions by thinking of people or situations that make you angry or lustful or afraid. The practice is to let the thoughts go and connect directly with the energy, asking yourself, "Who am I without these thoughts?" What we do with mindfulness-awareness practice is simpler than that, but I consider it equally daring. When emotional distress arises uninvited, we let the story line go and abide with the energy of that moment. This is a felt experience, not a verbal commentary on what is happening. We can feel the energy in our bodies. If we can stay with it, neither acting it out nor repressing it, it wakes us up. People often say, "I fall asleep all the time in meditation. What shall I do?" There are lots of antidotes to drowsiness, but my favorite is, "Get angry!"

Not abiding with our energy is a predictable human habit. Acting out and repressing are tactics we use to get away from our emotional pain. For instance most of us when we're angry scream or act it out. We alternate expressions of rage with feeling ashamed of ourselves and wallowing in it. We become so stuck in repetitive behavior that we become experts at getting all worked up. In this way we continue to strengthen our conflicting emotions.

One night years ago I came upon my boyfriend passionately embracing another woman. We were in the house of a millionaire who had a priceless collection of pottery. I was furious and looking for something to throw. Everything I picked up I had to put back down because it was worth at least $10,000. I was completely enraged and I couldn't find an outlet! There were no exits from experiencing my own energy. The absurdity of the situation totally cut through my rage. I went outside and looked at the sky and laughed until I cried.

In Vajrayana Buddhism it is said that wisdom is inherent in emotions. When we struggle against our own energy we are rejecting the source of wisdom. Anger without the fixation is none other than mirror-like wisdom. Pride and envy without fixation is experienced as equanimity. The energy of passion when it's free of grasping is discriminating awareness wisdom.

In bodhichitta training we also welcome the living energy of emotions. When our emotions intensify what we usually feel is fear. This fear is always lurking in our lives. In sitting meditation we practice dropping whatever story we are telling ourselves and leaning into the emotions and the fear. Thus we train in opening the fearful heart to the restlessness of our own energy. We learn to abide with the experience of our emotional distress.

Attention to the Present Moment

Another factor we cultivate in the transformative process of meditation is attention to this very moment. We make the choice, moment by moment, to be fully here. Attending to our present-moment mind and body is a way of being tender toward self, toward other, and toward the world. This quality of attention is inherent in our ability to love.

Coming back to the present moment takes some effort, but the effort is very light. The instruction is to "touch and go." We touch thoughts by acknowledging them as thinking and then we let them go. It's a way of relaxing our struggle, like touching a bubble with a feather. It's a nonaggressive approach to being here.

Sometimes we find that we like our thoughts so much that we don't want to let them go. Watching our personal video is a lot more entertaining than bringing our mind back home. There's no doubt that our fantasy world can be very juicy and seductive. So we train in using a "soft" effort, in interrupting our habitual patterns; we train in cultivating self-compassion.

We practice meditation to connect with maitri and unconditional openness. By not deliberately blocking anything, by directly touching our thoughts and then letting them go with an attitude of no big deal, we can discover that our fundamental energy is tender, wholesome, and fresh. We can start to train as a warrior, discovering for ourselves that it is bodhichitta, not confusion, that is basic.

Developing the Mind of Great Capacity

The Fourteenth Dalai Lama

The Fourteenth Dalai Lama explains the importance of generating bodhichitta, *the aspiration to attain enlightenment for the benefit of all beings, and describes two methods for cultivating this altruistic attitude.*

FROM ONE POINT OF VIEW, personal liberation without freeing others is selfish and unfair, because all sentient beings also have the natural right and desire to be free of suffering. Therefore, it is important for practitioners to engage in the practice of the stages of the path of the highest scope, starting with the generation of *bodhichitta*, the altruistic aspiration to achieve enlightenment for the benefit of all sentient beings. Once one has cultivated bodhichitta, all the meritorious actions that are supported by and complemented with this altruism—even the slightest form of positive action—become causes for the achievement of omniscience.

Omniscience is a wisdom that is able to perceive directly all phenomena, both the ultimate and the conventional natures, simultaneously. It is a state where all the potentials of one's wisdom are developed fully and where there is also a total freedom from all the obstructions to knowledge. It can be achieved only by purifying all the faults of one's mind, and only by complementing the practice of wisdom with the practices of method: bodhichitta, compassion, and so forth. Without bodhichitta, even though one might have great wisdom realizing emptiness, one will not be able to achieve the omniscient state.

In order to cultivate a genuine bodhichitta, you have to depend upon the proper methods and the instructions outlining these. There are two major systems of instructions, one the seven-point cause-and-effect method, the other the equalizing and exchanging oneself with others. The different methods will suit the various mental dispositions of different practitioners; some might find one more effective than the other. The tradition is that these methods are combined and practiced together.

The Seven-Point Cause-and-Effect Method

THE PRELIMINARY STEP OF CULTIVATING EQUANIMITY

The foundation for practicing the seven-point cause-and-effect method is cultivating a mind of equanimity. Without this foundation you will not be able to have an impartial altruistic view, because without equanimity you will always have partiality toward your relatives and friends. Realize that you should not have prejudice, hatred, or desire toward enemies, friends, or neutral persons, and thus lay a very firm foundation of equanimity.

To do this, first visualize a neutral person whom you do not know at all. When you clearly visualize that person, you will find that you don't feel any fluctuations of emotion, no desire or hatred—you are indifferent. Then visualize an enemy; when you visualize the enemy clearly you will have a natural reaction of hatred, feeling all sorts of ill will. Next, clearly visualize a friend or relative to whom you feel very close. With that visualization, the natural reaction will be a feeling of affection and attachment. With the visualization of your enemies, you will feel somewhat distant and will have hatred and a sense of repulsion. Reflect upon your justification in reacting so negatively to them. Although it is true that they have meted out much harm in this life, have they always done such things and been like this? You will find that they have not: in the past they must have engaged in actions beneficial to you and many others. Right now, because of being under the influence of ignorance, hatred, and so forth, they have these faults; it is not their essential nature.

Reflect that delusions are within your own mind also. Although there might be a difference in the force of these delusions, in terms of being delusions they are delusions equally. You should decide that there is not much point in emotionally reacting to the people you have categorized as enemies.

Then examine how you react, on the other hand, to your relatives and friends. Although it is true that they have been kind to you in this life, in the past they might have been your enemies, and even gone to the extent of taking your life. Therefore, there is no point in being absolutely or permanently attached to such people, categorizing them as your friends and relatives.

Thus, there is not much difference between enemies and friends as far as yourself is concerned. They have both had times of benefiting you and they have both had times of harming you. Your having partiality toward them is groundless. Therefore, develop the mind of equanimity directed toward all sentient beings. This mind cannot be brought about by meditating just once or twice, but rather through repeated meditations over months or years.

1. RECOGNIZING SENTIENT BEINGS AS HAVING BEEN ONE'S MOTHER

The first step of the seven-point cause-and-effect method is to cultivate the recognition of all sentient beings as having been one's mother. To do this, it is first necessary to reflect on your beginningless lives in this cycle of existence and that through many of your lives you have had to depend on your mothers. There is not a single living being that you can definitely point to as not having been your mother in the past. Perceive all sentient beings as having been your own kind mothers. If you are able to understand the beginningless-ness of your lives, you will be able to understand that you have taken many forms of life that require a mother. You will find that there is not a single sentient being that has not been your mother in the past.

Next, examine whether you stand to gain or lose by cultivating this recognition of others as mothers. Since you are concerned with cultivating bodhichitta, the altruistic aspiration, you should recognize that if you do not have this basic factor of recognition of others as having been your mothers, you will not have success in its cultivation. So by not developing this recognition you stand to lose.

A recognition of others as being your dearest ones need not be confined to recognizing them as mothers alone. As Maitreya recommends in his *Abhisamayalankara*, you can also view them as having been your best friends or closest relatives. For example, you can view all sentient beings as having been your fathers, if you relate better to your father than to your mother, or as children to whom you feel closest and for whom you have the deepest affection. The point is to bring about an effect within your mind and to develop a state of mind that will enable you to perceive all living beings as the closest objects of affection and kindness. That is how you cultivate the recognition of sentient beings as having been one's mother.

2. RECOLLECTING ALL BEINGS' KINDNESS

The next meditation is on the recollection of the kindness of all beings. For this, you should visualize the person to whom you feel closest—be it your mother or father—when she or he is quite old. Clearly visualize the person at an age when she or he depends upon others' cooperation and assistance. Doing this has a special significance, for it will make your meditation more powerful and effective.

Then think that your mother, for example, has been your mother not only in this lifetime, but also in past lives. Particularly in this life her kindness was boundless at the time of your birth, and before that during gestation she had to undergo all sorts of hard-ships, and even after birth her affection was such that she was able to surrender her own happiness and pleasure for the sake of the happiness and pleasure of her child. At the time of your birth she felt as joyful as if she had found a treasure, and according to her own capacities she has protected you. You were thus protected until you could stand on your own feet.

After reflecting upon the kindness of mothers, particularly of this lifetime, you should visualize other beings whom you find quite distant and repulsive, even animals, and take them as your object of visualization. Think that although these enemies are harmful to you and are your adversaries in this life, in past lives they must have been your most dear parents and must have even protected and saved your life countless times. Therefore their kindness is boundless. In such a manner you should train your mind.

3. Repaying Kindness

The meditation on the recollection of kindness should be followed by meditation upon repaying that kindness. The thought to repay the kindness of mothers will come about naturally when you have been successful in recollecting this kindness—it should come from the depths of your heart. Not to repay their kindness would be unfair and ungrateful of you. Therefore, you should work according to your own capacity for the benefit of others; doing this repays their kindness.

4. Cultivating Loving-Kindness

Having cultivated equanimity and the recognition of all sentient beings as having been one's mother, you will see all sentient beings as objects of affection and endearment. And the more forceful your feeling of affection toward them, the stronger will be your aspiration that they be free from suffering and enjoy happiness. So the recognition of others as having been one's mother is the foundation for the subsequent meditations. Having laid that proper foundation, recollected their kindness, and developed the genuine wish to repay it, you gain a state wherein you feel close to and affectionate toward all living beings. Now reflect that all these sentient beings, although they naturally desire happiness and wish to avoid suffering, are tormented by unimaginable sufferings. Reflect upon the fact that they are just like yourself in desiring happiness, but they lack this happiness. By such reflection, cultivate loving-kindness.

5. Cultivating Great Compassion

When you do the meditation on compassion, reflect upon the manner in which sentient beings undergo the experience of suffering. First, in order to have a very strong force of compassion, visualize a person undergoing active sufferings. You can visualize any situation that you find unbearable. Doing so will enable you to have a strong force of compassion and make it easier to develop a genuine universal compassion.

Then think about the sentient beings in other categories; they may not be undergoing manifest sufferings right now, but due to indulging in negative actions that will definitely produce undesirable consequences in the future, they are certain to face such experiences.

The wish that all sentient beings who lack happiness be endowed with happiness is the state of mind called universal love, and the wish that sentient beings be free of suffering is called compassion. These two meditations can be undertaken in combination, until there is some kind of effect or change in your mind.

6. Generating the Unusual Attitude

Your cultivation of love and great compassion should not be left in a state of mere imagination or wish alone; rather, a sense of responsibility, a genuine intention to engage in the task of relieving sentient beings of their suffering and providing them with happiness, should be developed. It is important for a practitioner to work for and take upon himself or herself the responsibility of fulfilling this intention. The stronger your cultivation of compassion is, the more committed you will feel to taking this responsibility. Because of their ignorance, sentient beings do not know the right methods by which they can fulfill their aims. It is the responsibility of those who are equipped with this knowledge to fulfill the intention of working for their benefit.

Such a state of mind is called the extraordinary attitude or special, unusual attitude. It is called unusual or extraordinary because such a force of compassion, committing oneself to taking on such a responsibility, is not to be found in the trainees of lower capacity. As the oral traditions explain, with this extraordinary attitude there is a commitment that one will take upon oneself the responsibility of fulfilling this aim. It is like striking a deal in business and signing a contract.

After generating the extraordinary attitude, ask yourself whether or not, although you have developed the strong courage and the determination to work for the benefit of other sentient beings, you really possess the capacity and capability to bring them genuine happiness. It is only by your showing living beings the right path leading toward omniscience, and by living beings on their part eliminating the ignorance within themselves, that they will be able to gain lasting happiness. Although you may be able to work for other sentient beings to bring them temporary happiness, bringing about their ultimate aims is possible only when these beings take upon themselves the initiative to eliminate the ignorance within themselves. The same is true of yourself: if you desire the attainment of liberation, it is your responsibility to take the initiative to eliminate the ignorance within yourself.

As I just mentioned, you must also show the right path to living beings—and for that, first of all, you must possess the knowledge yourself. So long as you yourself are not completely enlightened there will always be an inner obstruction. Therefore, it is very important that you work for your own achievement of the completely enlightened state. By thinking in such terms, you will be able to develop the strong belief that without attaining the omniscient state you will not be able to fulfill what you set out to do and truly benefit others.

7. Cultivating Bodhichitta

Based on the foundation of love and compassion, you should generate from the depths of your heart the aspiration to achieve the completely enlightened state for the benefit of all sentient beings. The cultivation of such a mind constitutes the realization of bodhichitta.

After the meditation on generating bodhichitta you should engage in the practice of cultivating bodhichitta that takes the result into the path. Visualizing the spiritual guru at your crown, imagine that the guru expresses delight, saying that it is very admirable and you are very fortunate that you have generated bodhichitta and have engaged in the path of cultivating it, and that he shall take you under his care. Imagine that, as a result of the guru's delight, he dissolves through your crown and into your heart. Then you dissolve into emptiness and from emptiness arise in the aspect of Buddha Shakyamuni. See yourself becoming inseparable from him, and rejoice. At your heart visualize all your virtues accumulated through the practice of bodhichitta. These emanate, in the form of light rays, toward all living beings and actively work for their benefit, relieving them of their suffering, placing them in the state of liberation and favorable rebirth, and eventually leading them to the omniscient state.

Equalizing and Exchanging Oneself with Others

Next follows the instruction on the cultivation of bodhichitta according to the method of equalizing and exchanging oneself with others. This meditation has five sections: (1) equalizing oneself with others; (2) reflecting on the disadvantages of the self-cherishing attitude from many perspectives; (3) reflecting on the advantages of the thought cherishing the welfare of others from many perspectives; (4) the actual exchange of oneself and others; and (5) giving and taking.

1. EQUALIZING ONESELF WITH OTHERS

This phrase refers to the practice of reflecting upon the equality of oneself and others in having the natural and spontaneous wish to enjoy happiness and avoid suffering. For the generation of this type of equanimity, the instruction by the late Kyabje Trijang Rinpoche on the nine-round meditation is very powerful and effective.

The nine-round meditation is comprised of training the mind in equanimity with a mental outlook based on the dual nature of things and events: the conventional and the ultimate. Based on different perspectives, the first in turn is divided into two sections, one from the viewpoint of others and the second from the viewpoint of oneself.

The rounds of visualization on cultivating equanimity from the viewpoint of others are divided into three:

a. Develop the thought that all sentient beings are equal insofar as the natural wish to avoid suffering is concerned and that therefore there is no point in being partial or discriminatory.
b. Reflect that all sentient beings equally desire happiness, and therefore there is no ground for discriminating between them when working for their benefit. The situation is analogous to one where you encounter ten equally wretched beggars who are desperately asking you to relieve their hunger. In such circumstances it is senseless to have any feeling of preference.
c. Develop an equanimity based on the reflection that all sentient beings are equal in lacking genuine happiness although they have the innate desire to possess it. Likewise all sentient beings are the same in having suffering and the wish to avoid it.

With the above three types of practice you train your mind in the attitude expressed as follows: "I shall never discriminate between beings and will always work equally to help them overcome suffering and gain happiness."

The next three rounds of meditation enforce the thought that there is no justification for discrimination between sentient beings from the point of view of oneself or from the viewpoint of others. This training is divided into three sections:

a. You might have the thought that although reflection upon the equality of others is fairly persuasive regarding the futility of your being discriminatory toward other beings, surely when viewed from your own side the situation will look quite different. After all, some people are friends and help you, whereas many others harm you. To counter this thought which attempts to give false grounds for being partial toward others, reflect that all sentient beings are equally kind to you: they have all been at one time or other your closest friends and relatives. Hence there is no rational basis at all for being biased toward or against any.

b. Perhaps you have the idea that although people have been your friends in the past, they have equally been your enemies and have caused harm as well. Such notions should be countered by reflecting that sentient beings' kindness to you is not confined to when they are friends and relatives alone; their kindness when they are your enemies is boundless. The enemy provides you with the precious opportunity to train yourself in the noble ideals of patience and tolerance, traits vital for the perfection of your generation of universal compassion and bodhichitta. For a bodhisattva who emphasizes the practice of bodhichitta, the training in patience is indispensable. Contemplating upon such lines of reasoning will persuade you that there are no grounds for neglecting the welfare of even a single sentient being.

c. Reflect that, as Shantideva wrote in *Bodhisattvacharyava-tara*, there is no sense in someone who is himself subject to suffering and impermanence being selfish and discrimina-tory toward others who are also tormented by the same fate.

The next three rounds of meditation deal with the cultivation of equanimity based on an insight into the ultimate nature of things and events. (This "ultimate" should not be taken to refer to the ulti-mate truth in terms of emptiness—rather, it means that the outlook adopted in these visualizations is deeper and hence relatively ulti-mate in comparison to the earlier meditations.)

a. Consider whether or not there are any "true" enemies in the real sense of the word. If there are, then the fully enlightened buddhas should perceive them as such, which is definitely not the case. For a buddha, all sentient beings are equally dear. Also, when you examine deeply, you will find that it is in fact the delusions within the enemies and not the enemies themselves that actually cause harm. Aryadeva said in his *Chatu-shataka Shastra*:

> Buddhas see the delusion as the enemy
> And not the childish who possess it.

Therefore, there is no justification at all for you to hold grudges against those who cause harm, and neglect the wel-fare of such beings.

b. Secondly, ask yourself whether these so-called enemies are permanent and will always remain as enemies or whether they are changeable. Concluding that they are not perma-nent will enable you to overcome your disinterest in their welfare.

c. The last meditation is a reflection upon the relative nature of "enemy" and "friend" and touches upon the ultimate nature of phenomena. Concepts of enemy, friend, and so forth are relative and exist only at the conventional level. They are mutually dependent, as are the concepts of long and short. A person may be an enemy in relation to one person while at the same time being a dear friend to another. It is your misapprehension of friends, relatives, and enemies as inherently existent that gives rise to your fluctuating emotions toward them. Therefore, by realizing that there is no such inherently existent enemy and friend, you will be able to overcome your biased feelings toward all beings.

2. Reflection on the Disadvantages of the Self-Cherishing Attitude

The next step is the contemplation—from many different perspectives—upon the disadvantages and faults of the self-cherishing attitude. As Geshe Chekawa said in his *Lojong dhon dun ma* ("Seven Points on Thought Transformation"): "Banish the one object of all blame." It is the self-cherishing attitude that is the source of all miseries and therefore is the only object to be blamed for all misfortune.

Since the self-cherishing and self-grasping attitudes abide strongly fortified within our minds, we have never been able to shake them in the least. We have so far not been able to disturb them even as much as a small pebble in a shoe would disturb a person.

If we remain with our present outlook and way of thinking, we will still be under the influence and command of these two factors. We should reflect that these factors have always caused our downfall in the past, and that they will do so in the future if we remain under their influence.

In deeper terms, we will find that all the sufferings and problems and anxieties of not finding what we seek, of being separated from our loved ones, of physical illnesses, of suffering from want, lack of contentment, quarrels, and so forth come about because of our underlying attachment to the self and the self-cherishing attitude that tries to protect such a self within ourselves. The more selfish a person is, the more sufferings and anxieties he or she will have. This self-cherishing attitude manifests in all sorts of ways, which results in problems and anxieties. Yet we never recognize the truth—that these are all the doings of the self-cherishing attitude. Rather, we have the tendency to blame others and external factors: "He did it, and if he had done something else, it wouldn't have happened."

3. REFLECTION ON THE ADVANTAGES OF THE THOUGHT CHERISHING THE WELFARE OF OTHERS

Having realized the enormous disadvantages of holding on to a selfish thought cherishing your welfare alone, you should now reflect upon the kindness of all mother sentient beings, as discussed earlier. The kindness of other beings toward us is boundless while we revolve in this cycle of existence. This is particularly true when we first embark upon a spiritual path and thus begin the process of untying the chains that bind us to this cyclic existence.

We find that if a person lives a very selfish life and is never concerned about the welfare of others, he will have few friends, and people will not take much notice of him. At the time of his death, there will not be many people who will regret his passing. Some deceptive and negative persons may be very powerful and wealthy, and therefore some people—for economic reasons and so forth— might portray themselves as friends, but they will speak against such persons behind their backs. When these negative persons die, these very same "friends" may rejoice at their death.

On the other hand, many people mourn and regret the death of a person who is very kind and always altruistic and who works for the benefit of others. We find that altruism, as well as the person who possesses it, is regarded as the friend of all, and it becomes the object of veneration and respect by others.

I often remark, partly in jest, that if one really wants to be selfish, one should be "wisely selfish" by working for others. By helping others, one will receive help and assistance in return, particularly when one is in a hard situation—the time when one needs assistance from others the most. But if one tries to be very selfish, then when one is in difficult circumstances, one will find fewer people who are willing to help and one will be left to resolve the situation and difficulty on one's own. It is the nature of human beings to depend upon the cooperation and assistance of others, particularly when facing difficult times; during such times and during hardship it is only true friends who will be beneficial and helpful. By living an unselfish life, one will be able to earn genuine friends, whereas selfish thoughts and a selfish life will never gain one genuine and true friends.

The essence of Mahayana practice is really to teach us the methods by which we will be able to succeed not only in this life but also in the future. Such instruction is, in fact, very practical and relevant to all—believers and nonbelievers alike. If we are able to derive practical benefits within this lifetime by living a virtuous life, we will be able to fulfill the wishes of future lifetimes as well.

4. THE ACTUAL EXCHANGE OF ONESELF WITH OTHERS

To exchange oneself with others is to reverse a former attitude: the thought of endearment and cherishing of oneself with its feeling of indifference toward others should now be reversed as follows. One should feel indifferent to oneself, reduce the force of clinging to oneself, and rather hold the welfare of other sentient beings as precious. That is the meaning of exchanging oneself with others. The degree of high value one feels toward oneself should now be turned toward others.

For this practice, one should also be knowledgeable about the commitments and precepts of thought transformation practices. If one undertakes such a practice one will be able to transform any adverse circumstances into favorable conditions of the path. In this age of degeneration when one meets with all sorts of problems and adverse circumstances, the practice of thought transformation is very effective. If someone lacks the practice of thought transformation, even though that person might be a very serious meditator he or she will meet with many hardships and hurdles.

5. GIVING AND TAKING

The practice of the actual exchange of oneself with others should be followed by the practice of giving and taking. The latter is begun by reflecting that although all mother sentient beings desire happiness, they lack it, and that although they do not desire suffering, they undergo it. Think that it is the ignorance of sentient beings that impels them to work for the fulfillment of their selfish aims.

You should develop the unusual, extraordinary attitude of wishing that all their sufferings ripen upon yourself. Induced by the strong sense of compassion for other sentient beings, visualize taking all their sufferings upon yourself; and then, induced by the strong wish of love, visualize giving away from the depths of your heart all your virtuous collections, happiness, wealth, possessions, even your body, to other sentient beings. If you can conjoin such practices with the breathing process—that is, imagining taking when inhaling and giving when exhaling—you will be able to engage in a powerful practice, leading you to the strong commitment that you will engage in the bodhisattva deeds. If you are able to engage in such a powerful practice, then due to the strong determination and commitment that you make as a result of cultivating bodhichitta, you will be able to alleviate the forces of the powerful and vast stores of negative actions committed in past lives, and also accumulate great stores of merit.

This is how you should undertake the practice of bodhichitta.

Looking Into Lojong, or Mind Training

Judy Lief

How do we bring our spiritual practice from the meditation cushion into the rough-and-tumble of daily life, where it can really benefit us as well as others? Judy Lief explains how the fifty-nine slogans on mind training serve as handy reminders that help us become more skillful and loving in our relationships.

THE TEACHINGS ON mind training, or *lojong,* are an invaluable aid to practitioners because they show us how the wisdom and skillful means of the Mahayana can actually be put into action. They show us how to make it real.

The lojong teachings include instruction in formless meditation, in the practice of "sending and taking" (*tonglen*), and in postmeditation practice—putting our meditation into action in our daily lives. These teachings are attributed to the great tenth-century Buddhist master Atisha Dipankara and became widely known after the Tibetan teacher Geshe Chekawa arranged and summarized them in a collection of fifty-nine mind-training sayings or reminders. Often referred to simply as the Atisha slogans, these encapsulate the essence of what it means to practice the Mahayana. The

Atisha slogans are a blueprint for practicing the bodhisattva path in fifty-nine easy steps.

The power of the slogans is that they break down the Mahayana ideal of loving-kindness for us. Rather than simply giving general guidelines on how to be a true practitioner, they actually spell it out in detail. They give specific guidelines both for how to approach meditation and how to awaken in daily life. It is easy to be vaguely compassionate and generally aware-ish, but when we actually look at what we are doing and how we interact with others, it is a different matter altogether. As the saying goes, the devil is in the details.

When I first encountered the practice of tonglen and the fifty-nine mind-training slogans attributed to Atisha, I was struck by their combination of down-to-earthness and profundity. I had already been taught about the importance of joining formal sitting meditation with postmeditation practice, but apart from a vague notion of trying to be more kind and aware, I was not at all sure how to go about it. These teachings gave me a way to unpack general notions such as compassion or wisdom into specific guidelines that I could apply to my life. They placed the practice of meditation, which was what had inspired me about the tradition to begin with, within a greater and more complete understanding of practice and what it means to be a practitioner.

Studying the mind-training slogans inspired me to look into my habit of dividing meditation from everyday life, regarding it as something special and apart. When I began to really take a look at that pattern I saw that it fostered a kind of leaky approach to practice. If meditation became too intense I could escape into everyday concerns; when daily life became too overwhelming I could escape into practice. There was lots of wiggle room for neurosis. Somehow it all seemed to come back to ego and its genius for co-opting everything to further its grip on power.

The scope of the fifty-nine Atisha slogans is extensive, and they can be applied to many levels of our activity. They provide guidelines for meditation, but their real focus is on relationships of all kinds: with our fellow humans, with the earth, with our colleagues, with our closest friends, with our enemies. At first glance some of them may seem like practical advice from your grandmother. Slogans such as "Don't wallow in self-pity" may seem moralistic or even simpleminded. At the other end of the spectrum, slogans such as "Examine the nature of unborn awareness" seem to be pointing beyond the ordinary to something more ultimate and perhaps even a bit obscure. Yet they are combined into one coherent system.

Altogether, the structure of the slogans is based on the two underlying themes of Mahayana Buddhism: skillful means and wisdom. If you are to travel on the path you need both. You need to see where you are going, and you also need a way to get there. The way to get there is what is referred to as skillful means. The cultivation of wisdom is essential, but as the old Zen saying goes, "Words don't cook rice."

With slogan practice, every situation is seen as complete, as an expression of both skillful means and wisdom. That means you do not need to look elsewhere to find the dharma, since it is present in every situation. On the other hand, it also means there is nowhere to hide. Once you have a glimpse of the extent of the teachings, they haunt you wherever you go.

Generally, no matter what you do, you need to learn how to go about it. Depending on what you want to achieve, you train in different ways. If you want to practice law, you go to law school; if you want to practice a trade, you go to trade school. And if you want to become a bodhisattva, you train in the six transcendent perfections (*paramitas*) through mind training and slogan practice.

In the Mahayana, the goal is to become a bodhisattva warrior who embodies wisdom, compassion, and openness, and the way to do that is by training in generosity, discipline, patience, exertion, and meditation. These five are the methods that will get you there, the skillful means. But those skillful means need to be joined with wisdom, or the vision to lead the way, which is *prajna,* or transcendent knowledge. Together, these six perfections are the Mahayana recipe for success on the path.

Working with the slogans begins to chip away at attitudes that hinder our relationships, our inner understanding, and our happiness. This chipping-away process begins with meditation practice, with the pacifying of our restless mind. With that foundation, we can begin the practice of tonglen. In tonglen, we practice reversing the habit of viewing everything purely through the lens of our own self-interest. Instead we begin to appreciate how we are continually in interchange with other beings. So tonglen opens up the possibility of relating in a more flowing and genuine way, one less caught up in fear and self-protection. We see that we do not have to just passively accept the relationship patterns we have fallen into. We can make changes.

In tonglen, we breathe out what we normally cling to and breathe in what we usually avoid. In doing so, we work with qualities within ourselves and with issues that arise in relating to others. The Atisha slogan related to this is number seven: "Sending and taking should be practiced alternately. These two should ride the breath."

It may seem crazy to practice breathing in what you do not want and breathing out what you desire, but rather than being self-destructive, this exercise is surprisingly liberating. You discover that the habit of trying to protect yourself by holding on to some things and getting rid of others does not really protect you; it just makes you mildly paranoid and defensive all the time. When you are not battling against whatever is bugging you at the moment but really breathe it in, you realize that you don't have to take everything that happens to you as a personal attack. It is just what is happening, and you can find a way to deal with it.

On the sending-out side, you begin to realize that you do not have to parcel out your limited store of goodness or health for fear of it running out, and you can let it flow more freely. The less you try to hold on to whatever virtue you have as your little treasure, the more there seems to be. Making it your possession has been like trying to drive with the parking brake engaged.

This practice is remarkable in its effects. When you are not so caught up in sucking in goodies and warding off threats, when you are not so attached to perfection and afraid of flaws, you can come to accept yourself and others in a new and fresh way. This reduces burnout and defeatism. When people encounter you, they sense that you are not trying to use them, even subtly, to further your own schemes. I think this is one reason that tonglen is such a healing force and is so helpful for people who work with pain and suffering in their line of work.

With slogan practice, we step-by-step liberate trapped energy, energy recruited to the project of propping up ego. That project is based on fear. Whenever we mess up we worry about being caught. We even worry about catching ourselves. So we waste a lot of energy covering up, being defensive, or making excuses.

According to slogan twelve—"Drive all blames into one"—most of our problems can be traced to one underlying cause: ego fixation. Until we start to deal with this level, we will only be treating symptoms. With this slogan we take responsibility for our own actions. Instead of hiding our mistakes, we face them and look for their underlying cause. And the more we look, the more we understand the power of ego-clinging and the damage it does. We begin to have a glimpse of what a difference it makes when we are not carrying around the hidden agenda of ego.

This slogan is also helpful when we are dealing with groups, where it is common to get into struggles about who is to blame, as though finding the guilty party will solve the problem. With this slogan you take on the blame yourself, no matter what the case. When you do so, the process can shift from one of finger-pointing to one of problem-solving, to the benefit of the whole organization. This does not mean that you do not try to discover where specific problems arise. In fact you are more apt to figure this out, since you have removed the need for others to cover up or to defend themselves from attack.

Another powerful lesson of slogan practice is how to relate to the ups and downs of life. Slogan forty-two—"Whichever of the two occurs, be patient"—is a reminder of how easily we are swept away by the excitement of things going our way or the disappointment of things not working out for us. When things are going well, we forget that it will inevitably change. Witness the optimism of the housing bubble. When things go downhill, we tend to get in a funk and see no way out. Witness the doomsday phenomenon.

This fluctuation in circumstances can take place on a grand scale or simply as the ups and downs of an ordinary day. Instead of just experiencing what we are experiencing, we either hope to get out of it or fear losing it. The practice of this slogan is to stay with present experience and not assume anything about what may follow. This allows us to find our ground in ever-shifting circumstances, and by example to provide that ground for others.

The Atisha slogans conclude with number fifty-nine: "Don't expect applause." When we are always looking over our shoulder to see how others think we are doing, it is hard to act directly and skillfully. The result of our need for recognition is that we feel disheartened, belittled, or furious when it does not materialize. It is hard to maintain steady effort when we give that power over to others, and we find that we are not really in tune with what we are doing. With this slogan, instead of looking for recognition from outside, we develop the confidence to trust the action itself for feedback. If outside recognition comes, that's great, but if not, it's no big deal.

The mind-training slogans skillfully prod us to lighten up and drop our pretentiousness. Instead of just talking about being loving or compassionate, they spell out how to do it. Their focus is on actions, not just attitude. We could have all sorts of loving and kind thoughts and feel all warm and fuzzy, but so what? The point is to help this world, ourselves, and others at the same time, and we have the means to do so. Every time we are pricked awake by one of the slogans and adjust our attitude or behavior, we expand our understanding of what it is to be skillful.

Working with the Atisha slogans is a wonderful way to bring practice into all aspects of your life. They work not by grand gestures but by the accumulation of many little interruptions to the momentum of ego confusion. In the midst of activity, a slogan pops up, and in an instant you change course. In that way, little by little, ordinary actions are liberated into bodhisattva activity. Because it is so easy to lose track of practice mentality and work from a more shallow and conventional fallback position, it is good that we have these handy reminders to wake us up on the spot. Through the power of mind training, we never run out of opportunities to flip our limited actions into the skillful methodology of the bodhisattva path, and our limited vision into the penetrating insight of prajna.

Meditation: Contemplating the Slogans

Choose one of the following lojong slogans to work with over a period of three days: "Be grateful to everyone"; "Always maintain only a joyful mind"; "Don't try to be fastest"; "Don't be swayed by external circumstances"; or "Always meditate on whatever provokes resentment."

On the first day, use the slogan to reflect on how you relate to your spiritual practice.

On the second day, bring the slogan to mind in reflecting on how you handle personal relationships.

On the third day, apply the slogan to your relationships with colleagues and your approach to your work.

You Can Do It!

Pema Chödrön

Pema Chödrön provides step-by-step instructions on tonglen, *the practice of "sending and taking," and describes how this meditation helps us to develop genuine compassion.*

THE FIRST STAGE in the practice of *tonglen*, or sending and taking, is a pause, a moment of stillness and space, a brief gap. If you need an image for this, you can reflect on any experience of wide-open space, such as gazing out at the ocean or looking up into a cloudless sky.

The second stage is a visualization, working with texture. As you inhale, breathe in hot, heavy, thick energy—a feeling of claustrophobia. Breathe it in completely, through all the pores of your body. Then, as you exhale, breathe out a sense of freshness, of cool, light, bright energy. Radiate it outward 360 degrees. Continue for a few minutes, or until the imagery is in sync with the in-breath and out-breath.

The third stage involves breathing in a specific painful situation, opening to it as fully as possible, then breathing out spaciousness and relief. Traditionally we begin tonglen for a person or animal we wish to help, but we can also begin with our personal experience in the moment—a feeling of hopelessness or anger, for example—and use that as a stepping-stone for connecting us with the painful feelings of others.

In the fourth stage, we extend tonglen further. If we're doing it for a friend with AIDS, we extend it to all of those with AIDS. If we're doing it for our alcoholic sister, we extend it to all alcoholics, to all of those suffering from addiction. If we're already doing tonglen for all of those experiencing the same pain we are, we can extend it to all of those, all over the world, who are suffering in any way, mentally or physically. And we can extend it still further to include all of us caught up in self-absorption, all of us tormented by our fixated minds and our inability to let go of hope and fear.

As a general guideline, we start tonglen practice with a situation that is immediate and real, not something vague or impersonal. Then we extend it to include more and more beings who are suffering in a similar way, as well as all of us suffering from ego-clinging, all of us suffering from resistance to uncertainty and impermanence.

If we ourselves have had even a glimmer of what egolessness feels like, of what awakening feels like, of what freedom feels like, then we want that for others too. When we see that they're hooked, instead of being critical and judgmental, we can empathize with what they're going through—we've been there and know exactly how they feel. Our wish for other people is the same as our wish for ourselves: to appreciate ourselves, to recognize when we're caught and disentangle ourselves from those feelings, to stop reinforcing the dysfunctional patterns that prolong our suffering, to reach out to others, to experience the goodness of being human.

Whether we do tonglen as a formal practice or on the spot, does it take time to get used to? Yes, it does. Does it take getting accustomed to the rawness of pain? Does it take patience and gentleness? Yes, it does. There's no need to get discouraged when the practice seems too hard. Allow yourself to ease into it slowly and at your own pace, working first with situations that are easy for you right now. I always remember what my teacher, Chögyam Trungpa, used to say when I was losing my confidence and wanted to give up. He'd sit up tall and smile broadly and proclaim, "You can do it!" Somehow his confidence was contagious, and when I heard those words, I knew I could.

I once read a poem about practicing tonglen in a time of war. The imagery was of breathing in bombs falling, violence, despair, losing your legs and coming home with your face burned and disfigured, and then sending out the beauty of the earth and sky, the goodness of people, safety and peace. In the same spirit, we can breathe in hatred and jealousy, envy and addiction—all the sorrow of the human drama—using our personal experience of that pain and extending tonglen to all others caught in the same way. Then we can breathe out flexibility, lightheartedness, nonaggression, strength—whatever we feel will bring comfort and upliftedness and relief. The pain of the world pierces us to the heart, but we never forget the goodness of being alive.

Chögyam Trungpa once said, "The problem with most people is that they are always trying to give out the bad and take in the good. That has been the problem of society in general and the world altogether." The time has come for us to try the opposite approach: to take in the bad and give out the good. Compassion is not a matter of pity or the strong helping the weak; it's a relationship between equals, one of mutual support. Practicing tonglen, we come to realize that other people's welfare is just as important as our own. In helping them, we help ourselves. In helping ourselves, we help the world.

Mahamudra and Dzogchen: Thought-Free Wakefulness

Chökyi Nyima Rinpoche

The ability to dissolve thoughts is essential to attaining liberation, says the renowned Dzogchen teacher Chökyi Nyima Rinpoche. Devotion and pure perception are two principles that can lead beyond confusion to thought-free wakefulness.

MEDITATION TRAINING, in the sense of sustaining the nature of mind, is a way of being free from clinging and the conceptual attitude of forming thoughts, and therefore free from the causes of samsara, the cycle of suffering: karma and disturbing emotions. Please do not believe that liberation and samsara is somewhere over there: it is here, in oneself. Thought is samsara. Being free of thought is liberation. When we are free of thinking, we are free of thought. The problem is that the causes for further samsara are being created continuously. We spin through the six realms and undergo a lot of suffering.

Compared to the other life forms in samsara, we human beings do not suffer that much. We don't experience the unbearable, overwhelming suffering that countless other beings do. But for some humans, their mental or physical pain may be unbearable. If we continue to allow our ordinary thinking to run wild, we cannot predict what is lined up for us in the future, where we will end up, in what shape or form.

The bottom line is this: *we need to know how to dissolve thoughts.* Without knowing this, we cannot eliminate karma and disturbing emotions. And therefore the karmic phenomena do not vanish; deluded experience does not end. We understand also that one thought cannot undo another thought. The only thing that can do this is thought-free wakefulness. This is not some state that is far away from us: thought-free wakefulness actually exists together with every thought, inseparable from it—but the thinking obscures or hides this innate actuality. Thought-free wakefulness is immediately present the very moment the thinking dissolves, the very moment it vanishes, fades away, falls apart. Isn't this true?

The Buddha described in detail that we can have 84,000 different types of emotions. In a condensed way, there are six root emotions and twenty subsidiary ones. An even shorter categorization of thoughts is that of the three poisons. Whatever the number of types of emotions or thoughts, the Buddha taught how to eliminate all of these by giving 84,000 sections of the dharma.

Perhaps you do not have the time to study and learn all these teachings, or maybe you don't have the desire, the ability, or the intelligence to do so. In this case, the Buddha and the bodhisattvas very skillfully condensed the teachings into a very concise form. This is called the tradition of pith instructions that deals with overcoming all the disturbing emotions simultaneously. The basic instruction here is to understand that all of these emotions are merely thoughts. Even ego-clinging and dualistic fixation is simply a thought. The pointing-out instruction given by a master to qualified students shows how to dissolve the thought and how to recognize the nature of the thinker, which is our innate thought-free wakefulness.

The root of confusion is thinking, but the essence of the thinking is thought-free wakefulness. As often as possible, please compose yourselves in the equanimity of thought-free wakefulness. It is said, "Samsara is merely thought, so freedom from thought is liberation." Great masters explain this in more detail, because simply being thoughtless is not necessarily liberation in the sense of thought-free wakefulness. To be unconscious, to faint, to be oblivious, is surely not liberation. If those states were liberation, attainment would be swift since it is very easy to be mindless. That would be a cheap liberation!

Simply suspend your thinking within the nonclinging state of wakefulness: that is the correct view. One important point about the teachings on mind essence is that they need to be simple and easy to train in. Particularly in Mahamudra and Dzogchen practice, the view is said to be open and carefree. The less you cling and grasp, the more open and free it is. It is the nature of things. The less rigid our conceptual attitude is, the freer the view.

The mind is empty, cognizant, united, unformed. Please make the meanings of these words something that points at your own experience. You can also say the mind is the "unformed unity of empty cognizance." These are very precious and profound words. "Empty" means that essentially this mind is something that is empty. This is easy to agree on: we cannot find it as a thing. It is not made empty by anyone, including by us—it is just naturally empty, originally so.

At the same time, we also have the ability to know, to cognize, which is also something natural and unmade. These two qualities, being empty and cognizant, are not separate entities. They are an indivisible unity. This unity itself is also not something that is made by anyone. It is not a unity of empty cognizance that at some point arose, remains for a while, and later will perish. Being unformed, it does not arise, does not dwell, and does not cease. It is not made in time. It is not a material substance. Anything that exists in time or substance is an object of thought. This unformed unity of empty cognizance is not made of thought; it is not an object of thought.

Whenever there is an idea based in time or substance, its upkeep becomes very complex; it takes a lot to sustain or maintain its validity. This unformed basic nature, however, is very simple, not complicated at all. So many complications are created based on concepts of time and substance—so much hope and fear. Honestly, substance and time never did exist; they never do exist, nor will they ever exist in the future, either. The conceptualization of time and substance is the habit of the thinking mind. Although right now time and substance do not exist, it seems to the thinking mind as if they do.

Concerning substance, if you look around, it seems like everything is solidly and precisely there. In the experience of a real yogi, time and substance do not exist, of course. Even a scholar can, through intelligent reasoning, feel convinced about this fact. When we think that which is not, is, then, it seems to be. As perceived by a buddha, however, all the experiences that samsaric beings have are no more substantial than dreams. It all looks like dreaming.

At the very foundation of Vajrayana practice lie two principles: devotion and pure perception. We should have devotion toward the unmistaken natural state, in the sense of sincerely appreciating that which is truly unmistaken, unconfused, never deluded. In reality, the nature of all things is totally pure. Impurity occurs only due to temporary concepts. That is the reason one should train in pure perception.

In this context, there are three levels of experience: the deluded experience of sentient beings, the meditative experience of yogis, and the pure experience of buddhas. Whenever there is dualistic mind, there is deluded experience. The deluded experience of sentient beings is called impure because it is involved with karma and disturbing emotions. In deluded experience, there is the attempt to accept and reject; there is hope and fear. Hope and fear are painful: that is suffering. Whenever there is thinking, there is hope and fear. Whenever there is hope and fear, there is suffering.

The meditative experience of a yogi is free of giving in to ordinary thought. It is something other than being involved in normal thinking. We can call it the state of *shamatha* or *vipashyana* or other names, but basically it is unlike ordinary thinking. The meditative experiences of a yogi are good and they become evident because of letting mind settle in equanimity. The most famous of these meditative moods are called bliss, clarity, and nonthought. They occur during vipashyana meditation, but they can arise even during shamatha practice. Through meditation training, the mind becomes more clarified, more lucid. But if we are not connected with a qualified master and if we do not know the right methods of dealing with these meditative states, we may believe that we are somehow incredibly realized beings. That becomes a hindrance; it can even turn into a severe obstacle.

The Mahamudra path is presented as the twelve aspects of the four yogas. These four yogas of Mahamudra constitute the path of liberation. The first of these, *one-pointedness*, essentially means that you can remain calmly undisturbed for as long as you want. The next yoga is *simplicity*, and it means to recognize your natural face as being ordinary mind, free from basis and free from root: "Simplicity is rootless and baseless ordinary mind." We need to develop the strength of this recognition; otherwise, we are as helpless as a small child on a battlefield. We train by means of mindfulness, first effortful, then effortless. We train in simplicity at lesser, medium, and higher levels, and then arrive at *one taste*, the third of the four yogas of Mahamudra. One taste means that the duality of experience dissolves, that all dualistic notions such as samsara and nirvana dissolve into the state of nondual awareness.

Having perfected one taste through the levels of the lesser, medium, and higher stages, the fourth yoga is *nonmeditation*. This is the point at which every type of conviction and the fixing of the attention on something completely dissolve. All convictions and habitual tendencies have dissolved and are left behind. One has captured the dharmakaya throne of nonmeditation.

In the beginning one needs to be convinced about how reality is: one needs to have confidence in the view. Ultimately, however, any form of conviction is still a subtle obscuration, still a hindrance. At the final stage of nonmeditation, all types of habitual tendencies and convictions need to be dissolved, left behind. There is nothing more to cultivate, nothing more to reach. One has arrived at the end of the path. All that needs to be purified has been purified. Karma, disturbing emotions, and the habitual tendencies have all been cleared up, so that nothing is left.

The path is necessary as long as we have not arrived. The moment we arrive, however, the need for the road to get there has fallen away. As long as we are not at our destination, then it is also necessary to have the concept of path in order to get there. But once the destination has been reached, once whatever needs to be cultivated has been cultivated and whatever needs to be abandoned has been left behind, the whole need for path is over. That is what is meant by nonmeditation, literally noncultivation. This is the dharmakaya [the formless body of ultimate reality, one of the three bodies (*kayas*) of Buddha] throne of nonmeditation. In Dzogchen, the exhaustion of all concepts and phenomena is the ultimate level of experience. This is the state of complete enlightenment. Both these levels of realization are equal to that of all buddhas.

At this point, for oneself, there is exclusively pure experience. At the same time, other beings are still perceived, along with their impure, deluded experiences. Take the example of the six classes of beings. When their experiences are compared with each other, each being will feel that his or her way of experiencing is more profound than the realm below. In general, everyone thinks that what they experience is real. The difference in the experiencing of the different realms is the difference in the density of their karma and obscurations. The less dense the karma, the closer to real experience. Compared to the ordinary samsaric sentient being, the meditative experience of a yogi is more real, more pure. But compared to that, the pure experience of a buddha is more real and more pure still.

We need to dissolve impure deluded experience. Deluded experience comes from not knowing the nature of mind; it comes from unknowing, from being ignorant of the natural state. When not knowing our nature, we are sentient beings. *Ignorance clears when knowing the natural state, the state of a buddha.* While not knowing, there is the forming of karma and disturbing emotions. While knowing, karma and disturbing emotions are not formed. If, in the very moment of knowing innate nature and sustaining the continuity of that, you were to never stray again, then you would be a buddha.

Buddhist philosophy has many splendid words to describe what happens. The Chittamatra, or mind-only school, presents a threefold classification of reality as the imaginary, the dependent, and the absolute. In the Dzogchen teachings, ignorance is described as having three aspects: conceptual ignorance, coemergent ignorance, and the single-nature ignorance. These are all very nice words. Basically, it is in the state of not knowing that confusion can take place. Not knowing our own essence is confusion. The essence of what thinks is dharmakaya. The thinking itself is not dharmakaya, but the identity of that which thinks is dharmakaya. Thinking is thought. Thinking is not the thought-free state. It is the identity of that which thinks that is thought-free.

Whether we use the terms mind essence, the primordially pure state of cutting through, original coemergent wisdom, or the Great Middle Way of definitive meaning, one point is true: *at the moment of not being involved in thought, you spontaneously have arrived at the true view, automatically.*

There are two ways to approach the view. One is through scriptural statements and reasoning, and the other is through experience. The first way is called "establishing the view through statement and reasoning." Although we want to train in Mahamudra or Dzogchen, still, without some feeling of certainty about the view obtained through studying and through our own reasoning, it is not that easy to be sure.

It is sometimes possible to transmit or communicate the view without using any scriptural statements, but this requires that a totally qualified master possessing the nectar of learning, reflection, and meditation meets with a qualified disciple who is receptive. There are three types of transmission. The first two, the mind transmission of buddhas and the symbolic transmission of the knowledge-holders, are like that. Mind transmission uses not even a single word or gesture, no sign. Yet something is communicated—

the wisdom of realization is communicated and fully recognized. Symbolic transmission uses no more than a word or sentence—no explanations, just a gesture—to point out the wisdom of realization and have it recognized. The third type is the hearing lineage, which uses a very brief spoken teaching.

In these times we are in, most people would have a hard time if we were only to use mind transmission, symbolic transmission, or hearing transmission with nothing else, no explanation. Explanation is generally necessary in order to point out the natural state. There are two ways to do so. One of these is the analytical approach of a scholar; the other is the resting meditation of a simple meditator. There are some people who can trust a master and be introduced to the natural state without any lengthy explanations. For other people, this is not enough. Then it is necessary to use scriptural references and intelligent reasoning in order to establish certainty in the view. But after arriving at the intellectual understanding of the true view, the scholar still needs to receive the blessings of a qualified master and to receive the pointing-out instruction from such a master.

PART FIVE

Keep Your Practice Going

Committing yourself to the practice of meditation brings a sense of reality, that the practice is no longer a myth. It's a real experience. And having become part of your lifestyle, the practice acts as a reminder, a way of looking at your heavy-handed thoughts, which are known as emotions. A complete new world, a new old world, of meditative life could be established. There is so much joy that goes with that, the joy of being connected with the earth.

—CHÖGYAM TRUNGPA RINPOCHE

NONMEDITATORS CAN'T BE blamed for sometimes thinking that sitting meditation hardly seems profound but *does* seem profoundly boring. And as at least one teacher in this next section tells us, it really *can* be boring. But after you've sat a bit and gained the sense that something meaningful really is happening here, meditation and its benefits in our lives become exciting, even—take this however you'd like to—liberating.

Still, sitting sometimes feels more like just "sitting there." In this section you'll find tips for building the excitement and energy needed to not only begin a meditation routine but to keep it going, even through difficult patches. You'll learn why sitting with others can be a boon to your practice, what to expect from an extended meditation retreat, and a good deal more. A new world awaits.

It's All in Your Mind

Sakyong Mipham Rinpoche

Through the practice of meditation we see past the mind's waves of discursiveness and begin to develop the noble qualities that we all naturally possess. Sakyong Mipham Rinpoche explains how working with the mind makes us stronger.

WHETHER WE ARE on the busy streets of New York or in the solitude of a mountain cave in Nepal, our happiness and contentment are completely in our own hands. Sitting meditation enables us to rest our mind in a present and cheerful way. At the base of that experience is a quality of happiness, which is not a sense of giddiness, but of relaxation. Wherever we are, life is going to be coming at us. But if we use our lives as an opportunity to develop and enhance our mind, we will always be able to acknowledge that we are in a precious situation.

When we sit, we make a direct relationship to the source of happiness, this wish-fulfilling jewel, the mind itself. Meditation gives us the ability to unpack the box in which the jewel is hidden. In effect, we're taking time out from our busyness to say, "I'm not going anywhere. I'm going to be right here." That is a profound step, because it means we're beginning to look at the truth and to trust it.

Our mind goes through a lot in the course of a day. Generally, our thoughts cycle between positive and negative. Either we're thinking about what upsets us or makes us anxious, or we're riding the wave of what inspires us and reminds of us of good things. If we don't work with the mind, the pattern tends to shift toward more disturbing thoughts and emotions. We get consumed by the negativity of the mind—fear and regret, anger and desire. When these thoughts and emotions come up, they completely obscure us and we're trapped by them.

By working with the mind in meditation, we learn to sit and watch all the ups and downs come and go like clouds in the sky. In the process, we gain more strength in terms of our clarity, insight, and wisdom. These are noble qualities that we all possess. In meditation we begin to recognize them. They are the lessons we learn from watching our discursiveness. But to develop those qualities takes more effort than just sitting on the cushion; we have to be proactive. If we don't apply ourselves, nothing is going to happen.

Yes, it's important to show up, to have the discipline to sit, but there is also the internal aspect of dealing with every thought, every emotion. That is how we learn that they are temporary. They are always arising, always falling away. We can look at our mind and try to figure out where the thoughts come from, but we'll never actually find that moment. The point is to learn to relax, to learn not to be absorbed in our discursiveness, because once we're lost in it, we can be lost in it for twenty minutes, half an hour, or twenty years. The mind is where we live. It is how we experience things. Whether we have a good day or a bad day really depends on our experience of the mind.

Sitting meditation gives us the confidence to acknowledge our thoughts without being hooked by them. We have the teachings and techniques to form the mind into something that is useful and pleasant. In terms of a spiritual tradition, we can say that we are developing our mind's potential to become buddha, to become awake. But in a very practical way, this level of practice is helpful to anybody. If we're going to live in this world we should at least have the ability to work with our mind. When we do yoga, for example, the more flexible and fluid our body becomes, the less of a nuisance it is. In meditation, we are putting the mind into a situation where it can become flexible, joyous, and less of a problem. It's that simple.

To practice successfully requires that we hold a view of what our mind really is. The idea I like to use is basic goodness. What are the aspects of basic goodness? There's compassion, virtue, wisdom, and other noble qualities. We meditate in order to become familiar with that good mind. Sometimes our meditation is fun; at other times, it can be boring. But overall, if we're holding this view and applying the technique, meditation makes us stronger. We're learning what the mind is and stabilizing ourselves in that reality. This ability gives us a very powerful tool.

Our mind is always becoming familiar with something. Most of the time we're becoming familiar with things that ultimately have little relevance to us. We get familiar with the fantasy of food, a relationship, or a holiday. Of course we may have to pay the rent— there are always concerns on which our mind can chew—but in our daily meditation, we practice unloading those concerns from our mind and experiencing the precious opportunity to become familiar with something more meaningful.

One way to ground ourselves in the view is to feel fortunate that we have the time and technique to meditate. We can say to ourselves, "I feel very fortunate to be able to follow my breath because, number one, I have a breath." It's not necessarily guaranteed. For us to sit here and not appreciate what's going on is ignorance, because we're taking our lives for granted.

What happens when we feel fortunate? Inspiration is born, and it grows. Without inspiration, we don't have any reason to return to the breath. Sitting is just an exercise. It's like working in a factory: we're just putting in the time until we can go home. Our noble qualities are not increasing. Without the view, our meditation is like a rock at the bottom of a lake. What happens to a rock at the bottom of the lake? No matter how much time passes, nothing happens. In a hundred years, it will still be a rock at the bottom of the lake.

Even though our understanding may be small, we should have confidence that the practice of sitting in this way and placing our mind on the breath is special. It's been handed down by people such as the Tibetan yogi Milarepa. He did not leave us the message that "Meditation's not really worth it" or "I looked in my mind and there's nothing really there, but it's a great way to lose weight." He didn't say that at all. Rather, he wrote 100,000 spontaneous songs that celebrate the basic goodness of our mind and the precious opportunity we have to develop our noble qualities. These are real. As our mind sticks with them, our level of *prajna,* or intelligence, rises.

When we meditate, we're not idly passing time. In following the breath and learning to deal with our thoughts, we're laying the foundation for a shift in attitude that has the power to change our lives in a truly meaningful way. There's a lot of darkness and aggression in our world. Developing our noble qualities has an immediate effect on ourselves and others. When we apply ourselves in practice, we're not only doing something very present; we're also creating the conditions for how our lives can move forward.

Bringing the Practice Home

Larry Rosenberg

How can a beginner take meditation practice beyond the exploratory phase? Larry Rosenberg explains the value of grounding your practice in the discipline of the lay precepts and describes what you might expect at an extended meditation retreat.

AT THE END OF every retreat, I always try to give the new people a few tips for taking the practice back home. It is best to sit every day and to have a place in your house or apartment that is quiet and removed from activity that you can reliably use for that purpose. I can't really say how long your sitting periods should be. When I teach beginners, I start with periods of fifteen to twenty minutes and gradually work up to forty-five minutes and more.

On retreats, sittings run between thirty and sixty minutes. The amount of time is less important than the regularity. It is good to sit a little longer than you want to so you see the part of your mind that resists practice, but you don't want to torture yourself. In the same way, it is important to sit even on days when you don't feel like it. If you sit only when you want to, you will know only the mind that likes to sit.

I can't emphasize enough, however, how helpful it would be to find a teacher and a place to do intensive practice. People often ask me how they will know if a teacher is good, and it is hard to say;

there is no mechanism for accreditation of Buddhist teachers in this country. You may be able to tell something from who that person's teachers have been and where he or she has studied. It is important to find a teacher who has been at the practice for a while, because long experience is what brings about real learning. Finally, you need to use the kind of discernment that you use in every other aspect of your life. If a person seems authentic and dedicated, start with him or her and see how it goes.

There are a number of meditation centers throughout the country, and a good way to find a teacher is to do a retreat at one of them. Often brochures will give descriptions of the teachers, and you can choose one who sounds like a good match for you. The kind of intensive practice that you do on retreat is extremely valuable and may be hard to do on your own.

Even if you live in a part of the country that is isolated from teachers and centers, regular trips to a center could, in effect, give you a teacher and a sangha (a group of practitioners). In ancient times, meditators often went off to practice by themselves for months at a time, traveling to see their teachers at regular intervals. Your practice could follow that model.

If you can't find a center, it is often helpful to start a sitting group on your own. Even if you can find only one other person who is interested, the two of you can get together once a week, do some sitting and walking meditation, perhaps listen to a tape by a teacher. It is extremely helpful to practice with other people. It gives support to your practice and helps you not to feel isolated. In time one other person might become two, then three. Substantial Buddhist centers have started in just that way.

It will also be a great help to your practice if you base it in an ethical standard of behavior. Buddhists for centuries have centered their practice on the five lay precepts, often declaring themselves Buddhists in ceremonies in which they take the precepts, agreeing not to kill, not to take what is not given, not to misuse speech, not to misuse sexual energy, not to use intoxicants. The precepts require a certain amount of interpretation, of course, but really, they are a bare minimum for civilized living.

The precepts are not intended as externally imposed rules but as guides to mindful living. Our innate wisdom gradually sees that these are sane and intelligent ways to behave. Thich Nhat Hanh sees them as guides in the same way that the North Star is a guide for a navigator. We never quite reach them—no one practices right speech all the time—but they give us an indication of the direction we want to go. They are like warning signs, letting us know that these are areas of behavior where human beings get in trouble.

In traditional Buddhist training, there are three areas of practice, and they are often thought of as successive. *Sila* is ethical training. *Samadhi* is the development of a stable, calm, clear mind. And *pañña* is the development of wisdom. Instruction begins with ethical training, centered around the five precepts, moves on to meditation instruction, and then finally arrives at the wisdom that is its true goal.

But these three aspects of practice are not really successive and cannot be so neatly compartmentalized. In order to practice the ethical precepts at all, we need a certain amount of wisdom. We need to see, for instance—in our efforts to practice right speech—that wrong speech leads to suffering. Otherwise the precepts will have no real meaning.

It also takes a certain amount of mindfulness to practice the precepts. You have to be aware when you are speaking that every moment of conversation is an opportunity for right or wrong speech. People cause a great deal of suffering by things they say. The breath can be a great help by giving you space around your words. Sometimes you are just moments from saying the wrong thing, but spending those moments with the breathing can give you the clarity to avoid it. In the same way, one of my students once told me of a situation in which he was perhaps thirty seconds away from committing a sexual indiscretion. He wanted to, and felt that the woman he was with did also. But in that brief period he was able to come to the breathing and bring himself back from a fantasy that had been very compelling. He had been carried away by a thought in the same way that he might have been on the cushion.

What he saw was that that sexual act would have violated a trust and caused him to be deceptive; it would very probably have hurt two families, his and that of the woman involved. In other words, he brought some wisdom to the situation. That is the kind of authority that the precepts can have, and it is the real reason for following them. You can save yourself from a lot of suffering.

There may be a time in our lives when we need to have rules imposed from the outside, but I have infinitely more confidence in a rule that is followed because a person sees the wisdom of it, because he or she has seen by looking into it that it is a good way to behave. The wisdom of the practice combines with the mindfulness we develop and eventually makes the precepts not exactly unnecessary, just perfectly obvious. Why would you do something that is going to lead to suffering for you and the people you love? However, until authentic spiritual maturity develops—and for many of us it can take a while—it is extremely helpful to have the precepts as reminders.

It is also helpful for meditators to develop a healthy fear of situations that will bring suffering and a healthy shame for things they've done that they know are wrong. Either of those feelings can become excessive, obviously. But when we have done something wrong, and remorse comes up, it is helpful to experience it fully, to be intimate with it just like any other emotion. Fully experiencing it helps us avoid unwise action in the future.

Ultimately the practice is not divorced from any part of our lives. It is not some fetish or obsession with the breathing; it's about learning how to live. I often suggest that my students ask themselves the simple question: Do I know how to live? Do I know how to eat? How much to sleep? How to take care of my body? How to relate to other people? One of the most valuable—and simultaneously humiliating—moments in my life was when I realized that I didn't know how to live. I was a grown man with a PhD and a professorship at a major university, but I didn't know how to live my life. So I set out to learn. I found that awareness can teach us everything we need to know.

It can be an especially valuable teacher in our relationships with other people. There is no area of human behavior that gets more attention nowadays, but much of it is the same old talk, the same tired thinking. Relationship is an extremely rich and viable part of practice, especially when you are able to use it as a mirror, so that you always see yourself in it.

Typically, we believe that other people make us angry, make us joyful or depressed. Buddhist psychology says simply: when A happens, B happens, which is different from saying that A causes B. When your partner does something and you become angry, you can see that as a valuable occasion for you to look at your anger, to bring your full attention to it. In time, as you keep bringing attention to a characteristic, it inevitably diminishes. Any relationship, even the most difficult one, can help you learn about yourself. And your learning is bound to affect the relationship.

The story is told that in one of G. I. Gurdjieff's communities, there was a man who was extremely obnoxious and was driving everybody crazy. Finally this person felt the hostility all around him, and left. But Gurdjieff chased after him and actually paid him to come back. He knew that the community could learn from that person in a way that they could from no one else. This isn't to say that you should stay year after year in a relationship that is hopeless or abusive. Obviously, wisdom would tell you to get out of such a situation. But it is to say that you don't need to tiptoe through life trying just to have "good" relationships.

One of my most vivid recollections from practice is when I was with my first Buddhist teacher, Soen Sunim, and he had decided to start a meditation center in New York. A group of us drove down with him in a car, and when we got to the place that he had picked out—a grim building on Fourteenth Street—we despaired. There were winos all around, drug users, drug pushers. It was exactly the kind of place we all would have run from on sight.

I will never forget his reaction. "No, listen. A bad situation is a good situation." He knew that there was a lot of energy in that place, even if at first the energy seemed to be negative. And he did start a successful center there. That didn't mean he was blindly positive. On another occasion in another place, he tried to start a center, saw after a few weeks that it was located in the wrong place, and immediately—without regret or any sense of failure—closed it down. He was able to see situations clearly. But he didn't make snap judgments from surface appearances. He knew that there is much beneath the surface that we are not seeing.

Seamless Practice

In other countries, Buddhist meditation is largely practiced by monks in monasteries, but in North America, for various reasons, meditation has been taken up in a major way by laypeople, who blend it in with the rest of their lives. It is a great help in that context. But it is also helpful—when you feel ready—to try a prolonged retreat.

I don't want to make exaggerated claims for retreats, but I do believe they deepen our practice as nothing else can. I lead many retreats as a teacher, but I also do a solo retreat every year, and in the early years of my practice I did many long retreats as a meditator, not as a teacher. I found them to be invaluable, and many of the students whom I work with on a regular basis have found a way to make retreats a part of their lives.

Retreats can take a variety of forms. At our center in Cambridge, we have daylong sittings, weekend retreats, and—on long holiday weekends—three-day retreats. The Insight Meditation Society (IMS) has some weekend retreats, but its most typical retreat, and the one I most often lead, lasts nine days. Meditators arrive on a Friday and leave a week from the following Sunday.

Full days at the retreat follow an invariable pattern. We rise early and have our first sitting at 5:45, followed by breakfast at 6:30 and a work period from 7:15 to 8:15. The morning is broken up into three periods of sitting and two of walking, as is the afternoon. In the evening there are two periods of sitting and one of walking, along with a dharma talk. Aside from individual interviews with teachers every other day, retreats are conducted entirely in silence, with no eye contact and no communication by note. We also ask that meditators not read or write. We are offering nine days for practitioners to stay entirely within their own consciousness.

Other traditions may set up their days somewhat differently, but all of the Buddhist traditions that focus on meditation offer some form of prolonged retreat. Experienced meditators can do a three-month retreat at the Insight Meditation Society, and in some traditions retreats last for years.

Obviously, this is a special environment, much different from the lives most of us normally lead. Different styles of retreats have been intricately designed through the years—through the centuries, actually—to give practitioners a unique opportunity to look at themselves. And just as obviously, sitting seems to be the star of the show. What most meditators wonder the first time they come is how they're possibly going to be able to sit that much. It does take some getting used to.

Walking meditation, I suppose, is the costar, or has at least a strong supporting role. There are also the work periods, tasty vegetarian meals, and breaks, and the evening dharma talk. But it is natural, especially for a beginner, to look at this schedule and think that sitting is what a retreat is all about. For many people, it is.

In addition to that dichotomy—sitting versus the rest of the day—students set up another one, thinking of retreats as intensive practice and time away from retreats as daily life. As I've said, there are some people who find intensive practice very attractive, almost addictive. They look forward to retreats as the most wonderful part of life and see daily life as a period to get through before the next retreat begins. It is the same as people on retreat who see sitting as the most important part and are just passing time the rest of the day.

This dichotomy—which is definitely a false one—is one of the knottiest problems of Buddhist practice. If teachers emphasize the importance of sitting, students think that sitting is the essence of Buddhism. It is the real practice and produces all the great realizations. If, on the other hand, we emphasize daily life, people start to neglect sitting and think that all they need to do is fully live their lives.

What is really difficult about this whole matter is that there is truth on both sides. Sitting is special and very important to practice, as countless teachers have said through the ages. On the other hand, you can't exaggerate the importance of daily life.

But I believe that these dichotomies are themselves the problem. What is preferable is a seamless practice that doesn't see any one aspect of life as more important than any other. I find retreats a particularly good place to teach, but I do so by emphasizing—and at first this sounds like a paradox—daily life on retreat. Because I believe that, in a real sense, there is only daily life.

After all, even though you are on retreat, you still have to wake up in the morning, brush your teeth, take a shower, get dressed. You have to go to the bathroom at regular intervals. You have to eat meals. You still have a job to do, and you have sitting practice (though the relative amounts of time you do these things are reversed). It's very different from your usual life, and it also isn't. It's the same old stuff.

"At least we don't have relationships!" people on retreat often say. One impossible burden has been lifted. But that isn't really true either, though relationships are definitely different when you can't talk. Some of the meditators at the Insight Meditation Society have roommates, and others work with people on work teams. They are definitely relating to those people.

There is also the notorious "dharma romance," in which meditators imagine a romantic relationship with someone else on retreat, only to realize at some point that it is all in their heads (and perhaps simultaneously realize that they have sometimes done the same thing out in the world). Some meditators work themselves into a frenzy because someone else was walking too slowly or wearing socks of different colors. So there may be no talking on retreat, but that doesn't mean there are no relationships.

I try to encourage meditators to see that there is daily life on retreat. Sitting is important, and walking is important, but so are meals and the breaks after meals. So is getting up in the morning and getting dressed. And so is the job that each meditator is assigned.

There are various ways of assigning these jobs. At some places where people do long-term practice, the teacher assigns the job as he or she gets to know the students. When I went to Korea, for instance, I was one of three Americans who were the first ever to practice Zen there. It was a big event, and people made quite a fuss over me, introducing me as a former professor and saying where I had taught. It was all quite impressive. So naturally, when it was time to give out the jobs, my teacher assigned me to the toilet.

It is also possible to let meditators pick their own jobs. That is what I used to do at IMS; people could pick work that was congenial to them. Someone who loved cooking could chop vegetables; those who liked to garden could work outside. I became aware in recent years that a fair number of veteran meditators were actually arriving hours early on the day that a retreat started, in the hope of getting their favorite jobs. Typically, an easy, enjoyable, and brief one.

I decided to change that procedure on recent retreats and have the jobs assigned entirely at random as meditators arrive, moving right down the list. People don't get to do their favorite jobs or have any choice at all. They find out as they arrive what work they will do (though we do make exceptions for medical considerations).

I wasn't doing this just to be mean. I was trying to remove the feeling a retreat has of being an overly protected environment where people control their destinies. After all, there are a hundred jobs on the list at IMS. Some are comparatively easy and rather enjoyable (chopping vegetables, dusting offices); others are not (cleaning bathrooms, scrubbing pots). Meditators who have hard jobs have been known to resent those with easy ones. Yet the emotions thereby aroused—anger, disgust, a feeling that this is unfair—tell us a great deal about ourselves and are ripe occasions for practice.

Insights don't come just when we are sitting on a cushion or doing formal walking meditation. When a contemplative is working, there are really two jobs. We're working on the vegetables or the toilet or whatever job we're doing. We're also working on ourselves.

So I encourage meditators on retreat to see it not as some specialized environment where something extraordinary is going to happen, but as another form of life, just this moment followed by that one, no activity more important than any other. Our challenge is always the same, to be with each moment as it is. That will be true even if we become enlightened; how could it be any different?

Sometimes, in order to encourage that attitude, I use the metaphor of the breath itself. Really to inhale, you need to have exhaled, to get all the old air out of your system to make room for new air. In the same way, in order to inhale a new experience, you need to have exhaled the old one. Maybe it was wonderful (a sitting where you were still and quiet and felt a deep peace), or maybe it was dreadful (one where you were restless and experienced a lot of pain), but however it was, it is over, and it is time to walk or go to lunch. If that old experience lingers, it will color the new one. And you won't fully have the experience that is before you.

If meditators encounter a retreat that way, they are better able to enter into their lives after the retreat. It can be disconcerting, after nine days of silence, to find yourself suddenly in the midst of downtown Boston or the hubbub of Logan Airport. It might be natural to compare that to the idyllic environment you've just come from, or to see with dismay the disintegration of the hard-earned samadhi that you've developed over nine days. But you can't hold on to samadhi—you can't hold on to anything—and in any case that airport, or that raucous urban setting, is your life in that moment. Your task is to be awake to it. Only when the retreat is exhaled can the airport be fully inhaled.

We practice different forms—sitting, walking, retreats themselves—but before any form, before Buddhism or the Buddha—is life itself, waiting to be lived. Life is the real teacher, and the curriculum is all set up. The question is: Are there any students? No form is unique, and on the other hand, every form is—sitting, walking, taking out the garbage, talking to a friend. Every form is unique, and so is every moment. When we see that, we are really beginning to practice.

My First Meditation Retreat: A Checklist

Karen Maezen Miller

There is no way to prepare for your first foray into extended sitting with others, says Karen Maezen Miller. You'll find her six tips helpful nonetheless.

How do you know if you are prepared to handle the silence, the physical rigors, the discipline, and the mental intensity of a prolonged meditation retreat?

Relax. You can't know. You don't need to know. There is no way to prepare. The very notion of preparation traps us in false expectation and self-evaluation. It shows us how often we are paralyzed by the feeling of inadequacy in our lives. We are never inadequate, but we are immobilized just the same.

A Zen retreat, which is the only kind of retreat I've experienced, is designed to cure you of that paralysis. It is intended to rid you of hobbling second thoughts and hesitation. I like to tell people to leave preparation aside and just bring readiness to a retreat. Readiness is no small thing. It can be quite compelling and even desperate, but it does not require preparation.

So here are a few tips on getting ready for a retreat:

1. The organizers will tell you when to come and what to bring. Follow those instructions to the letter. It is good practice for a retreat, which consists entirely of following instructions.

2. Find a pet sitter, a house sitter, a babysitter, and every other kind of sitter you think you need in order to leave home and its responsibilities completely. You are creating a trusted community to support you in your ongoing practice. Reliable surrogates may not relieve you of anxiety, but they rob you of excuses.

3. You may be inclined to read about retreats before you attempt one. This is natural, but it's not such a good idea. You are bound to form erroneous preconceptions about what you haven't yet experienced. I read Robert Aitken Roshi's *Taking the Path of Zen* before my first retreat, and of all the books I read it helped me to prepare the least.

4. Leave all books at home. Books aren't the subject of retreats, so you'll only be discussing it with yourself, probably on the cushion. Not helpful.

5. Leave your laptop, your phone, your every little ringing thing behind. (Except bring an alarm clock!) You are without a doubt central to the universe; you just aren't all that important. You can always be reached, but your retreat will be richly enhanced if your keypad is out of reach. In this way you can see how the dharma works by itself when we truly commit ourselves to doing nothing.

6. What's holding you back? Pack that in your suitcase and bring it along. You'll be bringing far more than you need, and next time you'll be unafraid to pack lighter.

Sangha: Practicing in Community

Gaylon Ferguson

If we expand our view of spiritual community, we can find inspiration in the compassionate activity of people all around us. Gaylon Ferguson explains how.

IN THE VARIOUS Buddhist traditions, *sangha* sometimes refers to the community of nuns and monks walking the path, but more generally it includes all those committed to waking up. So we could extend this view of practicing in community: let us receive inspiration from the examples of basic goodness we encounter around us, from the people who are manifesting bravery and compassion in everyday life. Whether they are religiously affiliated or not, surely these are spiritual warriors, and our own commitment to cultivating fearlessness is strengthened by their shining examples.

When we appreciate the kindness of a coworker or the thoughtfulness of a neighbor, we enter a virtuous gathering—whether we are in a zendo, temple, or meditation center at that moment or not. So, finding the noble community of the wakeful is in part a matter of perception. In this wider sense, traditional teachings on the supreme value of Noble Sangha are part of a "lion's roar" proclaiming the fundamental goodness of all beings, encouraging our appreciation of the sanity and warmth in the diverse communities around us.

Yet what about the neurotic confusion, the selfishness, and the greed we also see in our social environments? These too act as a mirror for us, reminding us of the strength of our own habitual patterns of delusion. There is something uncomfortably familiar in seeing others' acts of stupidity and aggression. Inner mindfulness is sparked to take note of our own thoughts, speech, and actions—and their harmful or helpful effects. As Jamgön Kongtrul the Great wrote: "Seeing bad qualities in others is like looking in the mirror at the dirt on one's own face." We are all engaged in a learning process together, and the feedback we receive from others (even if not always egolessly pure) can be very valuable in guiding our journey.

So the path here is to value our existing connections, whether it's as part of an environmental action group or hanging out with others after a strenuous yoga class. Our individual spiritual practice bears fruit in these collective human interactions.

The great meditation master Atisha often greeted his students this way: "Has your heart been kind?" How we are with others is a revealing mirror. We should be somewhat suspicious of any developing sense of "personal awakening" that does not show up as increased compassion and care for others' well-being. Wisdom shows its smiling face in the spontaneous joy of being with others.

Appreciating spiritual companionship means associating with any wakeful groups dedicated to compassionate activity. If slander and sarcasm are the daily bread of our communal meals, the determination to awaken gradually weakens and grows dim. Basic confidence and life-force energy decline. In a chapter in *Ruling Your World* called "Hanging Out with the Right Crowd," Sakyong Mipham put it this way: "Life is precious. Whom are we going to spend it with?"

Yoga Body, Buddha Mind

Cyndi Lee and David Nichtern

*A complete spiritual practice—or even just a healthy, satisfying life—
requires working with both body and mind. Cyndi Lee and David
Nichtern explain why yoga practice and Buddhist meditation make
the perfect mind-body combination.*

STRENGTH, STABILITY, AND CLARITY of mind are said to be the
fruits of mindfulness meditation. That sounds good, but if your
back is sore, your digestion is sluggish, and your nerves are fried, it's
tough to stabilize any kind of mental wakefulness or confidence.
Yoga is a path to these same fruits, but when your mind is jumpy,
sleepy, or full of angry thoughts, your body will reflect that with a
tight jaw, saggy shoulders, or a knot in your belly.

The body and mind need to work together in order to fully experience clarity of mind and radiant health. That's the recipe for
experiencing confidence, interest, and friendliness in our lives.
"Yoga Body, Buddha Mind" is a workshop that we have been teaching around the world. It began organically as a synthesis of Cyndi's
Tibetan Buddhist practice with the hatha yoga tradition that she
has studied and taught for over twenty-five years. Then we synced it
up with David's training in the teachings of Chögyam Trungpa
Rinpoche.

In our workshops, David presents the basic theme of each section, as well as how it applies to formal and in-the-field meditation practices. Cyndi follows this with a yoga session in which she weaves these ideas into how we work with our body, and elaborates on how to explore these principles in the movements and relationships of our daily lives. We will follow that structure here.

I. Making Friends with Yourself: Mindfulness Meditation

We start with our mind, because doesn't everything really start there? It seems strange, but many of us don't know our own mind. Often, without even realizing it, we avoid getting to know ourselves because we think we might not like what we find. Mindfulness provides a way to take a gentle and friendly look at oneself.

Meditation practice teaches us to recognize when our mind and body are dis-integrated: the body is right here, but the mind may be far away. We practice bringing mind and body together to develop a more harmonious, efficient, and creative relationship with ourselves and our world.

Since this process involves uncovering layers of discursive thoughts and habitual patterns, an important ingredient is to take an open and nonjudgmental attitude toward whatever we discover. Then that approach can be extended into our yoga practice, where the yogi is encouraged to work with her/his present situation without adding stress and ambition. Whatever body we have, whatever mind we have, we look at it with an open heart and a spirit of exploration.

David

Taking a look at our mind begins with our body—taking a strong and stable seat on our meditation cushion. Generally we take a cross-legged posture, but this can be done in a variety of ways, based on our flexibility and comfort level. We can also take a kneeling posture or even sit upright in a chair, with feet flat on the floor and the back upright and unsupported by the back of the chair. We can simply rest our hands palms down on our knees or on our thighs just above the knees.

Now we can pay attention to the position of our spine, stacking the vertebrae one on top of the other so that we have a good upright posture without straining. Our back is strong and stable and our front is soft and open. We can feel uplifted and dignified by sitting this way.

Our chin is tucked in slightly. There is a sense of containment and relaxation at the same time. The jaw is relaxed. The eyes remain open in a soft, downward gaze, focusing three to four feet in front. There is a feeling of relaxed awareness: we are seeing without looking too hard. We are awake and alert, but in a very peaceful and open way.

Having established our posture, we simply continue to breathe normally. There is no attempt made to manipulate the breath. Then we place our attention on our breathing in a very light and uncomplicated way. When our attention wanders, we simply bring it back to the breathing, time and time again. It's like taking a fresh start over and over.

Rather than creating an idealized or dreamy state of mind, we start with what we actually have, working with our thoughts and emotions as they arise and accepting the situation as it is. This is why we talk about making friends with ourselves. We start by accepting ourselves as we are, and gradually and peacefully bring our attention and breath together. This practice naturally creates more focus, clarity, and stability in our state of mind.

Cyndi

Yoga is an ideal bridge practice between formal meditation sessions and the rest of our life, when we move through the world, interacting with others. So much of what we fear, love, crave, push away, and ignore is stored in our physical body. Practicing yoga with a sense of alertness and curiosity can offer a complete program for getting familiar with our habits, creating space between stimuli and response, cultivating skillful means such as patience, and doing all this in an environment that includes other people.

But my observation is that this process does not automatically unfold through yoga practice. Without infusing friendly mindfulness into yoga practice, it is typical for overachievers to bring their aggression to the mat, while chronic underachievers wither from the required exertion. Both extremes are framed by a goal-oriented mentality focused on endpoints such as toe-touching. But once these postures are achieved, then what?

The Sanskrit word for posture is *asana*, which can be translated as "seat" or "to sit with what comes up." When yogis are invited to relax their agenda and open to the vibrancy of their immediate experience—lively sensations in hamstrings, inhalations massaging the low back, the shifting textures of the mind—they are finally practicing asana.

Getting curious about our personal experience (and practice isn't really practice unless it's personal), we begin to notice aspects of our process. Am I holding my breath and grasping? Or through full breathing, open eyes, and patient heart, could I slow down and wake up enough to create the conditions for fingers to touch toes? Whatever we notice is fodder for further exploration, both on the mat and after class.

This exploration offers us a nonjudgmental method of communication within our most primary relationship—that of our own mind and our own body. Just as we place our attention on our breath in meditation practice, we can do the same thing in yoga. Of course, when we're turning upside down and inside out, our breath shifts, but it shifts in life too, whenever we are challenged, excited, bored, sad. This is how yoga practice becomes fertile ground for cultivating a friendly attitude as we move through our day.

2. Not Too Tight, Not Too Loose

"It seems so easy—just sit and watch my breath. So why am I still having so many thoughts?" "I've been doing yoga for six months and even though I'm trying so hard, I still can't do a full backbend!" "I had a really good meditation—my mind was finally clear!" "I can't do that pose. Never, no way!"

These are all examples of how we can overexert or underapply ourselves in these practices. In order to have a balanced approach toward our effort, we need to recognize that equilibrium is dynamic and fluid, not at all a static process.

As we go deeper with our practice, we can begin to let go of what we think we are supposed to experience. Many students can do a full backbend after six months, but others—perfectly happy people—never do a backbend. Every meditation session is going to be different. The key is to cultivate discipline and exertion, and at the same relax our agenda.

David

Once we have started on the path of meditation, there are further refinements to the practice as we go along. In general, the teachings are like a roadmap or guidebook to a journey we have to undertake ourselves.

Beyond making friends with ourselves, we can develop greater stability and equilibrium in our state of being. In many cases our tendency is to think that we can achieve a particular state of mind (or body, for that matter) and hold it. I think this is the most common confusion that many meditators experience—that there is some absolute right way to do it, some ideal state of mind that we can achieve and sustain.

Actually, our situation is changing from moment to moment, and there is really nothing to hold on to at all. Impermanence is a fundamental fact of our existence. Whatever we experience seems to morph constantly, and it seems like every event, every perception, every thought, every situation is slipping away just as soon as we feel we are getting a handle on it. Our meditation practice is really a way to attune ourselves to this ever-changing experience of the present moment. It is training in the art of living as our life unfolds from moment to moment, like developing balance while standing on one leg on a windy cliff.

This approach is summed up by the slogan "Not too tight and not too loose." As we pay attention to our breathing, we use a light touch of awareness rather than a riveted and stiff kind of effort. On the other hand, if our effort is too loose, we simply wander around in a distracted state of mind, without developing any insight or clarity about how our mind works.

Developing equilibrium means that we ride the energy of our mind like a surfer rides the waves. If the surfer holds too tight, she will fall. If she hangs too loose, she will fall. Sometimes she needs to hang ten, sometimes none at all. Likewise, riding the energy of our mind is a dynamic and ongoing process.

Cyndi

Everybody gets "too tight" or "too loose" all the time. This is natural and normal. The yogic approach to balance integrates oppositional forces, the most basic elements being active and receptive. This is what distinguishes yoga as more than a mere exercise program and makes it a natural training ground for cultivating mindfulness.

When I begin teaching students how to do a handstand, most can't do it at all. In addition to the fear factor, they simply don't have the strength, coordination, and concentration required. They practice a few inch-high kicks up and leave it at that, a nice balance of reasonable physical effort and then mentally letting it go.

But intermediate yogis, who easily do handstands against the wall, start to crave balancing off the wall. They will jump up and fall back so many times they get in a bad mood. Here's what I say to them to help them shift their process: "If you hear a big boom when your feet hit the wall, you are using too much effort! Find out what is too little. Kick up, but don't touch the wall. Get familiar with the feeling of less. When you learn what is too much and what is too little, you can find just enough."

This is a revelation! When they were beginners they needed to kick hard to get even slightly airborne. With more strength and courage their balance will come from tighter mental focus and looser physical effort. Things have changed!

Without waking up to what is happening right now, yogis will literally continue to bang themselves against the wall. With the discovery of a middle path the practice really begins, because that sweet spot of stability is elusive—it won't be the same tomorrow.

It is tempting to want to establish a permanent balance point. But a reliable point of stability, or the amount of effort required to hold a handstand, or fairly manage your employees, or consistently discipline your children, will be different every day. In the *Yoga Sutra*, Patanjali advises us, "The asanas should be practiced with steadiness and ease." Doesn't that sound like a good recipe for life?

3. Obstacles as Path: Touch and Go

Actually, from one point of view there is no such thing as a path. We may have the feeling we are making some kind of journey and that it has shape and direction. We are going from here to there, with some specific idea of where we have been and where we are going. But this approach is based on an idealized version of our experience. In reality, our journey is unfolding as we go along.

Learning to bring our full attention to that journey could be called "path." So, as many dharma teachers have pointed out, "the path is the goal." That means that what we experience as "obstacles" along the way is usually just a sense of our own expectations falling apart. These same obstacles can be viewed differently, as the basis for reengaging our attention and working through whatever arises, whether it is a sense of purpose and satisfaction, or boredom and resistance, or a feeling of futility. Work with whatever arises.

David

Going further on our path, sometimes we will experience resistance to the practice itself. We may encounter strongly entrenched habitual patterns and it might feel difficult to move beyond them. Depression, resentment, anxiety, laziness, frivolity—to name a few—can make us feel there is no point in continuing to cultivate mindfulness and awareness.

A revolutionary approach we can take is to see that the obstacles can actually become the stepping-stones of the path. Our irritation, boredom, emotional upheavals, and wandering mind are the basis of the meditation practice itself. Without them, there is no meditation practice, just some kind of gooey, vague, and highly suspicious sense of well-being that lacks any real strength or foundation. We are just trying to pacify our mind in a superficial way, without working with ourselves as we really are—emotional, speedy, tired, anxious, spaced out, or whatever arises.

By touching in on these difficult aspects of our experience—really tasting them, and then allowing them to exist without judgment or manipulation—we are tuning in to a new kind of spaciousness that is refreshing and creative.

Here we can think of another slogan: "Touch and go." When we are trying to pay attention to our breathing and notice we are off in a daydream, nightmare, or drama of some kind, we simply label that "thinking" and come back to the breath.

There is no need to judge or evaluate the thoughts further. We simply let go, which is actually very profound. We do not need to repress or ignore the thought—that is the touch part. We can touch in on our thoughts and emotions and become more familiar with the patterns and movements of our mind. This exploration will of course include the ripples of "negative" thoughts and emotions that can sometimes grow into a tidal wave of resistance to the practice itself. Whenever our resistance solidifies like this, it can be helpful to remember why we started with the practice in the first place, and simply lean again into our effort.

Cyndi

People are always telling me that they don't do yoga because they are too stiff. No problem! Stiff bodies are perfect candidates for yoga, as is every other kind of body. No matter who you are or what yoga class you take, you'll find that some postures come naturally and some are beyond the realm of your current capacity or comprehension.

Typically, when we hit a yoga glitch, we try to identify an external reason: My arms are too long or too short; I'm too fat, too weak, too old, too short, too tall. Yet somehow those same arms are just the right size for that other easier pose. Hmmm . . . perhaps these obstacles aren't so solid after all.

I help students explore this through a pose called Utkatasana, nicknamed Awkward Pose. A "perfect" Utkatasana requires quadriceps strength; strong, loose shoulders and lower back; long, stretchy Achilles tendons; and cardiovascular stamina. But you don't need all that to work your way into it. You just need an open mind.

The first time in Utkatasana is fine—for a moment. But when I make the yogis stay longer than they expect, the resistance sparks start flying. Some students try an out-of-body experience—anything to ignore the intensity of this challenging pose. I bring them back with "What are you thinking? Where is your breath?"

Finally, I move them into a flowing sequence where Utkatasana becomes a happily forgotten memory, until I take them right back there again. This time I invite them to find their own way to make this pose workable. "What would it take for you to find ease? Perhaps you could widen your arms, bend your legs less, use less effort, observe your feelings changing."

Of course, the third time they come back to the pose they are ready and somehow it's not so bad. I tell them that *utkata* means "powerful" and ask them to figure out for themselves how they can feel power without being effort-full.

This goes on, and with each Utkatasana I can feel their attitude shift. The dreaded feeling of physical struggle transforms from an eye-rolling, here-we-go-again feeling, to a sense of possibility, to I-can't-believe-she's-doing-this-again, into laughing out loud! What would have happened if we'd only done one miserable Utkatasana?

4. Opening Your Heart: Maitri Practice

Our hearts are always fundamentally open. They're just covered up sometimes by doubt, hesitation, fear, anxiety, and all kinds of self-protective habitual patterns.

The practice of opening the heart is based on exploring and reversing some of these patterns. We cultivate openness while noting and dissolving the habits that obscure our natural sympathy and compassion for others.

At the physical and energetic level, we have an actual heart and surrounding area that can feel shut down and blocked up. So we can work on opening that area, bringing more *prana* and blood flow and breaking through the constriction and tightness that may have become normal for us.

David

Even though we might feel quite alone in our life and our practice, in the bigger picture we live in an interconnected web with others. The measure of success in our meditation practice is not how much we can transcend the pain and confusion of our own existence, but how much we can truly connect with our lives and with the others who share it.

After creating a proper ground by training our mind, it is a natural evolution of our practice to develop care and consideration for others. In fact, there are many meditation practices that are intended to develop kindness and compassion toward others as well as ourselves.

One such practice is called *maitri. Maitri* means loving-kindness or unconditional friendliness. It can be a natural outgrowth of mindfulness and awareness, but it is also a further step into overcoming and transforming our habitual patterns of selfishness and aggression. Maitri is a contemplative practice that encourages us to use our thoughts and imagination creatively. We actually use the thinking mind to help us develop sympathy toward others.

In some sense, we have already trained ourselves to be self-centered, uptight, jealous, and short-tempered. We can also train ourselves to be expansive, open, generous, and patient, because our thoughts are not as solid as we have made them out to be. They actually come and go in a somewhat haphazard fashion, with a tendency to repeat certain patterns that have become comfortable and familiar. It is entirely possible to step out of these patterns altogether, and through contemplation develop more positive habits that benefit oneself and others.

In maitri practice, we start by tuning in to somebody we love and wish well. Then, through the power of directing our thoughts and intentions, we try our best to extend that loving feeling toward our indifferent group, then even to our enemies, and then gradually to all beings everywhere. We recognize that none of these categories of friend, enemy, and don't-care is really solid anyhow. They are all changing year to year, day by day, and even moment to moment.

The traditional form that our good wishes take is contained in these four slogans:

May you be safe.
May you be happy.
May you be healthy.
May you be at ease.

We bring our loved one to mind, then ourselves, then the neutral person, and then the "enemy" or irritating person. In each case we simply repeat these slogans or contemplate their meaning. In this way we can deliberately cultivate and direct our goodwill and positive intentions toward ourselves and others.

Cyndi

There's good news right off the bat here for yogis, because just the fact that you've come to yoga class is an act of kindness toward yourself. Asana practice is an unparalleled method for removing energetic obstructions that make it tough to feel good or to have energy for yourself and others.

In yoga the primary activity of the arms is to support the function of the heart and lungs, the heavenly internal organs associated with feelings, vision, and the primary channels of life force, or prana. When our breath and blood are circulating freely, we feel fully alive and more available to ourselves and others.

Circulate is what we want our emotions to do, too. A sunken chest, slumped shoulders, and drooping chin inhibit energy flow and wholesome feelings. They're depressing. The opposite is equally true—if your chest, back, and heart muscles are supported, spacious, and mobile, you will breathe better and feel cheerful.

Loving-kindness asana practice focuses on heart-opening poses. We rotate our shoulders, open our ribs, and do backbends that release chest muscles and unlock sensation in the heart center. Some of these poses are challenging, but they can be done with curiosity and gentleness. One way I try to make them fun is by creating community.

Partnering exercises such as supported backbends or holding shoulders in a group tree pose teaches us how to support and be supported by others. When everybody falls over we laugh! It's a clear example that if something doesn't work for everybody, it doesn't work. It's an immediate reminder that our minds and hearts truly extend past the apparent boundary of our body. The sense of "other" starts to dissolve. We can experience interdependence right there on the yoga mat.

Traditional yoga theory emphasizes ahimsa, or nonharming. By applying maitri to how we work with relationships in yoga class, we grow the seed of ahimsa into an active blossoming of seeing others and consciously connecting to them. This shows up in our class etiquette: Can I move my mat over to make more space for a latecomer? Can I pass you a tissue? Yoga class becomes a safe haven for practicing kindness with like-minded seekers and gives us the skills to handle what we meet when we walk out the door.

When we started teaching "Yoga Body, Buddha Mind," it appeared to be a somewhat unique offering in both the yoga and the Buddhist communities. In general, the yoga community in the West was not familiar with Buddhist practice and Buddhists were not particularly interested in hatha yoga practice.

But although yoga is a wonderful method for getting a strong and fluid body, it can also be a way to solidify habits of attachment and aversion. And even though you might be able to sit on your meditation cushion for a month, when you try to get up after thirty days—or thirty minutes—it might take just as long for your legs to start working again. That's why we find that the practices of yoga and Buddhism complement each other so well.

Yoga and meditation are not ends in and of themselves. You may not ever put your leg behind your head, but you might find yourself having more patience with your children. You may only have ten minutes a day to practice meditation, but you might find that wakeful energy and compassionate outlook creeping into your staff meetings at work.

No matter what your job is, who your family is, what country you live in, or what planet you live on, your body and mind will always be with you. Our identities are all tightly linked with how we feel about our body and our mind—Am I fat? Am I smart? Perhaps this integration of meditation and yoga will inspire you to get to know your body and mind better—maybe not the body you had when you were twenty or the mind you had when you got that high score on your SAT—but the good body and mind you have right now.

Stabilize Your Practice

Andy Karr

If you're finding it difficult to establish a stable daily practice, Andy Karr has a simple, effective method for getting over the hump and onto the cushion every day.

PERHAPS THE MOST DIFFICULT part of meditation is getting yourself onto the cushion (or wherever you sit). For those of us trying to practice while working in the world, establishing a regular practice is challenging.

After I had been practicing for about fifteen years, I woke up one morning and realized that I didn't have a daily practice. I would do retreats and practice at home, but then wouldn't get around to meditating for days at a time, even though the Buddhist path was the most important thing in my life. Seeing this contradiction caused a wave of embarrassment to crash over me. As I lay in bed feeling shitty, I remembered hearing a friend say that Trungpa Rinpoche had told him to sit for at least ten minutes a day. When he mentioned that, it sounded pretty wimpy, but reflecting back, I realized that no matter how busy I was, there would never be a day when I could honestly say that I couldn't find ten minutes to sit. Before getting out of bed that morning I committed to not let another day go by without practicing for at least ten minutes.

That commitment was surprisingly effective. Sometimes I would come home, tired from work, and force myself to sit for a few minutes. Sometimes, on a business trip, my head would be about to hit the pillow and I would remember I hadn't practiced that day. It might be one o'clock in the morning, but I would spring up in bed and sit there like an idiot. It would be an exaggeration to say that I actually meditated at those times, but I certainly made an effort.

I went ten or fifteen years without missing a day, just because the commitment was so clear-cut. Eventually, I found that practicing had become a habit. Now, not practicing feels as unreasonable as missing morning coffee. For me it was an important stepping-stone. The point is, you don't need to depend on inspiration to meditate. Inspiration comes and goes. You don't have to be inspired to brush your teeth. You just need to know why it is a good idea and then get into the habit.

After getting onto the cushion, the next-hardest thing about developing a regular meditation practice is learning to stay there. Most of us start practicing with enthusiasm and a certain amount of naive optimism. This wears out fairly quickly when we discover the boredom, agitation, emotionality, drowsiness, aches, pains, and general cluelessness that we experience when we begin to sit with ourselves for any length of time. Unfortunately, there is really no way around this. You just have to sit through it.

There are three things that will help you. The first is a certain amount of faith in the dharma, which comes from understanding that this is a reliable path that is worth pursuing. The second is the aspiration to become a good practitioner, which comes from understanding the benefits of meditation. The third is good old-fashioned exertion.

If you keep practicing with your difficulties, eventually things will shift. The things that caused so much discomfort before will begin to recede, and you will have subtle experiences of physical and mental well-being. There is a good Tibetan word for this stage: *shinjang*, which means "suppleness," "pliancy," or "thoroughly trained." This is what we experience when we get over the hump. It is not a great revelation, just a feeling of wholesomeness when we practice.

Building Your Mental Muscles

Thanissaro Bhikkhu

Meditators and musclemen don't seem to have much in common, but Thanissaro Bhikkhu says the techniques of strength training can teach us a lot about how to develop a meditation practice.

MEDITATION IS THE MOST useful skill you can master. It can bring the mind to the end of suffering, something no other skill can do. But it's also the subtlest and most demanding skill there is. It requires all the mental qualities involved in mastering a physical skill—mindfulness and alertness, persistence and patience, discipline and ingenuity—but to an extraordinary degree. This is why, when you come to meditation, it's good to reflect on any skills, crafts, or disciplines you've already mastered so that you can apply the lessons they've taught you to training of mind.

As a meditation teacher, I've found it helpful to illustrate my points with analogies drawn from physical skills, and a particularly useful comparison is strength training. Meditation is more like a good workout than you might have thought.

The Buddha himself noticed the parallels here. He defined the practice as a path of five strengths: conviction, persistence, mindfulness, concentration, and discernment. He likened the mind's ability to beat down its most stubborn thoughts to that of a strong man beating down a weaker man. The agility of a well-trained mind, he said, is like that of a strong man who can easily flex his arm when it's extended or extend it when it's flexed. And he often compared the higher skills of concentration and discernment to the skills of archery, which—given the massive bows of ancient India— was strength training for the noble warriors of his day. These skills included the ability to shoot great distances, to fire arrows in rapid succession, and to pierce great masses—the great mass standing here for the mass of ignorance enveloping the untrained mind.

So even if you've been pumping great masses instead of piercing them, you've been learning some important lessons that will stand you in good stead as a meditator. Here are a few of the more important ones.

Read Up on Anatomy

If you want to strengthen a muscle, you need to know where it is and what it moves if you're going to understand the exercises that target it. Only then can you perform them efficiently.

In the same way, you have to understand the anatomy of the mind's suffering if you want to understand how meditation is supposed to work. Read up on what the Buddha had to say on the topic and don't settle for books that put you at the end of a game of telephone. Go straight to the source, the words of the Buddha himself. You'll find, for instance, that the Buddha explained how ignorance shapes the way you breathe, and how that in turn can add to your suffering. This is why most meditation regimens start with the breath, and why the Buddha's own regimen takes it all the way to nirvana. So read up to understand why.

Start Where You Are

Too many meditators get discouraged at the beginning because their minds won't settle down. But just as you can't wait until you're big and strong before you start strength training, you can't wait until your concentration is strong before you start sitting. Only by exercising what little concentration you have will you make it solid and steady. So even though you feel scrawny when everyone around you seems big, or fat when everyone else seems fit, remember that you're not here to compete with them or with the perfect meditators you see in magazines. You're here to work on yourself. Establish that as your focus and keep it strong.

Establish a Regular Routine

You're in this for the long haul. We all like the stories of sudden enlightenment, but even the most lightning-like insights have to be primed by a long, steady discipline of daily practice. That's because the discipline is what makes you observant, and being observant is what enables insight to see.

Don't get taken in by promises of quick and easy shortcuts. Set aside a time to meditate every day and then stick to your schedule, whether you feel like meditating or not. Sometimes the best insights come on the days you least feel like meditating. Even when they don't, you're establishing strength of discipline, patience, and resilience that will see you through the even greater difficulties of aging, illness, and death. That's why it's called practice.

Aim for Balance

The "muscle groups" of the path are threefold: virtue, concentration, and discernment. If any one of these gets overdeveloped at the expense of the others, it throws you out of alignment, and your extra strength turns into a liability.

Set Interim Goals

You can't fix a deadline for your enlightenment, but you can keep aiming for a little more sitting or walking time, a little more consistency in your mindfulness, a little more speed in recovering from distraction, a little more understanding of what you're doing. If you're approaching meditation as a lifetime activity, you've got to have goals. You've got to want results. Otherwise the whole thing turns into mush, and you start wondering why you're sitting here when you could be sitting at the beach.

Focus on Proper Form

Get your desire for results to work for you rather than against you. Once you've set your goals, focus not on the results but on the means that will get you there. It's like building muscle mass. You don't blow air or stuff protein into the muscle to make it larger. You focus on performing your reps properly, and the muscle grows on its own.

If, as you meditate, you want the mind to develop more concentration, don't focus on the idea of concentration. Focus on allowing this breath to be more comfortable, and then this breath, this breath, one breath at a time. Concentration will then grow without your having to think about it.

Pace Yourself

Learn how to read your pain. When you meditate, some pains in the body are simply a sign that it's adapting to the meditation posture, others that you're pushing yourself too hard. Learn how to tell the difference. The same principle applies to the mind. When the mind can't seem to settle down, sometimes you need to push even harder and sometimes you need to pull back. Your ability to read the difference is what exercises your powers of wisdom and discernment.

Learn how to read your progress. Learn to judge what works for you and what doesn't. You may have heard that meditation is nonjudgmental, but that's simply meant to counteract the tendency to prejudge things before they've had a chance to show their results. Once the results are in, you need to learn how to gauge them, to see how they connect with their causes so you can adjust the causes in the direction of the outcome you want.

Vary Your Routine

Just as a muscle can stop responding to a particular exercise, your mind can hit a plateau if it's strapped to only one meditation technique. This is why the Buddha taught supplementary meditations to deal with specific problems as they arise. For starters, there's goodwill for when you're feeling down on yourself or the human race—the people you dislike would be much more tolerable if they could find genuine happiness inside, so wish them that happiness. There's contemplation of the parts of the body for when you're overcome with lust—it's hard to maintain a sexual fantasy when you keep thinking about what lies just underneath the skin. And there's contemplation of death for when you're feeling lazy—you don't know how much time you've got left, so you'd better meditate now if you want to be ready when the time comes to go.

When these supplementary contemplations have done their work, you can get back to the breath, refreshed and revived. So keep expanding your repertoire. That way your skill becomes all-around.

Watch Your Eating Habits

As the Buddha said, we survive on both mental food and physical food. Mental food consists of the external stimuli you focus on, as well as the intentions that motivate the mind. If you feed your mind junk food, it's going to stay weak and sickly no matter how much you meditate.

Show some restraint in your mental eating habits. If you know that looking at things in certain ways, with certain intentions, gives rise to greed, anger, or delusion, look at them in the opposite way. As Ajaan Lee, my teacher's teacher, once said, look for the bad side of the things you're infatuated with and the good side of the things you hate. That way you become a discriminating eater, and the mind gets the healthy, nourishing food it needs to grow strong.

As for your physical eating habits, this is one of the areas where inner strength training and outer strength training part ways. As a meditator, you have to be concerned less with what physical food you eat than with why you eat. Give some thought to the purposes served by the strength you gain from your food. Don't take more from the world than you're willing to give back. Don't bulk up just for the fun of it, for the beings—human and animal—that provided your food didn't provide it in fun. Make sure the energy gets put to good use.

Don't Leave Your Strength in the Gym

If you don't use your strength in other activities, strength training simply becomes an exercise in vanity. The same principle applies to your meditative skills. If you leave them on the cushion and don't apply them in everyday life, meditation turns into a fetish, something you do to escape the problems of life while their causes continue to fester.

The ability to maintain your center and to breathe comfortably in any situation can be a genuine lifesaver. It keeps the mind in a position where you can more easily think of the right thing to do, say, or think when your surroundings get tough. The people around you are no longer subjected to your greed, anger, and delusion. And as you maintain your inner balance in this way, it helps them maintain theirs. So make the whole world your meditation seat. You'll find that meditation on the big seat and the little seat will strengthen each other. At the same time, your meditation will become a gift both to yourself and to the world around you.

Never Lose Sight of Your Ultimate Goal

Mental strength has at least one major advantage over physical strength: it doesn't inevitably decline with age. It can keep growing up to and through the experience of death. The Buddha promises that it leads to the deathless state, and he wasn't a man to make vain, empty promises.

So when you establish your priorities, make sure that you give more time and energy to strengthening your meditation than you do to strengthening your body. After all, someday you'll be forced to lay down this body, no matter how fit or strong you've made it, but you'll never be forced to lay down the strengths you've built into the mind.

Keeping It Real:
Working with Boredom and
without Self-Deception

Carolyn Rose Gimian

*Great meditators before us have laid out the path, but how can
we be sure we're following it genuinely? There are no guarantees—
but Carolyn Rose Gimian has some tips.*

SITTING ON THE CUSHION for a lot of years (if I tell you how many,
it will be really embarrassing) has yielded some results. I have wit-
nessed a whole circus of bizarre fantasies, emotions, and extreme
mental states, starring anger, lust, hatred, delusion, arrogance,
pride, depression, anxiety, and a host of other amazing performers.
I've made friends with Speedy, Distracted, and Lazy, three of the
seven dwarfs of meditation for small-minded people. However, I do
have one genuine accomplishment: I have gotten completely and
totally bored.

Boredom is my great achievement. Isn't that what you aspire to
in your meditation practice? To be totally, fully bored with yourself,
your practice, your life, your fantasies, etc., etc., etc.? No?

The topic I sat down to write about is genuineness. *Genuine* is a term that is bandied about quite a lot these days, and it can mean many things, depending on the context. Through my search engine, I found that a lot of advertising companies use the word *genuine* in the title of their companies and websites. Suspicious. I also noticed that popular searches with *genuine* as the first word were mainly for car parts. If you're going to drive an automobile, you would like it to have genuine parts, I'm sure. But this was not what I associate with genuineness in spiritual practice.

On the other hand, my word processor tells me that synonyms for *genuine* include real, authentic, indisputable, true, unadulterated, actual, legitimate, and valid. As far as the practice of meditation is concerned, these sound pretty good. I would definitely like my meditation to be real, authentic, indisputable, true, unadulterated, actual, legitimate, and valid.

Okay, so how are we going to achieve that? And what are the pitfalls? Simple. To be genuine, you have to be honest with yourself first, and then with others. Don't make anything up. Just do it. Just be it. It's pretty straightforward. But being honest with yourself is not so easy. There's a little thing called self-deception that gets in the way.

Now that we've introduced that scary word, self-deception, we have our work cut out for us. In the realm of overcoming self-deception, it's probably better to have no goal in your practice, but that's a very difficult thing. Since meditation actually works, it's hard not to have a goal. It actually does make you kinder, more aware, less speedy, happier, more mindful, more efficient, more peaceful, more in the moment, and so on. I'm not belittling these. They are important and valid outcomes of meditation. There are many studies and self-reports that support this. I'm a fan, a true believer. But this doesn't specifically address genuineness.

In fact, when it comes to being genuine, it may be better to have one of those definite but perhaps limited purposes and let genuineness, which is all-pervasive, take care of itself. Indeed, unwittingly, you do manifest genuineness through the practice of meditation.

You become more transparent and available to yourself, your thoughts are less fixed, you discover both natural strength and natural gentleness, and you're able to see through preconceptions.

I presume you're waiting for the "but," the pitfall. Here it comes, and it's a big one. Largely, it's attachment to credentials.

Sometimes experience comes blessedly, with no connection to credentials. If out of nowhere you have an experience of openness, joy, compassion, or awareness, an experience that doesn't seem causally connected to anything particular in your life, then it is largely free from credentials. It's a gift. It's just what it is. Enjoy it for what it is, while it lasts.

But as soon as you become a "meditator," whether you have been meditating for one hour, one week, one retreat, or twenty years, you may begin to feel the need to label your meditation experiences and to communicate them to others. That's the beginning of gaining your spiritual credentials. You've just done your first meditation retreat. You go home and tell your family and friends about it: "Oh, it was fantastic. I had a really hard time for a few days, and my body hurt and I couldn't control my thoughts, but then I had the most amazing (or insert other adjective) experience." Whatever it was. Well, what else are you going to say? "Nothing happened. It was a complete waste of time, but I want to keep doing this." Huh? We have positive experiences, and we want to share them with others. That's an ordinary and acceptable thing to do. Pretty benign.

A little less benign is that, internally, we are looking for confirmation, signs that something is happening in our practice. We are looking for results, progress on the path. That also may be natural, but it's a little more dangerous because after a while we may tend to manufacture results or jump on things in our practice. If we have a "good" (that is, peaceful) meditation session, we are pleased and we try to repeat that. Another time we are frustrated when our mind is a roaring freight train of thoughts and emotions. Or we are experiencing huge upheavals in our life, yet nothing is coming up when we're on the cushion. Shouldn't they manifest in our meditation?

We may try to manufacture emotionality and crisis in our practice. There are many other examples of how our expectations manifest in our meditation practice.

All these concerns about our practice and our various meditation experiences are genuine signs of—wait for it—confusion. Actually, the recognition of confusion is quite helpful. Seeing our confusion is an important and, dare we say, genuine discovery. If we look into our experience, we see that we are very, very confused in some fundamental way. That may be the most authentic realization that comes up over and over in our meditation practice. If we are willing to acknowledge confusion, at the beginning, in the middle, and at the end, then the path and the teachings are real, even if we may not seem to be getting anywhere.

Give up any hope of fruition. This slogan from the *lojong* (mind training) tradition is another way of putting it. This is the idea of our practice being anti-credential, or free from credentials—through and through, start to finish. That is why boredom, our starting point, is so helpful. It's really not a very good credential. If someone asks what you have achieved after three days, or three years, or three decades of meditating, it's not that impressive to say, "I'm thoroughly bored." To prepare for writing this article, I looked at ads for spiritual paths and retreats, and not one of them said, "Come sit with us. We'll make you completely bored."

But boredom is actually a great sign, if it is genuine, complete boredom that includes being bored with your confusion, your anger, your arrogance, your everything, your you. I'm probably letting the cat out of the bag a bit, but if you commit yourself fully to your practice and discipline, you eventually wear out a lot of things—they begin to seem quite unnecessary and quite boring.

Boredom is genuinely helpful in ventilating our minds. The point of meditation is obviously not to encourage or enshrine our confusion, so getting really bored with our story lines, positive and negative, helps us clarify our confusion immensely. Of course, the path of meditation is not designed to deter us from commitment, confidence, and positive achievements in life. Meditation is not a nihilistic enterprise. But the approach of collecting credentials rather than wearing them out is problematic. It is very dangerous to try to con buddha mind, hoping to find a shortcut. It's not dangerous to buddha mind itself, but it may lead to self-deception, the opposite of being genuine.

This is often a problem the longer you have been practicing, especially if you become an instructor or a spiritual model of some kind for others. Then you really feel that you have to demonstrate some accomplishment, and you may begin to panic if you don't find anything in yourself that qualifies. People are looking to you for advice. They may be watching your every move, or so you think. They may ask you, "What was it like when you were just a beginner like me?" "How did you become so wise, kind, open, generous, blah blah blah?" And you start to think, "Well, I must have accomplished something. Yes, I am wiser, kinder, more open, more generous, more blah blah blah." You may try to fulfill people's expectations because you actually want to help them. But you also want to avoid embarrassment.

The interesting thing is that people actually see right through one another, so really we could relax about the whole thing. It's an open secret. Or as Leonard Cohen wrote, "Everybody knows." Everybody really does know their own and others' little secrets. We know, that is, if we admit to ourselves what we see, what we really know. We perceive what is truly genuine.

Unfortunately, it's not so easy to relax with that in ourselves. We have a lot of resistance to simply being ourselves, without pretense or adornment, with all our warts and wrinkles. It is quite uncomfortable. So often we put on a little show for ourselves and others, thinking that's what is required. We try to give the people what they want. We try to give ourselves what we think we want. It's actually very sad, and in the long run it doesn't help ourselves or others. But in the short run, it's a pretty good con.

But while everybody may know, that's not a license for telling other people what's wrong with them or what's good for them. To do that, you'd have to really know. You'd have to be able to see others not just as schmucks or charlatans, devils or angels, but also as the immaculately genuine human beings they are. That has to start in one's own practice. Sitting with ourselves without expectation, viewing practice as practice, as life's work rather than a race to the finish line. In that way, we leave space so that buddha mind, genuine mind, can shine through at the most unexpected moments.

Genuineness is actually that simple. But I have to confess that I fall short most of the time, failure that I am.

A little voice pops up: Give it up. Abandon any hope of fruition. I yield to the little voice.

Signs of Spiritual Progress

Pema Chödrön

The concept of success on the spiritual path is pretty suspect. After all, isn't it a journey without goal? But there are ways, says Pema Chödrön, we can tell if our practice is working.

IT IS TEMPTING TO ASK ourselves if we are making "progress" on the spiritual path. But to look for progress is a setup—a guarantee that we won't measure up to some arbitrary goal we've established.

Traditional teachings tell us that one sign of progress in meditation practice is that our *kleshas* diminish. Kleshas are the strong conflicting emotions that spin off and heighten when we get caught by aversion and attraction.

Though the teachings point us in the direction of diminishing our klesha activity, calling ourselves "bad" because we have strong conflicting emotions is not helpful. That just causes negativity and suffering to escalate. What helps is to train again and again in not acting out our kleshas with speech and actions, and also in not repressing them or getting caught in guilt. The traditional instruction is to find the middle way between the extreme views of indulging—going right ahead and telling people off verbally or mentally—and repressing: biting your tongue and calling yourself a bad person.

Now, to find what the middle way means is a challenging path.

That is hard to know how to do. We routinely think we have to go to one extreme or the other, either acting out or repressing. We are unaware of that middle ground between the two. But the open space of the middle ground is where wisdom lies, where compassion lies, and where lots of discoveries are to be made. One discovery we make there is that progress isn't what we think it is.

We are talking about a gradual awakening, a gradual learning process. By looking deeply and compassionately at how we are affecting ourselves and others with our speech and actions, very slowly we can acknowledge what is happening to us. We begin to see when, for example, we are starting to harden our views and spin a story line about a situation. We begin to be able to acknowledge when we are blaming people, or when we are afraid and pulling back, or when we are completely tense, or when we can't soften, or when we can't refrain from saying something harsh. We begin to acknowledge where we are. This ability comes from meditation practice. The ability to notice where we are and what we do comes from practice.

I should point out that what we're talking about is not judgmental acknowledging, but compassionate acknowledging. This compassionate aspect of acknowledging is also cultivated by meditation. In meditation we sit quietly with ourselves and we acknowledge whatever comes up with an unbiased attitude—we label it "thinking" and go back to the out-breath. We train in not labeling our thoughts "bad" or "good," but in simply seeing them. Anyone who has meditated knows that this journey from judging ourselves or others to seeing what is, without bias, is a gradual one.

So one sign of progress is that we can begin to acknowledge what is happening. We can't do it every time, but at some point we realize we are acknowledging more, and that our acknowledgment is compassionate—not judgmental, parental, or authoritarian. We begin to touch in with unconditional friendliness, which we call *maitri*—an unconditional openness toward whatever might arise. Again and again throughout our day we can acknowledge what's happening with a bit more gentleness and honesty.

We then discover that patterns can change, which is another sign of progress. Having acknowledged what is happening, we may find that we can do something different from what we usually do. On the other hand, we may discover that (as people are always saying to me), "I see what I do, but I can't stop it." We might be able to acknowledge our emotions, but we still can't refrain from yelling at somebody or laying a guilt trip on ourselves. But to acknowledge that we are doing all these things is in itself an enormous step; it is reversing a fundamental, crippling ignorance.

Seeing but not being able to stop can go on for quite a long time, but at some point we find that we can do something different. The main "something different" we can do begins with becoming aware of some kind of holding on or grasping—a hardness or tension. We can sense it in our minds and we can feel it in our bodies. Then, when we feel our bodies tighten, when we see our minds freeze, we can begin to soften and relax. This "something different" is quite doable. It is not theoretical. Our mind is in a knot and we learn to relax by letting our thoughts go. Our body is in a knot and we learn to relax our body, too.

Basically this is instruction on disowning: letting go and relaxing our grasping and fixation. At a fundamental level we can acknowledge hardening; at that point we can train in learning to soften. It might be that sometimes we can acknowledge but we can't do anything else, and at other times we can both acknowledge and soften. This is an ongoing process: it's not like we're ever home free. However, the aspiration to open becomes a way of life. We discover a commitment to this way of life.

This process has an exposed quality, an embarrassing quality. Through it our awareness of "imperfection" is heightened. We see that we are discursive, that we are jealous, aggressive, or lustful. For example, when we wish to be kind, we become more aware of our selfishness. When we want to be generous, our stinginess comes into focus. Acknowledging what is, with honesty and compassion; continually training in letting thoughts go and in softening when we are hardening—these are steps on the path of awakening. That's how kleshas begin to diminish. It is how we develop trust in the basic openness and kindness of our being.

However, as I said, if we use diminishing klesha activity as a measure of progress, we are setting ourselves up for failure. As long as we experience strong emotions—even if we also experience peace—we will feel that we have failed. It is far more helpful to have as our goal becoming curious about what increases klesha activity and what diminishes it, because this goal is fluid. It is a goalless exploration that includes our so-called failures. As long as our orientation is toward perfection or success, we will never learn about unconditional friendship with ourselves, nor will we find compassion. We will just continue to buy into our old mind-sets of right and wrong, becoming more solid and closed to life.

When we train in letting go of thinking that anything—including ourselves—is either good or bad, we open our minds to practice with forgiveness and humor. And we practice opening to a compassionate space in which good/bad judgments can dissolve. We practice letting go of our idea of a "goal" and letting go of our concept of "progress," because right there, in that process of letting go, is where our hearts open and soften—over and over again.

GLOSSARY

bodhichitta (Skt.): The mind of enlightenment; the compassionate aspiration to attain liberation in order to free others from suffering.

bodhisattva (Skt.): One who seeks enlightenment not primarily for oneself but for the benefit of all beings.

Dzogchen (Tib.): "Great Perfection," the main teaching of the Nyingma school of Tibetan Buddhism.

jhana (Pali): A state of blissful tranquillity or absorption that may arise as a result of meditation practice.

kinhin (Jap.): The Zen practice of walking meditation.

klesha (Skt.): Disturbing emotion; defilement.

koan (Jap.): A story, phrase, or anecdote used in the Zen tradition as a means to help the practitioner's mind transcend dualistic thinking.

lojong (Tib.): "Mind training"; teachings propagated by the Indian master Atisha Dipankara on how to develop bodhichitta and reduce self-cherishing.

Mahamudra (Skt.): "Great Seal"; the meditation practice of the Tibetan Kagyu school which involves looking directly at the mind in order to help us realize emptiness, free ourselves from suffering, and to recognize the inseparability of both.

Mahayana (Skt.): The "Great Vehicle" tradition of Buddhism; the path of the bodhisattva, who seeks enlightenment in order to benefit all beings.

maitri (Skt.; "metta" in Pali): Kindness, loving-kindness, friendliness.

metta: *See* maitri.

mudra (Skt.): Hand gestures that correspond to certain qualities to be cultivated in meditation practice, often seen in Buddhist iconography.

pañña (Pali; "prajna" in Skt.): Wisdom or insight.

paramita (Skt.): The "perfections," or virtues, cultivated by a bodhisattva, including generosity, discipline, patience, exertion, meditation, and wisdom.

prajna (Skt.): *See* pañña.

prana (Skt.): Energy or life force.

Rinpoche (Tib.): "Precious jewel"; an honorific for a Tibetan lama or teacher.

Rinzai (Jap.): Along with Soto, one of the two primary schools of Ch'an and Zen. The Rinzai school emphasizes the practice of koan introspection.

Roshi (Jap.): "Old [venerable] master"; an honorific for a Zen teacher.

samadhi (Skt.): Meditative concentration.

sampajañña (Pali): Self-awareness.

samsara (Skt.): The cycle of suffering and rebirth from which Buddhists seek liberation.

sati (Pali): Mindfulness, recollection.

sesshin (Jap.): An extended Zen meditation retreat.

shamatha (Skt.): "Calm-abiding"; meditation to cultivate stillness and mental tranquillity.

shamatha-vipashyana (Skt.): A meditation practice that joins calm-abiding meditation with insight meditation.

shikantaza (Jap.): "Just sitting"; along with koan introspection, one of two main meditation practices of the Zen school.

sila (Pali): Ethical conduct; discipline.

Soto (Jap.): Along with Rinzai, one of the most important schools of Zen Buddhism. Founded in China, the Soto school flourished in Japan under Dogen Zenji.

Theravada (Pali): The oldest school of Buddhism, practiced widely in Southeast Asia and providing a bedrock of teachings on vipassana practice in the West.

tonglen (Tib.): "sending and taking"; a meditation for developing bodhichitta and diminishing self-cherishing.

Vajrayana (Skt.): "Diamond Vehicle"; the tantric teachings of the Mahayana, a path of method practiced chiefly by Tibetan Buddhists, with students guided through practice and formal initiations by a master or guru.

vipashyana: *See* vipassana.

vipassana (Pali; "vipashyana" in Skt.): Meditation to develop insight into the true nature of mental and physical phenomena.

zabuton (Jap.): A mat placed under a zafu to cushion the legs and feet in meditation.

zafu (Jap.): A cushion for seated meditation.

zazen (Jap.): Zen meditation.

zendo (Jap.): Zen meditation hall.

CONTRIBUTORS

Sᴙʟᴠɪᴀ Bᴏᴏʀsᴛᴇɪɴ, PʜD, has been a psychotherapist since 1967 and a dharma teacher since the mid-1980s. She is a cofounding teacher at Spirit Rock Meditation Center in Woodacre, California, and the author of several books on Buddhism and mindfulness, including *Happiness Is an Inside Job.*

Jᴏʜɴ Dᴀɪsʜɪɴ Bᴜᴋsʙᴀᴢᴇɴ was ordained as a Zen priest in 1968, and teaches at both the Zen Center of Los Angeles and the Ocean Moon Sangha in Santa Monica. He is a licensed psychoanalyst and the author of *Zen Meditation in Plain English.*

Aᴊᴀʜɴ Cʜᴀʜ (1918–1992) was part of a movement to establish simple monastic communities in the remote forests of Thailand; over 100 such forest monasteries look to his teaching as their inspiration. His teachings have been collected in such volumes as *Food for the Heart* and *Being Dharma.*

Pᴇᴍᴀ Cʜöᴅʀöɴ received full ordination as a Buddhist nun in 1981 and has since become one of America's most important Buddhist teachers. She is the author of several best-selling books, including *The Wisdom of No Escape* and *The Places That Scare You.*

Tʜᴇ Fᴏᴜʀᴛᴇᴇɴᴛʜ Dᴀʟᴀɪ Lᴀᴍᴀ, Tenzin Gyatso, is considered the foremost Buddhist leader of our time. The exiled spiritual head of the Tibetan people, he is a Nobel Peace Laureate, a Congressional

Gold Medal recipient, and a remarkable teacher and scholar who has authored over one hundred books.

AJAAN LEE DHAMMADHARO (1906–1961) was a forest monk who became one of Thailand's most renowned teachers of Buddhist meditation.

GAYLON FERGUSON is the author of *Natural Wakefulness*. He teaches religious and interdisciplinary studies at Naropa University in Boulder, Colorado, and is a senior teacher in the Shambhala Buddhist tradition.

NORMAN FISCHER is a Zen teacher and poet and the founder of the Everyday Zen Foundation. He served as abbot of the San Francisco Zen Center from 1995 to 2000. He has written many books of prose and poetry, including *Training in Compassion*.

JAMES ISHMAEL FORD is a guiding teacher of Boundless Way Zen and a Unitarian Universalist minister. He is the author of *Zen Master Who?* and *If You're Lucky, Your Heart Will Break*.

CAROLYN ROSE GIMIAN is a senior editor of the works of the late Chögyam Trungpa Rinpoche, including *The Collected Works of Chögyam Trungpa* and *Smile at Fear*.

BHANTE GUNARATANA was ordained as a Buddhist monk in Sri Lanka at the age of twelve and earned his PhD in philosophy from American University. He has led meditation retreats, taught Buddhism, and lectured widely throughout North America, Europe, and Australia. He is the author of several books, including *Mindfulness in Plain English*.

THICH NHAT HANH is one of the most renowned Buddhist teachers of our time. He is a Zen master, poet, prolific author, and founder of the Engaged Buddhism movement. Still actively traveling and teaching in his eighties, he resides at Plum Village, a practice community in southern France.

BLANCHE HARTMAN is a Soto Zen teacher practicing in the lineage of Shunryu Suzuki and the former abbess of the San Francisco Zen Center. She was the first woman to assume such a leadership position at the center.

ANDY KARR is a longtime Buddhist meditator and amateur photographer. He is the author of *Contemplating Reality* and *The Practice of Contemplative Photography*.

JACK KORNFIELD is one of the leading Buddhist teachers in America. A practitioner for over forty years, he is one of the key teachers to introduce mindfulness and vipassana meditation to the West. His books include *A Path with Heart* and *The Buddha is Still Teaching*.

GEN LAMRIMPA was born in Tibet in 1934, and spent most of his life in meditative retreat in Dharamsala, India. He is the author of *How to Realize Emptiness* and *How to Practice Shamatha Meditation*.

CYNDI LEE is the first female Western yoga teacher to fully integrate yoga asana and Tibetan Buddhism in her practice and teaching. She is the author of *May I Be Happy*.

NOAH LEVINE teaches meditation classes, workshops, and retreats nationally as well as leading groups in juvenile halls and prisons. He is the author of *Dharma Punx*, *Against the Stream*, and *The Heart of the Revolution*.

JUDY LIEF has been teaching on the subject of lojong, or mind training, for more than thirty years. Author of *Making Friends with*

Death, she teaches on applying a contemplative approach to facing death and working with the dying, and leads an annual retreat for women touched by cancer called "Courageous Women, Fearless Living."

Melvin McLeod is the editor-in-chief of the *Shambhala Sun* and *Buddhadharma: The Practitioner's Quarterly*. He is also the editor of several books, including *Mindful Politics* and *The Best Buddhist Writing* series.

Karen Maezen Miller is a Zen Buddhist priest and teacher at the Hazy Moon Zen Center in Los Angeles. She is the author of *Momma Zen* and *Hand Wash Cold*.

Sakyong Mipham Rinpoche is the spiritual leader of Shambhala International, a network of meditation centers founded by his father, Chögyam Trungpa Rinpoche. He is the author of *Turning Your Mind into an Ally* and *Running with the Mind of Meditation*.

David Nichtern is a senior teacher in the Shambhala Buddhist lineage. A composer, author, and meditation teacher, he works with OM Yoga Center founder Cyndi Lee to develop and lead meditative yoga workshops.

Chökyi Nyima Rinpoche is the abbot of Ka-Nying Shedrub Ling monastery in Kathmandu, Nepal. Eldest son of the late Dzogchen master Tulku Urgyen Rinpoche, he also teaches annually at Rangjung Yeshe Gomde, his retreat center in northern California.

John Powers received his PhD from the University of Virginia and specializes in Indian and Tibetan intellectual history. He is currently Professor of Asian Studies at Australian National University, and has published many books, including *Introduction to Tibetan Buddhism*.

LEWIS RICHMOND is an ordained disciple and lineage holder of Zen master Shunryu Suzuki. He leads the Vimala Zen Center Sangha in Mill Valley, California, and is the author of *Work as a Spiritual Practice*, *Healing Lazarus*, and *A Whole Life's Work*.

LARRY ROSENBERG is founder and resident teacher of the Cambridge Insight Meditation Center in Cambridge, Massachusetts, and a guiding teacher at the Insight Meditation Society in Barre, Massachusetts. He is the author of *Breath by Breath* and *Three Steps to Awakening*.

SHARON SALZBERG cofounded the Insight Meditation Society with Jack Kornfield and Joseph Goldstein, and is the author of several books, including *Real Happiness* and *Lovingkindness*.

CLARK STRAND is a former Zen Buddhist monk and a contributing editor to *Tricycle: The Buddhist Review*.

SHUNRYU SUZUKI ROSHI (1904–1971) was the founder of the San Francisco Zen Center and the Tassajara Zen Mountain Center. He is the author of *Zen Mind, Beginner's Mind* and *Branching Streams Flow in the Darkness*, and is the subject of the biography *Crooked Cucumber* by David Chadwick.

JOHN TARRANT is the director of Pacific Zen Institute, which conducts retreats devoted to koans, inquiry, and the arts. He is the author of *The Light Inside the Dark* and *Bring Me the Rhincoeros*.

THANISSARO BHIKKHU (born Geoffrey DeGraff) is a senior monk in the Thai forest tradition of Theravada Buddhism and the abbot of Metta Forest Monastery in San Diego County, California. Free digital versions of his teachings are available at Dhammatalks.org.

CHÖGYAM TRUNGPA RINPOCHE (1940–1987) was a holder of the Kagyu and Nyingma lineages of Vajrayana Buddhism and founder of Shambhala International, Naropa University, and the *Shambhala Sun*. He is the author of several classics, including *Cutting Through Spiritual Materialism*, *Born in Tibet*, and *Shambhala*.

TSOKNYI RINPOCHE has been teaching students about the innermost nature of mind, as taught in the Tibetan tradition, for more than twenty years. He is the author of *Carefree Dignity*, *Fearless Simplicity*, and *Open Heart, Open Mind*.

SAYADAW U PANDITA is the founder and abbot of Panditarama Forest Meditation Center near Yangon, Myanmar.

CREDITS

PART I
───

Let's Get Started

Melvin McLeod, "Basic Breath Meditation: It Doesn't Get Simpler Than This." From the July 2012 issue of *Shambhala Sun*. www .shambhalasun.com

Clark Strand, "On Motivation: Meditate as a Hobby, Not as a Career." Excerpted from *Meditation without Gurus: A Guide to the Heart of Practice.* Copyright © 1998 by Clark Strand. Permission granted by SkyLight Paths Publishing, Woodstock, Vt. www.skylightpaths.com.

Norman Fischer, "Getting Started." From the September 2010 issue of *Shambhala Sun*. www.shambhalasun.com

Bhante Henepola Gunaratana, "What Meditation Isn't." Excerpt adapted from *Mindfulness in Plain English*, by Bhante Gunaratana. Copyright © 2011 by Bhante Gunaratana. Reprinted with permission of The Permissions Company, Inc., on behalf of Wisdom Publications. www.wisdompubs.org.

Sharon Salzberg, "Dedicating Your Practice." Excerpted from *Real Happiness: The Power of Meditation.* Copyright © 2011 by Sharon Salzberg. Used by permission of Workman Publishing, Co., Inc., New York. All rights reserved. www.workman.com.

PART 2

Cultivating Calm and Insight (and More)

Ajaan Lee Dhammadharo (Thanissaro Bhikkhu, translator), "Working with Method 2." From *Keeping the Breath in Mind and Lessons in Samadhi* by Ajaan Lee Dhammadharo, translated from the Thai by Thanissaro Bhikkhu. This and many other related publications are freely available via http://www.dhammatalks.org.

Sylvia Boorstein, "Developing Insight." From the July 2012 issue of *Shambhala Sun*. www.shambhalasun.com

Thich Nhat Hanh, "Getting Grounded through Walking Meditation." From the July 2012 issue of *Shambhala Sun*. www.shambhalasun.com

Noah Levine, "Compassion and Loving-Kindness Meditation." From *Against the Stream: A Manual for Spiritual Revolutionaries* by Noah Levine. © 2007 by Noah Levine. Reprinted by permission of Harper Collins.

PART 3

A Taste of Zazen

Blanche Hartman, "This Life Which Is Wonderful and Evanescent." From the May 2001 issue of *Shambhala Sun*. www.shambhalasun.com.

John Daishin Buksbazen, "Sitting Zen." Adapted from *Zen Meditation in Plain English* by John Daishin Buksbazen. © 2002 by Zen Center of Los Angeles. Reprinted with permission of The Permissions Company, Inc., on behalf of Wisdom Publications. www.wisdompubs.org.

James Ishmael Ford, "The Practices of Zen." From *Zen Master Who?* by James Ishmael Ford. Copyright © 2006 by James Ishmael Ford. Reprinted with permission of The Permissions Company, Inc., on behalf of Wisdom Publications. www.wisdompubs.org.

Lewis Richmond, "Going Nowhere." From the January 2000 issue of *Shambhala Sun*. www.shambhalasun.com.

John Tarrant, "The Power of Koan Practice." From the May 2003 issue of *Shambhala Sun*. www.shambhalasun.com.

Shunryu Suzuki, "Study Yourself." From *Zen Mind, Beginner's Mind* by Shunryu Suzuki. Protected under the terms of the International Copyright Union. Reprinted by arrangement with Shambhala Publications, Inc., Boston, Mass. www.shambhala.com.

PART 4

Indo-Tibetan Innovations

John Powers, "What the Practice Can Do." From *A Concise Introduction to Tibetan Buddhism* by John Powers. © 2008 by John Powers. Reprinted by arrangement with Shambhala Publications, Inc., Boston, Mass. www.shambhala.com.

Pema Chödrön, "Relaxing with the Truth." Adapted from *The Places That Scare You: A Guide to Fearlessness in Difficult Times* by Pema Chödrön. © 2001 by Pema Chödrön. Reprinted by arrangement with Shambhala Publications, Inc., Boston, Mass. www .shambhala.com.

Tenzin Gyatso, the Fourteenth Dalai Lama, "Developing the Mind of Great Capacity." Adapted from *The Path to Bliss* by Tenzin Gyatso, the Fourteenth Dalai Lama, translated by Thupten Jinpa. © 2003 by H.H. the Dalai Lama, Tenzin Gyatso. Reprinted by arrangement with Shambhala Publications, Inc., Boston, Mass. www.shambhala.com.

Judy Lief, "Looking Into Lojong, or Mind Training." From the July 2012 issue of *Shambhala Sun*. www.shambhalasun.com.

Pema Chödrön, "You Can Do It!" From *Living Beautifully with Uncertainty and Change* by Pema Chödrön. © 2012 by Pema Chödrön. Reprinted by arrangement with Shambhala Publications, Inc., Boston, Mass. www.shambhala.com.

Chökyi Nyima Rinpoche, "Mahamudra and Dzogchen: Thought-Free Wakefulness." From *Present Fresh Wakefulness: A Meditation Manual on Nonconceptual Wisdom* by Chökyi Nyima Rinpoche. © 2003 by Chökyi Nyima Rinpoche. Reprinted by arrangement with Rangjung Yeshe Publications.

PART 5

Keep Your Practice Going

Sakyong Mipham Rinpoche, "It's All in Your Mind." From the November 2006 issue of *Shambhala Sun*. www.shambhalasun.com.

Larry Rosenberg, "Bringing the Practice Home." From *Breath by Breath: The Liberating Practice of Insight Meditation* by Larry Rosenberg. © 1998 by Larry Rosenberg. Reprinted by arrangement with Shambhala Publications, Inc., Boston, Mass. www.shambhala.com

Karen Maezen Miller, "My First Meditation Retreat: A Checklist." Originally published on www.shambhalasun.com.

Gaylon Ferguson, "Practicing in Community." Adapted from "Community: Extending the View of Sangha," from the Spring 2010 issue of *Buddhadharma: The Practitioner's Quarterly*. www.thebuddhadharma.com.

Cyndi Lee and David Nichtern, "Yoga Body, Buddha Mind." From the March 2007 issue of *Shambhala Sun*. www.shambhalasun.com.

Andy Karr, "Stabilize Your Practice." From *Cultivating Reality: A Practitioner's Guide to the View in Indo-Tibetan Buddhism* by Andy Karr. © 2007 by Andy Karr. Reprinted by arrangement with Shambhala Publications, Inc., Boston, Mass. www.shambhala.com.

Thanissaro Bhikkhu, "Building Your Mental Muscles." From *Head and Heart Together, Essays on the Buddhist Path* by Thanissaro Bhikkhu.

ABOUT THE EDITOR

ROD MEADE SPERRY is an editor and writer for the *Shambhala Sun*, the leading Buddhism-inspired magazine. He was a founding member of what would become Boundless Way Zen, a rapidly growing Buddhist community based in New England. He is the creator of TheWorstHorse.com, which began in 2005 to document interesting collisions—both meaningful and amusingly meaningless—of Buddhism and pop culture. He lives in Halifax, Nova Scotia.

1/23/15